THE
MASTERS

Also by JANN S. WENNER

Lennon Remembers

Garcia: A Signpost to New Space

Gonzo: The Life of Hunter S. Thompson
(with COREY SEYMOUR)

Like a Rolling Stone

THE MASTERS

CONVERSATIONS WITH
BONO, BOB DYLAN, JERRY GARCIA,
MICK JAGGER, JOHN LENNON,
BRUCE SPRINGSTEEN,
PETE TOWNSHEND

JANN S. WENNER

Little, Brown and Company   NEW YORK · BOSTON · LONDON

Copyright © 2023 by Jann S. Wenner

Hachette Book Group supports the right to free expression and the value of copyright. The purpose of copyright is to encourage writers and artists to produce the creative works that enrich our culture.

The scanning, uploading, and distribution of this book without permission is a theft of the author's intellectual property. If you would like permission to use material from the book (other than for review purposes), please contact permissions@hbgusa.com. Thank you for your support of the author's rights.

Little, Brown and Company
Hachette Book Group
1290 Avenue of the Americas, New York, NY 10104
littlebrown.com

First Edition: October 2023

Little, Brown and Company is a division of Hachette Book Group, Inc. The Little, Brown name and logo are trademarks of Hachette Book Group, Inc.

The publisher is not responsible for websites (or their content) that are not owned by the publisher.

Photographs in the insert are credited to the following:

Bono (2017), by Mark Seliger; Bruce Springsteen, by Danny Clinch; Bob Dylan, by Elliott Landy / Magnum Photos; Jann Wenner, by Annie Liebovitz; Jarry Garcia, by Annie Liebovitz; John Lennon, by Annie Liebovitz; Mick Jagger, London, 1995 © Peter Lindbergh (courtesy Peter Lindbergh Foundation, Paris); Pete Townshend, by David Montgomery.

ISBN 9780316571050
Library of Congress Control Number: 2023941506

Printing 1, 2023

LSC-C

Printed in the United States of America

For dearest friends Bette and Michael

CONTENTS

INTRODUCTION

MY SEARCH FOR ROCK AND ROLL

Forms and rhythms in music are never changed without producing changes in the most important political forms and ways... The new style quietly insinuates itself into manners and customs and from there it issues a greater force. It goes on to attack laws and constitutions displaying the utmost impudence and it ends by overthrowing everything, both in public and private.

— PLATO

RALPH J. GLEASON quoted those words from Plato to preface an essay he wrote in 1967 for *The American Scholar*, a piece he titled "Like a Rolling Stone." Ralph helped me found *Rolling Stone*, and his essay laid out our esthetic and ethical underpinnings.

To us the artists were the moral compass of society, the

gatekeepers of truth. Introducing our first issue, I quoted the Lovin' Spoonful, saying that the magazine was for anyone who believed that rock and roll was "the magic that can set you free."

It was unequivocally Black music, rooted directly in slavery, and therefore unequivocally American music. This music was from the cotton fields of the Mississippi Delta, whence sons of slaves and sharecroppers, like Muddy Waters and Howlin' Wolf, migrated north and electrified the blues. The music was also rooted in the gospel of the Black churches where souls were stirred and lifted up in mighty clouds of joy. Elvis, Jerry Lee Lewis, and Little Richard grew up infused by gospel and sang it all their lives. Rock and roll became this country's native, original art and it conquered the civilized world. The music was one of the most significant cultural and social forces to cause the walls of segregation to crumble — white kids who loved Black music.

That there are no women or Black musicians in this collection is reflective of the prejudices and practices of the times. As a white middle-class kid in the Fifties and Sixties, and as a more aware college student, I didn't hear such songs as Sam Cooke's "A Change Is Gonna Come" (1964) as part of my zeitgeist. It was an inspirational and transporting anthem, but I didn't internalize it as part of my struggle. My loss.

This music in its infancy and teenage years was irredeemably male. Even for the girl groups it was all about the leader of the pack. As the teen idol tide receded, the audience I saw was overwhelmingly male and enthralled with gunslinging guitar players and microphone-swinging singers. It was macho to the core. The girl singers were stuck in the lane of teenage innocence and irrelevance. The Sixties began to welcome women like Janis Joplin, Grace Slick, and Cass Elliot as powerful equals in the new rock and roll bands. This discrimination was another barrier that rock would tear down.

If you look for it, the theme of feminization of behavior and values can be traced through the history of rock, not as a sexual pursuit, but as a liberating of gender, in search of a society where the insensitivity and brutality of male energy are restrained and balanced by nurture and compassion. Elvis and Little Richard wore eyeliner and coiffed themselves with care. The Beatles epitomized androgyny. Long hair — an in-your-face sign of femininity — was now a principal, flag-waving symbol of rock stardom. It was an early cry for equality and shared humanity.

The music was everywhere, day and night, at home, in school, and in your car, in every city and suburb, from sea to shining sea. Local Top 40 stations were joining powerful regional radio signals broadcasting from the South and the big cities. *American Bandstand* was a national teenage television ritual. The new technologies of the 45 rpm single, the transistor, the portable radio, the long-playing record, the cassette tape, and then the compact disc, and now streaming, led to a level of instantaneous and universal communication never seen in the history of the world.

We were the first generation of Americans weaned on this music. From first kisses to last dates, from crushes to car crashes, lyrics, if often partially disguised, addressed adolescent concerns. It wasn't only the sympathetic articulation of youthful yearnings, but the physical language of the music itself that spoke to self-discovery. I was eleven years old when I first heard Jerry Lee Lewis tell me, "Too much love drives a man insane." It was the dance. Rock embraced the open sexuality of the Black rhythm. The body found expression and freedom, the ecstasy and abandon of the tribal and the primal as well as the slow dance, with its invitation to intimacy. It captured both soul and body. This was not bobby socks and big bands. It was going to church.

Rock and roll was our own secret language and code. It was also freely available, for anyone, including adults, who wanted to listen and understand. It was open-source code. But the reaction was neither embracing nor curious. It was threatened, derisive, and hostile. There were organized record-smashing rallies, church-led denunciations, and congressional hearings. Today this hatred and fear of social change is called "culture wars."

It was a conversation, a dream, a shout for joy and attention and community that began speaking to and for me when I was eight, and has only become more powerful to me as I turn toward eighty.

The Masters collects the major interviews I conducted over my fifty years as the editor of *Rolling Stone:* conversation with seven artists whom I listened to with awe and joy. The talent level is prodigious. I think that to read these seven, as a collection, gives us a deeper understanding of the art of rock and roll, it's shared purpose, and a broader knowledge of the era that these artists defined.

The people whom I interviewed were part of my search for rock and roll, for its meaning and its power over me. My selection was intuitive. I wanted to join a community that was being shaped by this music and to play a role in that community. The span of these interviews, 1968 to 2023, is a chronology of my own maturation as a person, and my role as an historian and well-traveled reporter. I was a full-time fan and proselytizer. I gave myself to the music as it gathered glory and power. We all had an awareness of the serious stakes, of the sway of the music over a generation, and its hold on American culture.

Bob Dylan was nineteen years old when he dropped out of the University of Minnesota and drove to New York City. On October 26, 1963, he debuted at Carnegie Hall, singing, "Your sons and your daughters are beyond your command, for the times they are a-changin'." One month later John F. Kennedy's brains were blown out in Dallas, Texas. Our beautiful young president was murdered in front of our eyes. Another song Dylan performed that night at Carnegie Hall was "With God on Our Side." One year later, Joan Baez sang it to thousands of students on the University of California campus in Berkeley as they assembled for the first of the mass student protests of the Sixties. I was in the crowd that day.

The Beatles and the Rolling Stones had by then begun their

conquest of London society, and quickly engulfed British culture. Rock music was a "completely new form," Mick Jagger said to me. "I was there at the beginning. You felt like you were one of the chosen few, one of the only ones in the world who would get to play with this new toy. We had evangelistic fervor. No one knew where it was going or if it was going to last. Rock history is full of songs hoping rock would never die."

Jan Morris, one of the keenest historians of the British Empire, wrote: "Almost at a stroke, the advent of the Beatles altered the entire national attitude toward class, toward appearances, toward achievement and the nature of success. The kingdom seemed to be rejuvenated. In all the long centuries of British history there have been few decades more invigorating than the Sixties."

Pete Townshend put it this way: "As individuals these people were nothing. They were England's lowest common denominators. Not only were they young, they were also lower-class young. As a force, they were unbelievable. That was England's 'Bulge'; all the war babies, all the soldiers coming back from war and screwing until they were blue in the face. This was the result: thousands and thousands of kids, too many kids, not enough teachers, not enough parents, not enough pills to go around."

The Beatles led an armada to liberate America. It was called the British Invasion. It was not a conquest, it was the formation of an international alliance, the forces of liberation. The Beatles appeared on *The Ed Sullivan Show* on February 9, 1964. The show was watched by 73 million people, tuned in by half of all television households in the United States, less than three months after the assassination of President Kennedy. America surrendered the day after. That morning, after seeing the Beatles, Bruce Springsteen bought his first guitar.

The stage was set.

———————

It was Bob Dylan who singularly and forever changed music and the culture of modern times. Nothing was ever the same afterward. He had a gift that was wide and deep. His voice had profound expressiveness, the ability to convey the full range of human feeling. Bob's insight into the human condition, his vision of America, and the genius of his language set him apart. Not since Walt Whitman, not since Lincoln and the Civil War, had anyone spoken like this to America. That voice came through the jukebox and over the radio into every corner of the land.

Bob Dylan was "showing me a version of my country that I knew was true but had not been whispered to me previously," Bruce Springsteen told me. "Bob was the guy that came in, pulled the veil away, and said, 'This is where and what I'm living really looks like to me,' and it feels like, 'I know that person and I know this place. This place is my home, and this is who I am.'"

When the baby boomers began to enter college, they were the largest generational cohort in Western civilization — also the wealthiest, and one which had been molded by a vast government-financed system of public education. We were leaving to be on our own, no direction home.

We quickly saw that America was on the cusp of a spiritual crisis. Too many genies and monsters had been unloosed in the cauldron of a world war, chief among them the atomic bomb. Man's inhumanity to man was ascendant.

My most vivid memories of grammar school are the wail of "Heartbreak Hotel" ("Down at the end of Lonely Street, I've found a new place to dwell") and the strange mornings when we were told to hide under our desks, cover our heads, and wait for the sudden flash of blinding light and then a thundering boom just before shattered glass would come flying at us. Even then, adults were lying to us: there was no safety under a desk. We were all going to die.

What does it do to a child, to a generation, to a country, or to a world to know that your death and the death of your family are not just inevitable, but indeed imminent, just a shot away? Nuclear war had now been joined by looming environmental destruction, reinforcing our sense of perishability, displacing the church-taught promises of immortality. It was this brave new world which gave birth and sustenance to rock and roll.

The Sixties began with a murder most foul. The hopes and dreams of a generation would never fully recover. What followed was a decade of war in Vietnam, which eroded a generation's faith in the government and the leaders of the country. The horrors of America's racism were surfacing. We too had concentration camps. The chickens were coming home to roost.

Next came the whipsaw of 1968: the assassinations of Martin Luther King Jr. and Bobby Kennedy, looting and burning throughout the cities of Black America, and a police riot at the Democratic National Convention in Chicago, and Nixon's election. Within the "counter culture," naïve fantasies were upended by events of its own making, Altamont and the Manson Family. Young people were stigmatized for their hairstyles, and the "War on Drugs" was officially declared against the use of the harmless marijuana, criminalizing the lifestyle of a generation.

Some recent historians call it the "Long Sixties," but mark the dates as 1955 to 1973, which suggests a flawed history, neglecting the centrality of the conflicts that drove and divided our society in a way that they hadn't since the Civil War. The real Sixties began in 1963 and ended in 1976 with the election of Jimmy Carter, a successful presidential campaign initially funded by the Allman Brothers.

The actual politics incompletely explains the era. Television and mass communication meant that popular culture became a window into society and ultimately shaped the debate. The soundtrack was rock and roll, it was the voice of the opposition, the soundtrack of a generation. The debate became widely accessible to the ordinary citizen. The irrelevance and ignorance of adults — the evil manifested in their deeds — proved youthful poets and prophets to be right. Graphic violence proved plain truths. Adults had lost the basis of their authority.

Because politics had become so corrupt and apparently impotent, to participate in the charade was delusional and pointless. The new radical politics of the left had no real-world applications. Bomb-throwing was abhorrent. Only rock and roll — and the values implicit in its whole stance — made sense.

I think of it as the Era of Rock and Roll in an Age of Consequences. Rock and roll became a metaphor for everything. Popular culture overtook politics and the pulpit as the righteous forum for discussions of ethics and morality. It was the new gospel and it preached democratic values.

Bob Dylan's incandescent and spiritually profound songs ("And if my thought-dreams could be seen, they'd probably put my head in a guillotine") gave permission to and challenged songwriters and poets to step up, with language and visions about their own souls and the real world. They were called to tell their own truth. Jerry Garcia said to me, "Whether he intended it that way or not, is completely unimportant."

I see the rock and roll era — roughly the second half of the twentieth century — in a larger framework, as one of those moments in world history when the genetic wheels of chance bring together a handful of creative geniuses, whose work interacts in specific socioeconomic circumstances and causes some kind of chain reaction.

In Paris of the 1920s, Matisse, Picasso, and Léger overturned and discarded the formal art that had become so irrelevant to the new postwar world. "There do seem to be constellations, electromagnetic moments when there is a concentration of creative forces... It's possible that creation sometimes has the effect of implosion... instead of exploding, creative forces are concentrated, move toward a hidden center," wrote the literary critic George Steiner.

The same constellation of electromagnetic forces (perhaps they were flaring solar storms) occurred in Elizabethan England, which saw the great flowering of poetry, music, and literature of the Shakespearean era. A century earlier Florence had been the center of the Renaissance, the rediscovery of humanism and human achievement. Fifth-century Athens was dominated by the playwrights Sophocles, Euripides, and Aeschylus, while Socrates and Plato and Aristotle walked the same streets. Perhaps such talent randomly exists at all times in history, and it takes an institutional or political watershed to catalyze those voices. Athens, Florence, and England were dominant world powers, mighty and rich. Because of modern communications and jet travel, it was no longer necessary to have a singular incubating geography.

America was the victor in two world wars and a near-infinite storehouse of capital and natural resources. The ideological norms that guarded America's immense wealth and power for the chosen few came to be challenged by its own heirs. Once plugged in, new technology proved to be an uncontrollable accelerant. We didn't start the fire.

Our own precedent to the Sixties was the Twenties, when an earlier generation of the young returned home with their eyes opened to European culture and their minds scrambled by an overseas war. They returned to a country suddenly unified by new technology, like automobiles, radios, and telephones. Fifty years later, we had vastly more powerful technology. The bland, gray-suited, three-martini Fifties were pushed aside in favor of bikinis, long hair, pot, and LSD.

The Masters is a collection of interviews with artists engaged in their work at the highest levels. We took rock and roll seriously, so I wanted to discuss it in philosophical terms with each of "the masters," to get to the sources of its power and depth. I wanted to understand the common threads of their youth, and their world. How did they discover rock? Whom had they heard and what did it mean to them, then and now? I wanted them to be introspective. I wanted to ask about the sources of their creativity, their technique and craft, their insights into this new art form, and, perhaps most importantly, what was this noise all about?

To get a good interview, you present yourself as a person who is sympathetic, knowledgeable, and deeply engaged with the work. You must have mutual respect. I tried to represent my reader in the room. In editing these, I've left various small pieces of the casual and conversational to present a dimensional voice and person. I have tried to preserve an encounter that was uniquely personal and privileged.

The interviews are presented here in chronological order to impart a historical evolution. One can get a feel for the hubris and pissed-off attitude that characterized Pete Townshend in the early days of a young man's life, and in rock itself, along with a sense of his introspection and seriousness. He was already imagining a rock opera. He embodied the spirit of the British Invasion.

I sat with Bob Dylan in 1969, after he had taken a long break from physical and mental exhaustion at the height of his rock and roll fame. He spoke carefully, warily, about his own singular role and popularity. I was an acolyte, trying to be cool. I was struck by his handling of my hard-to-conceal naïveté. He was gracious, honest, funny, every bit a gentleman. I have tried to preserve that element here.

John Lennon's interview surely put an end to the brief, shining age of the Beatles, Camelot as a rock fairy-tale soap opera. For me and everyone who read it, it felt like a dive into an active volcano. This is a backstage visit *extraordinaire*.* In judging Lennon's commentary, we should remember how brutalized he was by the unrelenting, unforgiving eye of fame. We shouldn't forget that the Beatles never really had — other than screaming teenage girls — the chance to know or to interact with their audience other than from a recording studio.

Jerry Garcia was the central musical and moral influence in the

---

* The full-length, unedited transcript is in print as a book, *Lennon Remembers*.

San Francisco rock scene of the sixties. Our interview feels a lot like sitting around a late-night campfire, having a few tokes, and talking about the good old days. The Grateful Dead operated as a commune, and wanted to have a communal relationship with their audience. They created a style and presentation to sustain that audience and that life for themselves. Jerry was revered by his musical peers. The ideals of the Dead inspired groups everywhere. Jerry and John Lennon talk about drugs, especially LSD and how intertwined rock and roll and psychedelics were in this era. The vocabulary and sound of rock were openly and indelibly influenced by pot and especially LSD. Jerry stressed the need to have fun: "Well, good times is the key to this all."

After Garcia, I didn't touch the tape recorder for another thirty years, by which time it was replaced by compact digital technology. What had been a rebellious social and artistic movement led by people in their twenties was now a multibillion-dollar business largely in the hands of newly minted adults. To have reached the summit of any human endeavor was now known as becoming a rock star. Despite the seductions of success, the soul, the spirit, and the sound seemed stronger than ever. Rock and roll had become certain, sure footed, and had conquered mainstream culture and mores. Naysayers, whether adult haters or baby bomb-throwers from within, like Kurt Cobain, couldn't convincingly challenge its fundamental integrity. With success came strength; with integrity came power.

These artists used the language and form of rock to express their restless creativity. They spoke in their unique voices, but they also were a symphony with a common vision. Bob brought the traces and memories of an old-time, small-town rural America; Jerry Garcia emerged from an urban, multiracial bohemian family; Mick and Pete were the sons of the respectable middle class; Lennon, the child from the ignored lower rungs of Liverpool. Likewise, Springsteen was stuck in a place with little future, a forgotten New Jersey union town. Bruce's lifetime work was to tell the stories of that childhood home, the men and women who lived, loved, and died in that mythical place.

He drew the strength of his ideas and the necessity for economic justice from that world.

Bono, born Paul David Hewson, two decades after Dylan and Lennon, was steeped in their work, which he heard as prayers and questions for God. To be Irish was to be raised in and by the Church, to have the Scripture and the spiritual imbedded for life. It was the window through which he discovered the evangelistic potential of rock. He told me, "It's such an extraordinary thing, music. It is how we speak to God, finally, or how we don't. Even if we're ignoring God, it's the language of the spirit. If we believe we contain within our skin and bones a spirit that might last longer than your time breathing in and out, if there is a spirit, music is the thing that wakes it up. It's how we communicate on another level."

I look at this collection as a whole, one ongoing conversation I had been having. It is also a colloquy among the artists themselves, speaking to one another. I think everyone had a sense that they were also speaking to history and its institutional voice, *Rolling Stone*.

The founders of rock and roll, the young men who first split the atom and set off the "Big Bang," came of age in the Fifties. Chuck Berry was twenty-nine when he recorded "Roll Over Beethoven" in 1956. Buddy Holly was twenty when he wrote "Peggy Sue" in 1957. The energy they unleashed was unknowable and proved formidable. One could call it radioactive, or perhaps "radio-active."

The masters were the inheritors. Nurtured in powerful sounds and emotions, they began to create a new *lingua franca* to catalyze their own times, their needs as young adults and what they discovered in the world around them. It could say everything for them. They took the tools and tradecraft of the new language and created a new literature.

Humanity could no longer survive a world war. The atomic bomb called not just for new treaties, but for a transfiguration of human behavior. "Today we no longer have a choice between violence and nonviolence," said Dr. Martin Luther King Jr. "It is either nonviolence or nonexistence." Rock and roll called for love and peace. That might have seemed painfully and hopelessly naïve to some, but to me it seemed a strategy for survival. "Love is the absolute power," King said. It was gospel in the Church of Rock and Roll.

The broad claims I have made for rock and roll, a loud and disrespectful art that had emerged from the poorest economic places in society, leave me vulnerable to charges that could range from historical myopia to infatuation, blindness, naïveté. Did every leper get cured? No. Every exception to the rule, like the Monkees, will be thrown at me. I will be told to "grow up." But it's too late to stop now. Rock and roll didn't speak to or for every member of the baby boom generation, nor did every great musical artist address morality or geopolitics. They didn't need to. Rock and roll was riding the tide of history. It had spoken to and for the masses.

Inconceivable social progress has been made over the last fifty years. During those years, we have spoken the language of youth, sung the song of rock and roll, we have marched to the beat; we now spit the rhymes and drop the beats of hip-hop. Music has been the glue holding generations together.

"I associate music with emancipation and freedom for myself," Bono told me. "If rock and roll means anything to me, it's liberation. Not just for yourself — your sexuality, your spirituality — but also for others."

The idea of liberation, expressed in the lyric or in the inexpressible power of the musical note, is at the heart of the modern dilemma. Rock spoke to this yearning. It had language and tools especially attuned to a modern technological society. It had the technology itself at its back.

Is it too much to make such a sweeping assertion of power for this art, to claim that it is something without precedent in Western civilization? Rock has asserted itself in global affairs — disease, poverty, the political rights of self-determination. In every presidential election since 1972, it has been a meaningful national constituency in the Democratic Party and in support of environmental, human, and civil rights.

Did we solve every problem? No. But we didn't turn our backs or stay silent. We spoke and we acted. Our job was not to finish the work, but to get it under way.

And all the while speaking intimately and privately to our deepest hearts.

THE
MASTERS

PETE TOWNSHEND

[1968]

PETE ARRIVED at my loft just after 1 a.m., still pumping adrenaline, straight from his show at the Fillmore, in the heart of the San Francisco ghetto. Bill Graham had been booking all the English rock groups on their small, exploratory tours of America. Of all the cities, it was San Francisco that was considered the most important stop — we had the hippest audience; the most influential national music critic, Ralph J. Gleason; the groundbreaking "underground radio" station KMPX-FM; and *Rolling Stone*.

I had seen The Who at Monterey Pop Festival in 1967, just a few months before launching *Rolling Stone*. They existed for me in a magic circle of enchantment I found there: Jimi Hendrix, Otis Redding, Janis Joplin, the Mamas and Papas. Unlike the mostly beaded, bearded musicians in leather boots and sandals — this was a hippie festival to be sure — The Who came out in ruffled shirts, silk scarfs, jackets, and exquisite capes, true Carnaby Street costumes. As Otis Redding similarly did in his lime-green silk suit, they blew away everyone with a real rhythm and blues–rock show. "My Generation" and "Summertime Blues" were irresistible, Keith Moon blasting away, Roger Daltrey swinging his mic in wide loops, and Pete windmilling as he played, something he told me was his attempt to look "lethal."

A few months later, The Who came to San Francisco to play the Cow Palace, a ten-thousand-seat venue built in 1940, on a multi-act tour headlined by Herman's Hermits. I wanted to do some kind of review for an early issue of the magazine and ended up spending the afternoon with Pete in his dressing room while he waited between shows. I was not much more than a bright fanboy, but he was eager to talk, polite and charming, a genuine English rock star. He was obviously very smart and he was quite happy to have the company.

Pete and The Who took their role as "mod" icons seriously. They looked like and led their audience, widely thought of in England as a powerful and aggressive army of teenagers. Talking about "my generation" was no joke. Pete meant it when he said, "I hope I die before I get old." The idea of rebellion as led by a rock and roll group had special urgency for me. I saw it clearly linked — despite the difference in clothes and pills — to what we were doing in San Francisco.

Pete is a thinker and a talker, very clever, very intense, rather the opposite of laid-back. In response to my own youthful but very serious interest, he colorfully laid out how the music and style of The Who had helped galvanize the brewing baby boom ("the bulge") in England, his own musical processes, and why he thought rock and roll was so powerful.

I asked him what he planned to work on next and he

proceeded to describe a multipart work, a "rock opera." This would be a completely new and ambitious form for rock. He wanted to call it *Deaf, Dumb and Blind Boy*. He said he didn't know if he could explain it correctly "in my condition," but the idea for it was all there, the first time he had ever catalyzed the bits and pieces of it into what would shortly become the fully realized *Tommy*.

The next morning, as I drove him to the airport, he said he knew he had let loose in an assertive and uncensored way. He said letting the idea for a rock opera flow felt like he had been in a dream. He wanted to know if I had spiked his orange juice with LSD. Pete was twenty-three and I was twenty-two.

I imagine it gets to be a drag
talking about why you smash your guitar.

No, it doesn't get to be a drag to talk about it. Sometimes it gets [to be] a drag to do it. I can explain it, I can justify it, and I can enhance it, and I can do a lot of things, dramatize it and literalize it. Basically it's a gesture which happens on the spur of the moment. I think, with guitar smashing, just like performance itself, it's an act, it's an instant, and it really is meaningless.

When did you start smashing guitars?

It happened by complete accident the first time. We were just kicking around in a club which we played every Tuesday and I was playing the guitar and it hit the ceiling. It broke and it kind of shocked me because I wasn't ready for it to go. I didn't particularly want it to go but it went.

And I was expecting an incredible thing, it being so precious to me, but nobody did anything, which made me kind of angry in a way, and determined to get this precious event noticed by the audience. I proceeded to make a big thing of breaking the guitar. I pounced all over the stage with it and I threw the bits on the stage and I picked up my spare guitar and carried on as though I really meant to do it.

Were you happy about it?

Deep inside I was very unhappy because the thing had got broken. It got around and the next week the people came up to me and they said, "Oh, we heard all about it, man; it's 'bout time someone gave it to a guitar" and all this kind of stuff. It kind of grew from there, we'd go to another town and people would say, "Oh yeah, we heard that you smashed a guitar." After that I was into it up to my neck and have been doing it since.

**Was it inevitable that you were going
to start smashing guitars?**

It was due to happen because I was getting to the point where I'd play and I'd play and I mean, I still can't play how I'd like to play. When The Who first started we were playing blues, and I dug the blues and I knew what I was supposed to be playing, but I couldn't play it. I could hear the notes in my head, but I couldn't get them out on the guitar. It used to frustrate me incredibly. I used to try and make up visually for what I couldn't play as a musician. I used to get into very incredible visual things where in order just to make one chord more lethal, whereas really it's just going to be picked normally. I'd hold my arm up in the air and bring it down so it really looked lethal, even if it didn't sound too lethal. Anyway, this got bigger and bigger and bigger until eventually I was setting myself incredible tasks.

How did this affect your guitar playing?

In fact, I forgot all about the guitar because my visual thing was more my music than the actual guitar. I got to jump about and the guitar became unimportant. I banged it and I let it feed back and scraped it and rubbed it up against the microphone, did anything. It didn't deserve any credit or any respect. I used to bang it and hit it against walls and throw it on the floor at the end of the act. And one day it broke. It just wasn't part of my thing and ever since then I've never really regarded myself as a guitarist. When people come up to me and say, like, "Who's your favorite guitarist?," I say, "I know who my favorite guitarist is, but asking me, as a guitarist, forget it because I don't make guitar-type comments. I don't talk guitar talk, I just throw the thing around." Today still I'm learning. If I play a solo, it's a game to me because I can't play what I want to play. That's the thing: I can't get it out because I don't practice. When I should be practicing, I'm writing songs.

**You said you spend most of your time writing songs
in your basement.**

A lot of writing I do on tour. I do a lot on airplanes. At home, I write a lot. When I write a song, what I usually do is work the lyric out first from some basic idea that I had and then I get an acoustic guitar and I sit by the tape recorder and I try to bang it out as it comes. Try to let the music come with the lyrics. If I dig it, I want to add things to it, like I'll add bass guitar or drums or another voice. This is really for my own amusement that I do this.

The reason "I Can See for Miles" came out good was because I sat down and made it good from the beginning. The fact that I did a lot of work on arrangements and stuff like that doesn't really count. I think that unless the actual song itself is good, you know, you can do all kinds of incredible things to it, but you're never going to get it. Not unless the meat and potatoes are there.

Although I do fuck around in home studios and things like that, I think it's of no importance; I don't think it's really got anything to do with what makes The Who The Who.

When you work out an arrangement and figure out the bass line and the various voices, is that just directly translated onto a record that would be released?

More or less, but then we don't really take it that grimly. What happens is I will suggest the bass riff on the demonstrations record, John [Entwistle] takes up and goes from there. I use the piano or drum — simple and effective as possible, putting the song across to the group.

Instead of me hacking my songs around to billions of publishers trying to get them to dig them, what I've got to do is get the rest of the band to dig my number. I know that I've got to present it to them in the best light. That's why I make my own recordings: so when they first hear it, it's not me stoned out of my mind plunking away on a guitar trying to get my latest number across.

Do you ever think of using the demo version instead of the group version?

A lot of the demos have been so good in fact that it's scared us out of making recordings. "I Can See for Miles" and "Magic Bus" both had demos which were very, very comparable to the finished releases. They were just so exciting and so good that for a long time we didn't ever dare attempt to make singles because we were blackmailing Kit Lambert, our producer, into doing them better. So we always put it off until Kit was very sure of himself. The same with "Magic Bus" — we didn't want to do it. I listened to the demo and I thought that demo was good but that we're never going to catch it on record. It's going to bring us all down. Kit was going, "No, we're going to do it, every little precious thing in the demonstration record, you're going to catch and you're going to copy it if necessary." What happened is in the end we gave up and we went down and we did it completely differently.

How does a session start?

We walk in, we set up our equipment, and through the talkback will come, "Can we hear the bass guitar, please?" And then for quarter of an hour it's *clang, clang*, where the bass guitar microphone is corrected and so on. Then "Can we hear the bass drum, please?," and *clang, clang*, another quarter of an hour, and "Can we hear the top kit?," and Keith plays the top kit, and "Can we hear the guitar?" The guitar's always good. The guitar really is good the first time.

But by this time, of course, you're pissed off at the whole proceedings. All you want to do is go out for a drink so that's usually what happens. We all go out for a drink and come back in and we seem to have screwed up the balance a bit. So "Just a quick check on the bass guitar" and a "quick check" on bass rhythm and you go through the whole proceedings again. "Okay, we're ready to go!" Then you find that you've forgotten something, and so by the time you've worked the routine out, the balance is lost again and you have to start all over again. This is the way The Who record.

What's happened when you've tried spontaneous recording so far?

It wasn't music, it wasn't a happening, it wasn't an event, it wasn't a musical situation, it wasn't a beginning, and it wasn't an end. It was just roughly parallel musical statements. There was none of the constriction of thought or anything; it was all analytical. And if a thought went along a song, it came in A and went out a Z. With grooving or jamming or whatever you want to call it, you just pick up your guitar and — okay, you might have a very complicated lyric in front of it — you just play the lyric out. The music becomes far more realistic. In today's time sequence, you got to make something which adds up like the present. Albums are only going to be played once or twice.

What other ideas do you have?

Well, the album concept in general is complex. I don't know if I can explain it in my condition, at the moment. But it's derived as a result of quite a few things. We've been talking about doing an opera; we've been talking about a whole lot of things, and what has basically happened is that we've condensed all of these ideas, all this energy, and all these gimmicks, and whatever we've decided on for future albums, into one juicy package. The package I hope is going to be called *Deaf, Dumb and Blind Boy*. It's a story about a kid that's born deaf, dumb, and blind and what happens to him throughout his life. The deaf, dumb, and blind boy is played by The Who, the musical entity. He's represented musically, by a theme which we play, which starts off the opera itself and then there's a song describing him. But what it's really all about is the fact that because the boy is deaf, dumb, and blind, he's seeing things basically as vibrations which we translate as music. That's really what we want to do, create this feeling that when you listen to the music you can actually become aware of the boy, and aware of what he is all about, because we are creating him as we play.

And the whole album is about his experience?

Yes, it's a pretty far-out thing, actually. But it's very, very endearing to me because the thing is that inside, the boy sees things musically and in dreams and nothing has got any weight at all. He is touched from the outside and he feels his mother's touch, he feels his father's touch, but he just interprets them as music. His father gets pretty upset that his kid is deaf, dumb, and blind. He wants a kid that will play football and God knows what.

One night he comes in and he's drunk and he sits over the kid's bed and he looks at him and he starts to talk to him, and the kid just smiles up, and his father is trying to get through to him, telling him about how the other dads have a kid that they can take to football and they can teach them to play football and all this kind of crap, and he starts to say, "Can you hear me?" The kid, of course, can't hear him. He's groovin' in this musical thing, this incredible musical thing, he'll be out of his mind. Then there's his father outside, outside of his body, and this song is going to be written by John. I hope John will write this song about the father who is really uptight now.

The kid won't respond, he just smiles. The father starts to hit him and at this moment the whole thing becomes incredibly realistic. On one side you have the dreamy music of the boy wasting through his nothing life. And on the other you have the reality of the father outside, uptight, but now you've got blows, you've got communication. The father is hitting the kid; musically then I want the thing to break out, hand it over to Keith — "This is your scene, man, take it from here."

And the kid doesn't catch the violence. He just knows that some sensation is happening. He doesn't feel the pain, he doesn't associate it with anything. He just accepts it.

A similar situation happens later on in the opera, where the father starts to get the mother to take the kid away from home to an uncle. The uncle is a bit of a perv. He plays with the kid's body while the kid is out. And at this particular time the child has heard his own name, his mother called him. And he managed to hear these words: "Tommy." He's really got this big thing about his name, whatever his name is going to be, you know, "Tommy." And he gets really hung up on his own name. He decides that this is the king and this is the goal. Tommy is the thing, man.

He's going through this and the uncle comes in and starts to go through a scene with the kid's body, and the boy experiences sexual vibrations, sexual experience, and again it's just basic music, it's interpreted as music and it is nothing more than music. It's got no association with sleaziness or with undercover or with any of the things normally associated with sex. None of the romance, none of the visual stimulus, none of the sound stimulus. Just basic touch. It's meaningless. Or not meaningless, you just don't react, you know. Slowly but surely the kid starts to get it together, out of this incredible simplicity in his mind. He starts to realize that he can see and he can hear, and he can speak; they are there and they are happening all the time. And that all the time he has been able to hear and see. All the time it's been there in front of him, for him to see.

This is the difficult jump. It's going to be extremely difficult, but we want to try to do it musically. At this point, the theme, which has been the boy, starts to change. You start to realize that he is coming to the point where he is going to get over the top, he's going to get over his hang-ups. You're going to stop monkeying around with songs about people being tinkered with, and with Fathers getting uptight, with Mothers getting precious and things, and you're going to get down to the fact of what is going to happen to the kid.

The music has got to explain what happens, that the boy elevates and finds something which is incredible. To us, it's nothing to be able to see and hear and speak, but to him, it's absolutely incredible and overwhelming; this is what we want to do musically. Lyrically, it's quite easy to do it; in fact, I've written it out several times. It makes great poetry, but so much depends on the music. I'm hoping that we can do it. The lyrics are going to be okay, but every pitfall of what we're trying to say lies in the music, lies in the way we play the music, the way we interpret, the way things are going during the opera.

The main characters are going to be the boy and his musical things; he's got a mother and a father and an uncle. There is a doctor involved who tries to do some psychiatric treatment on the kid which is only partly successful. The first two big events are when he hears his mother calling him and hears the word "Tommy," and he devotes a whole part of his life to this one word. The second important event is when he sees himself in a mirror, suddenly seeing himself for the first time: he takes an immediate step back, bases his whole life around his own image. The whole thing then becomes incredibly introverted. The music and the lyrics become introverted and he starts to talk about himself, starts to talk about his beauty. Not knowing, of course, that what he saw was him, but still regarding it as something which belonged to him, and of course it did all of the time anyway.

It's a very complex thing and I don't know if I'm getting it across.

You are.

Because I don't feel at all together.

On *The Who Sell Out*, there's a boy with pimple problems and a girl with perspiration troubles and so on.

Most of those things just come from me. Like this idea I'm talking about right now comes from me. These things are my ideas; it's probably why they all come out the same. They've all got the same fuckups, I'm sure.

I can't get my family together. My family were musicians. They were essentially middle-class, and I spent a lot of time with them when other kids' parents were at work, and I spent a lot of time away from them when other kids had parents. That was the way it came together. They were always out for long periods. They were very respectable — nobody ever stopped making me play the guitar and nobody ever stopped me smoking pot, although they advised me against it.

They didn't stop me from doing anything that I wanted to do. I had my first fuck in the drawing room of my mother's house. The whole incredible thing about my parents is that I just can't place their effect on me and yet I know that it's there. Fucked if I know; musically, I can't place it, and I can't place it in any other way. I don't even feel myself aware of a class structure, or an age structure, and yet I perpetually write about age structures and class structures. On the surface I feel much more concerned with racial problems and politics. Inside I'm much more into basic stuff.

> **You must have thought about where it comes from if it's not your parents. Was it the scene around you when you were young?**

One of the things which has impressed me most in life was the mod movement in England, a movement of young people, much bigger than the hippie thing, the underground, and all these things. It was an army, a powerful, aggressive army of teenagers with transport, with these scooters, and with their own way of dressing. It was acceptable. This was important; their way of dressing was hip, it was fashionable, it was clean, and it was groovy. You could be a bank clerk, man. It was acceptable.

You got them on your own ground. They thought, "Well, there's a smart young lad." And also you were hip, you didn't get people uptight. That was the good thing about it. To be a mod, you had to have short hair, money enough to buy a real smart suit, good shoes, good shirts; you had to be able to dance like a madman. You had to be in possession of plenty of pills all the time and always be pilled up. You had to have a scooter covered in lamps. You had to have like an army anorak to wear on the scooter. And that was being a mod. That was the end of the story.

The groups that you liked when you were a mod were the Who. We were mods and that's how we happened. That's my generation, that's how the song "My Generation" happened: because of the mods. The mods could appreciate the Beatles' taste. They could appreciate their haircuts, their peculiar kinky things that they had going at the time.

Music was as much a fashion as the fashion it created. It was an incredibly flippant fashion. It was as flippant as the girls in the group drinking liebfraumilch in the 1920s. Music was just a feather. You went from record to record and you went from group to group, but you always dug The Who, because they were always down at the local dance. They were mods and we're mods and we dig them. We used to make sure that if there was a riot, a mod-rocker riot, we would be playing in the area. That was a place called Brighton.

> The mods seemed to have graduated
> from "My Generation" and "The Kids Are Alright"
> to very ordinary people, with very ordinary problems.

I'm also going through the same changes. I'm becoming more and more ordinary as I go along. This is the natural progression, this is the natural progression of boring maturity and boring spirituality and boring ascendance of the evolutionary path. The thing is that you become simpler and more and more down to the simple ways of life, to be able to blunder through life without getting anybody uptight at all.

When I write today, I feel that it has to tell a little story. Seriously. And I can't shake this. Like "Odorono" I dug because it was a little story, and although I thought it's a good song, it was about something groovy, like it was about underarm perspiration. I still did make a story out of it, just like it was a literary piece and there's no need to make "Odorono" a story. "My Generation" is a story; in fact, I'm getting storier and storier until now, as I just told you, the next album is just a huge, complicated, complex story, with lots and lots of aspects which I hope are going to come out in the future.

You see, as individuals these people were nothing. They were

England's lowest common denominators. Not only were they young, they were also lower-class young. They had to submit to the middle class's way of dressing and way of speaking and way of acting in order to get the very jobs which kept them alive. They had to do everything in terms of what existed already around them. That made their way of getting something across that much more latently effective, the fact that they were hip and yet still, as far as Granddad was concerned, exactly the same. It made the whole gesture so much more vital. It was incredible. As a force, they were unbelievable. That was the bulge, that was England's baby boom; all the war babies, all the soldiers coming back from war and screwing until they were blue in the face — this was the result. Thousands and thousands of kids, too many kids, not enough teachers, not enough parents, not enough pills to go around. Everybody just grooving on being a mod.

I know the feeling of what it's like to be a mod among two million mods and it's incredible. It's like you're the only white man in the Apollo. Someone comes up and touches you and you become black. It's like that moment, that incredible feeling of being part of something which is much bigger than race. It was impetus. It covered everybody, everybody looked the same, and everybody acted the same and everybody wanted to be the same.

It was the first move that I have ever seen in the history of youth towards unity, towards unity of thought, unity of drive, and unity of motive. Youth has always got some leader or other, some head man. The head man was Mr. Mod. It could be anyone. Any kid, however ugly or however fucked up, if he had the right haircut and the right clothes and the right motorbike, he was a mod. He was mod! There was no big Fred Mod or something. You could get all the equipment at the local store, you get the haircut at the barber's; there was nothing special. You just needed a job in order to get you into the stuff, and that was the only equipment you needed. It was an incredible youthful drive. It really affected me in an incredible way because whenever I think, "Oh, you know, youth today is just never going to make it," I just think of that fucking gesture that happened in England. It was the closest to patriotism that I've ever felt.

A lot of people try to imbue rock and roll with spirituality, give it very deep meaning.

You can take "I'm Dreaming of a White Christmas" at any spiritual level if you want to. It is, in effect, a spiritual song, and it's effective on every spiritual level and it's a complete and wonderful musical effort because it can't be criticized; it's got to be accepted for what it is, it's a piece of pure existence. You've got to work from the lowest level, and let...let the spiritual people get the spiritual bag out of what you're doing.

Primarily, by itself, the record's got to entertain; it's so simple and so beautiful. It's just a piece of entertainment, like life itself. If life ceases to entertain, what do you want to do? You want to commit suicide. It's got to entertain.

You can't create something as huge as rock and roll and then come along and say, "Well, I'm going to do the follow-up now, which is going to be spirituality." Rock and roll is enormous. It's one of the biggest musical events in history. It's equal to the classical music, the weight of the feeling.

It's like saying, "Get all the pop music, put it into a cartridge, put the cap on it, and fire the gun." You don't care whether those ten or fifteen numbers sound roughly the same. You don't care what periods they were written in, what they mean, what they're all about. It's the bloody explosion that they create when you let the gun off. That's what rock and roll is. It is a single force. It is a single impetus and threatens a lot of the crap which is around at the moment in the middle class and in the middle-aged politics or philosophy.

It blasts it, out of its sheer brashness, its sheer realisticness. It's like suddenly everybody getting hung up on a bum trip: Mother has just fallen down the stairs, Dad's lost all his money at the dog track, the baby's got TB. In comes the kid, man, with his transistor radio, grooving to Chuck Berry. He doesn't give a shit about Mom falling down the stairs. He's with rock and roll.

That's what rock and roll says to life: it says, you know, "I'm hip, I'm happy, forget your troubles and just enjoy!" And, of course, this is the biggest thing it has to offer, the biggest single thing it has to offer. At the same time it can have content if... if one desires content in something as incredible as it is already. The rock and roll songs I like, of course, are songs like "Summertime Blues" — man, that's beautiful. It says everything: Don't have the blues, it's summertime. You don't get the blues in summertime! There is no such thing. That's why there's no cure for them.

Can you pin down some of the elements that make rock and roll what it is, starting with the basic elements? It's got the beat.

The reason it's got to have a beat is the fact that rock and roll music has got to have that bounce; it's got to have that thing to make you swing; it's got to swing in an old-fashioned sense. In other words, it's got to undulate. It doesn't have to be physical because when you think of a lot of Beatles music, it's very nonphysical. *Sgt. Pepper's* is an incredibly nonphysical album.

But when I hear something like "Summertime Blues," then I do both, then I'm into rock and roll, then I'm into a way of life, into that thing about being that age and, like, not being able to get off work early and not being able to borrow the car because Dad's in a foul mood. All those frustrations of summer so wonderfully and so simply, so poetically, put in this incredible package, the package being rock and roll.

Is it because you start to take yourself seriously?

You don't want to take things seriously, you just let things pour out. You might be thinking that you're keeping things light and you're keeping things groovy and you're just making your own musical statement and life's a ball. But on the outside they'll think it's probably fucked up, loaded with meaning, obviously a nostalgic bit, obviously the story has got something to do with your first sexual relationship. You know, obviously it's got some spiritual significance: "Does Pete Townshend think he's Jesus?" It can all be read into it. I'm sure a lot of it is there, but one doesn't know because one is trying to avoid this. We, of all people, have got to be afraid of seriousness in The Who, because if The Who were serious, we'd admit that we don't like each other. But because we're not serious, we don't have to admit it.

You talked about settling down.

I always used to work with the thought in my mind that The Who were going to last precisely another two minutes. If the taxman didn't get us, then our own personality clashes would. I never would have believed that The Who would still be together today and, of course, I'm delighted and love it. Nothing can be better really than waking up in the morning and everything is still the same as it was the day before. That's the best thing you can have in life: consistency.

It always amazes me. As an individual, it's given me an incredible freedom. I know that I don't have to do things like I used to. Our manager will create artificial pressures to try and get me to operate, but I know they are artificial so they don't work like they used to. "My Generation" was written under pressure. Someone came to me and said, "Make a statement, make a statement, make a statement," and I'm going, "Oh, okay, okay," and I get "My Generation" together very quickly, like in a night.

The whole structure of our early songs was very, very simple. Now, with less pressure, I have to create the pressures for myself. I have to excite myself: this is what The Who are going to do. The Who are the impetus behind the ideas. Now our music is far more realistically geared to the time in which our audience moves. If you slow down just a little bit and gear yourself to your audience, you can give them 100 percent. If you do a slightly longer set on the stage, you can give all instead of having to cram a lot of unused energy into guitar smashing.

What groups do you enjoy the most?

I like to watch a band with a punch, with drive, who know what they're doing, with a tight sound. I used to like to watch Jimi Hendrix; sometimes he worries me now because he often gets amplifier hang-ups and stuff — I can't stand that, it kills me. I used to like to watch Cream until they got sad and fucked up. I still dig to watch a group like the Young Rascals, who just walk on with their incredibly perfect sound and their lovely organ and they're so easy, the way their numbers flow out, just to watch a group stand and go through their thing so beautifully. I dig Otis Redding and Aretha Franklin. She's been standing still and singing the blues all night and then when she's really into it she'll do a tiny little dance and just get her little feet going, very slightly, just a little jog, and in terms of what she's doing with her voice, it's an incredible gesture and really goes mad. I dig Mick Jagger, who I think is an incredible show, and Arthur Brown I think is an incredible show, too.

What I dig in a performance is to be communicated to, to feel part of an audience. I like to feel that I'm being effective as a member of the audience. I don't mind being asked to clap my fucking hands, let's get that straight. It doesn't get me uptight if someone says "Clap" or "Sing" or "Shout" or "Scream" or "Do what you want to do." That's exactly what I want to do and if I feel like jumping up and down and dancing, I don't want everyone telling me that I'm bringing them down or that they can't listen to the music or something. People should be an audience, and if it's get up and dance time, everybody should do it at the same time.

What about the sexual content in rock and roll?

It embodies it, it's part of its life. Life revolves, if not around it, within it, if not within it, rock and roll has everything to do with sex. The process of sex is embodied in just the rock and roll rhythm. Just banging the table is like it's the demand and it's also the satiation as well. You bang on the table and in the same process you masturbate. At the end of the show you're finished, you've had it. You've come your lot and the show's over.

Did you read my interview with Booker T. & The M.G.'s?

Fantastic. It was in such a relaxing and realistic manner. Being such a huge fan of Steve Cropper, I expected the first article about him that I ever saw to be incredible. He's been here all your life, folks, on your Otis Redding albums, on your Booker T. specials. Here he's been, Steve Cropper, hiding from you, the most incredible guitarist in history.

When I met them, they were straight and they were beautiful. I went up to Booker T. — I'd really like to see this in print — who was my absolute idol, my absolute top man. No music gives me as much pleasure as listening to Booker T. "Green Onions" is my ultimate record of all time, and the guitar work is so tasteful; it's everything that I want to do.

They're so soulful without knowing it. They are playing them straight and they are playing them off-the-cuff, as they come, the sounds which appeal to them and the sounds which go down with them, things which they groove to, things which they think other people will groove to. They just happen to be totally right. They don't know this, because nobody expects to be totally right.

Can we digress for a moment and talk about your nose?

This seemed to be the biggest thing in my life: my fucking nose, man. When I was in school the geezers that were snappy dressers and got chicks like years before I ever even thought they existed would always like to talk about my nose. Whenever my dad got drunk, he'd come up to me and say, "Look, son, you know looks aren't everything" and shit like this. He's getting drunk and he's ashamed of me because I've got a huge nose and he's trying to make me feel good. I know it's huge and of course it became incredible and I became an enemy of society.

I had to get over this thing. I've done it, and I never believe it to this day, but I do not think about my nose anymore. And if I had said this when I was a kid, if I ever said to myself, "One of these days you'll go through a whole day without once thinking that your nose is the biggest in the world, man," you know, I'd have laughed.

It was huge. At that time, it was the reason I did everything. It's the reason I played the guitar — because of my nose. The reason I wrote songs was because of my nose, everything. I eventually admitted something in an article where I summed it up far more logically in terms of what I do today. I said that what I wanted to do was distract attention from my nose to my body and make people look at my body, instead of at my face — turn my body into a machine.

What is interesting is the fact that it was me versus society, until I could convince them that there was more to me than what they thought.

What is your life like today?

Mainly laughs, actually, mainly laughs. The Who on tour is a very difficult trip; it's a delicate one and it could be dangerous. So it's best to keep this on the humorous side.

Life is fun and it's fun because we make it fun. Playing is enjoyable because we make it enjoyable. We're experienced at enjoying life as it is for us now. Whether we do a bad show to a bad audience, whether we can't make the gig, or whether we play on someone else's amplifiers or whether our clothes didn't come from the cleaners or whether we've just heard that our whole families have been wiped out in a car crash, we still know how to enjoy life.

Some people say to be a performer what you have to do is go on the stage and be able to forget all your troubles, go up there and smile. It's a privilege, man, to be able to do that — when you're down, to be able to go on the stage and forget and elevate yourself back to what it's all about, to basic simple communication.

To put it in my own terms, I think that performers are just damn lucky to have the chance. It's a perfect way of enjoying life, when you're on the stage, nothing, nothing goes wrong. Life is just heaven on the stage. "Life is heaven onstage with The Who" — that would be true, actually.

How is it to be a rock and roll star, people coming on all the time, people that want to lay their trip on you?

It can be a big drag, man. One of the hang-ups is that people won't be normal, and if they won't be normal, they won't be themselves. You can sense it. You can sense professional groupies because they're at ease. Me, personally, I don't want to know about them anyway.

It's the kids mostly and the inexperienced people that have preconceptions about you, that have read articles by you or seen what you've said or what you've written and put weight on your words. Pre-loaded, pre-emphasized meetings. Like tonight, when I walk out of an auditorium and there's a thousand kids left in the place and one of them turns around and says, "Hey, you're Peter Townshend," and sticks out his fucking hand and gets hold of my hand so tight that I know I'm not going to get away. I don't know who he is. But he knows everything about me. It's a weird feeling.

The difference between the way Lennon and McCartney behave with the people that are around them is incredible. What Lennon does is he sits down, immediately acknowledges the fact that he's John Lennon and that everything for the rest of the night is going to revolve around him. He completely relaxes and lets everybody feel at ease and just speaks dribble little jokes. Everybody gets into his thing and also has a generally good time.

But Paul McCartney worries. He wants a genuine conversation, a genuine relationship, starting off from square one: "We've got to get it straight that we both know where we're both at before we begin." One of them is fucking Paul McCartney, a Beatle, the other one is me, a huge monumental Beatle fan who still gets a kick out of sitting and talking to Paul McCartney. And he's starting to tell me that he digs me and that we're on an even par so that we can begin the conversation, which completely makes me even a bigger fan. That's all it serves to do. The conversation comes to no purpose and all he serves to do is to confuse himself. He's trying to say, "Oh, you know, you know where you're at. I know where I'm at, we're both really just us and let's talk." So what do you say? "I'm a fantastic fan of yours, man."

Can you break it down in somebody? If you see it happening in somebody, can you break it down?

Sometimes. If you just blatantly snap people out of it and say, "Look, man, no need to put on a phony English accent for me," because you know the best thing to say is "It gets me uptight."

It's just one of the things, the unreality you get from a lot of kids. They don't know what you're all about; their first words are test questions. Questions they've read the answers to a million times in every fucking godforsaken paper in the world, they've seen it. "Why do you break the guitar?" They know why. "Do you really break them?" They know. "What were the words to this?" They know the fucking words. "What's your latest record?" and they already read it. Test questions to see if you're really interested in knowing anything about them, in telling them anything, in performing any kind of service outside of performing on the stage.

I've often ended up in conversations with people who, if my first words to them were "Fuck off, I don't want to talk to any little creep like you," they would have gone. But in fact, because I sat down and talked to them, they ended up telling me that I'm a fool and an idiot and they're going to go and get a Coke.

What kind of people do you like?

The breed of people that I like the most around me, in music, are the ones from whom I get what I would call — I know this is a weird thing but I've had it before — what I would call a positive assistance vibration. It is the difference between someone having a role in what you're doing and being there as an ornament or as an object of the performance. People who have a purpose.

The audience out there, on the other hand, are playing a part. And we're playing a part because we're the fucking group and you're playing a part because you're writing an article about it. But they seem to have no role at all and I can never understand it. How can anyone be content to just act as the parasites of the glory, parasites of the booze, parasites of the grass, parasites of everything? I could never understand them. They're a breed apart from me. Once a fucking groupie gets it together and does something constructive, then I'm back with them again.

I'm not a total believer, to be quite honest, in "The world turns and everything comes together." I think the world turns if you turn it and that if you don't turn it it's going to fucking sit there. You can wait for eons for judgment day and it's never going to come. You've got to get to it yourself.

What is going to happen to rock and roll?

I'm looking to a couple of people. I've heard some of the Rolling Stones' tracks and although I dig them, I don't think they're anything more than what they are, which is incredible, delicious, and wonderful rock and roll and well overdue from them. The Rolling Stones should always be a nonprogressive group. I don't think that the Rolling Stones should be concerned with what they're doing in pop. That's what I dig about them. Dylan, for example, could create a new thing. I think if he made his next record with the Big Pink, that could be interesting. Dylan's thing about writing the lyric and then picking the guitar up and just pumping out the song as it comes out is a direct guide to what will happen in music.

People are going to want music to be more realistic, more honest, and more of a gift from the heart rather than a gift from the lungs, as it were. Instead of wanting to go and watch Ginger Baker run six miles before your very eyes, you'd rather dig what he's doing. I think this is what's happening.

It's going to be the case that the Stones are going to groove along. A lot of other groups are going to groove along and make good music, in a transitional period, but they're going to be part of the transition and the transition is going to be very delicate. It's going to be, believe it or not, become a kind of a broad, unified thing. Rock and roll is going to embody itself.

Explain that.

It's so hard to explain. I'm trying to talk about a change, to describe how I feel a change is going to come about. There's going to be no visible change. I don't think the way the people perform is going to change. The lyrics won't change or anything, but rock and roll is going to change. It might be that new artists come along;

anything can happen. But it's going to be something noticeable, something big. It's going to be something which comes within terms of pop now.

There has got to be a landmark, a milestone before one could get anything together. Something will emerge out of what already exists in music. In other words, instead of having to say, "Well, we're going to have to completely scrap what we've got and get a completely new bag together," rock and roll gives us the ingredients for the next major musical crisis, to encounter the next musical starvation or whatever is happening.

Music is going to swing, is going to be simple, is going to be impulsive. People are far more concerned now with honesty, with quite simply someone playing what they dig and with playing impulsively and realistically, than with people's hang-ups and people's image, with people's so-called talent or genius. So okay, poor Eric is going to be a god again. But he was born to be a god and he always will.

Rock and roll is going to become down-home, it's going to become realistic. It's going to become the answer to the day's problems. It's going to become part of everybody's life from now on. You can't switch it off, you can't change what it is so far. You can't change the old classics, you can't stop the classics being born.

What are the modern classics? What are the classic rock and roll songs since the Beatles?

"Wild Thing," "I Got You Babe," "Satisfaction," "My Generation." There's lots more, lots more. I'm just trying to think. "Eleanor Rigby." "Reach Out I'll Be There" I thought was incredible. It's difficult to say, because everything is so fucking good. There are a lot of classics and there is a lot of good rock and roll and it is one of the reasons it's going to have enough impetus to carry it through to the next transition.

**People are always trying to find a parallel with jazz.
Do you see what happened to jazz happening here?**

No. Jazz totally absolutely boiled down to a different kettle of fish. Because of the audiences. Audiences were a different breed entirely. If you're talking about the days when the people used to do the black bottom, then maybe you're getting nearer to what pop music is equivalent to today.

Jazz, in its entirety — modern jazz, progressive jazz — hasn't had the effect on the world in fucking twenty-five years that pop has had in one year today. Geniuses like Charlie Parker are completely unrecognized by the world and yet groups like the Rolling Stones — very normal, very regular guys — are incredibly well-known. This is true of everything. The whole system is a different thing entirely. This is what the jazz listener was like. Okay, he'd have a few beers and he'd go down to the fucking Village Gate and shout out one "Yeah" in a night, when he thought that someone had played something quite clever. But he didn't know what they were into. I just about know what they're into today, listening to some recordings that Charlie Parker made nearly twenty-five years ago. God knows what people thought then.

The audiences then were smaller, they became snobbish, racist. They were pompous jazz audiences. They became slow to catch on to new ideas. They became prejudiced, dogmatic, everything bad. While pop music is everything good.

Pop is everything; it's all sugar and spice, it really is. Pop audiences are the cream of today's music listening audiences. They're not the classical snobs who sit by their poxy Fisher amplifiers and listen to Leonard Bernstein conducting. Not knowing that Leonard Bernstein is completely stoned out of his crust and grooving to high heaven, thinking, "What a fine, excellent recording this is, what a fine conductor Leonard Bernstein is, really fine," and not knowing what the fucking hell is going on.

Pop's audience is right alongside; they know what's happening.

Pop hasn't yet confused anybody, it really hasn't. It's kept up with the people, it's kept in time with the people. The panic now is that the people feel it going out of step. They felt it go out of step in England and completely rebelled.

People just felt that pop was getting out of their hands; groups like the Pink Floyd were appearing, scary groups, psychedelic. So they completely freaked out. Nothing like the down-home Rolling Stones who used to have a good old-fashioned piss against a good old-fashioned garage attendant. This Pink Floyd — what were they all about? With their flashing lights and all taking trips and one of them's psycho. "What's this all about? That's not my bag."

So they all turn over to good old Engelbert Humperdinck, who is a phenomena of our age in England. Yet it's a sign of the revolt; it's a sign of the fact that the music got out of step with the people.

Why did it happen in England?

Europe is a piss place for music and it's a complete incredible fluke that England ever got it together. England has got all the bad points of Nazi Germany, all the pompous pride of France, all the old-fashioned patriotism of the old Order of the Empire. It's got everything that's got nothing to do with music. All the European qualities which should enhance, which should come out in music, England should be able to benefit by, but it doesn't.

And just all of a sudden, *bang! Wack! Zap-swock!* Out of nowhere, there it is: the Beatles. Incredible. How did they ever appear then on this poxy little shit-stained island? Out of the Germans you can accept Wagner, out of the French you can accept Debussy, and even out of the Russians you can accept Tchaikovsky. All these incredible people. Who's England got? Purcell? He's a gas but he's one of the only guys we've got, and Benjamin Britten today who copies Purcell. There's so few people.

And all of a sudden there's the Beatles, with their little funny "We write our own songs." "Don't you have ghostwriters?"

It's difficult to talk about rock and roll. It's difficult because it's essentially a category and a category which embodies something which transcends the category. The category itself becomes meaningless. The words "rock and roll" don't begin to conjure up any form of conversation in my mind because they are so puny compared to what they are applied to. But "rock and roll" is by far the better expression than "pop." It means nothing.

It's a good thing that you've got a machine, a radio that puts out good rock and roll songs and it makes you groove through the day. That's the game, of course: when you are listening to a rock and roll song the way you listen to "Jumpin' Jack Flash," or something similar, that's the way you should really spend your whole life. That's how you should be all the time: just grooving to something simple, something basically good, something effective, and something not too big. That's what life is.

Rock and roll is one of the keys, one of the many, many keys to a very complex life. Don't get fucked up with all the many keys. Groove to rock and roll and then you'll probably find one of the best keys of all.

BOB DYLAN

[1969]

I T WAS my dream to interview Bob. He said he would meet me and we could talk about doing one. He was going to check me out first. He showed up at my hotel room in New York City one fall morning, just himself, like a normal person. I don't know what version of him I was expecting, but it wasn't a plainspoken, reserved young man just a few years older than me, carefully taking a measure of the kid with the new rock paper from San Francisco that was named after one of his songs.

Bob had given few big interviews in his early career; full of hilarious mythmaking and paradox. He had also held a few press conferences that were a buffet of improv comedy and obfuscation. He was not known for his love and respect for reporters.

Bob had a motorcycle accident in 1966 and had been in seclusion for two years. There had been no records or performances. The interview I was asking him for would be a big scoop for us, scrutinized and decoded throughout the Dylan world.

It took another eight months to set a date, which turned out to be the one on which Judy Garland's funeral was taking place at the Frank Campbell Funeral Chapel, around the corner from the Stanhope Hotel, where we met for the interview. We could hear the Judy fans waiting in the streets below as we sat upstairs and talked.

I liked him immediately. He was prepared to do this interview seriously and respectfully. There was no way I was going to obtain a searching examination of his life and genius, his gift from God. One doesn't discuss this kind of stuff, although it is exactly what you want to know. My life was catalyzed by his music and poetry. It changed me forever. He spoke my truth. I was just one of thousands. How to act around him? How can you not tell him this? Not ask him, "Who are you? What does it mean, Bob?"

That was not the road I was going down. This was going to be a check-in, a series of snapshots, not a portrait. I thought the way in was through the music and his records, though you do not ask what a song is about or what a lyric means. I intended to ask about his image, his business, and how he handled the intensity with which people regarded him, and the weird energy that came with it.

Bob doesn't discuss all this, even if he has given it a lot of thought, as I am sure he had. He will answer in his way, honestly but deflecting. He is witty, as can be easily seen in his writing. If he doesn't want to answer, he just won't. No matter how long you wait, or how you rephrase the question, he doesn't budge. In his reply to my question about his then-manager Albert Grossman, observe carefully how much fun he has dancing around the answer. When I reread this interview fifty years later, what stands out is his humor and honesty, his playful spirit. His answers were simple and straight. He looked you in the eye and his twinkled.

Bob Dylan is an incandescent moral and literary figure as well as a musical genius. Bob is someone who was — and still is — the most profound writer of our times. He transformed popular art, particularly music, forever; and he forever transformed America and our understanding of our own country.

––––––––––––––

Why haven't you worked in so long?

Well, I do work, but working on the road...Jann, I'll tell you, I was on the road for almost five years. It wore me down. I was on drugs, a lot of things. A lot of things just to keep going. And I don't want to live that way anymore. I'm just waiting for a better time, you know what I mean?

What would you do that would make the tour that you're thinking about doing different from the ones you did do?

Well, I'd like to slow down the pace a little. The next show's going to be a lot different from the last show. The last show, during the first half of what was about an hour, I only did maybe six songs. My songs were long, long songs. That's why I had to start dealing with a lot of different methods of keeping myself awake, alert because I had to remember all the words to those songs. Now I've got a whole bag of new songs. I've written them for the road. They're going to sound a lot better than they do on record. My songs always sound a lot better in person than they do on the record.

On *Nashville Skyline*, who does the arrangements? The studio musicians or . . .

Boy, I wish you could've come along the last time we made an album. You'd've probably enjoyed it, because you see right there how it's done. We just take a song; I play it and everyone else just sort of fills in behind it. No sooner you got that done, and at the same time you're doing that, there's someone in the control booth who's turning all those dials to where the proper sound is coming in, and then it's done. Just like that.

On Nashville Skyline, do you have any song that you particularly dig?

"Tonight I'll Be Staying Here with You." There's a movie out now called *Midnight Cowboy*. You know the song on the album "Lay Lady Lay"? Well, I wrote that song for that movie. I like "Tell Me That It Isn't True," although it came out completely different than I'd written it. It came out real slow and mellow. I had it written as sort of a jerky, kind of polka-type thing. I wrote it in F. That's what gives it kind of a new sound. There's not many on that album that aren't in F. I had those chords which gives it a certain sound. I try to be a little different on every album.

I'm sure you read the reviews of Nashville Skyline.
Everybody remarks on the change of your singing style.

Well, Jann, I'll tell you something. There's not too much of a change in my singing style, but I'll tell you something which is true: I stopped smoking. When I stopped smoking, my voice changed so drastically, I couldn't believe it myself. That's true. I tell you, you stop smoking those cigarettes [laughter] and you'll be able to sing like Caruso.

How many songs did you go into Nashville Skyline with?

The first time I went into the studio I had, I think, four songs. I pulled that instrumental one out... I needed some songs with an instrumental... then Johnny [Cash] came in and did a song with me. I wrote one in the motel and then pretty soon the whole album started filling in together, and we had an album. We didn't go down with that in mind. That's why I wish you were there. You could've really seen it happen. It just manipulated out of nothing.

**What did you do in the year between *Blonde on Blonde*
and *John Wesley Harding*?**

Well, I was on tour part of that time, Australia, Sweden. Then I came back home. *Blonde on Blonde* was up on the charts at this time. I had a one-month vacation and I was going to go back on the road again. I had a dreadful motorcycle accident...which put me away for a while. I still didn't sense the importance of that accident till at least a year after that. I realized that it was a real accident. I thought that I was just going to get up and go back to doing what I was doing before...but I couldn't do it anymore.

What change did the motorcycle accident make?

It limited me. It's hard to speak about the change, you know? It's not the type of change that one can put into words besides the physical change. I had a busted vertebrae — neck vertebrae. And there's really not much to talk about. I don't want to talk about it.

**You must have had time to think. That was the ABC-TV
show? What happened to the tapes of that?
How come that never got shown?**

Well, I could make an attempt to answer that, but...[laughs]... I think my manager could probably answer it a lot better.

I don't think he answers too many questions.

Doesn't he? He doesn't answer questions? Well, he's a nice guy. He'll usually talk to you if you show some enthusiasm for what you're talking about. As far as I know, it will be sold, or a deal will be made. That's what I'm told. But you see, Jann, I don't hold these movie people in too high a position. You know this movie *Don't Look Back?* Well, that splashed my face all over the world. I didn't get a penny from that movie. So when people say why don't you do this and why don't you do that, people don't know half of what a lot of these producers and people, lawyers do. I'm an easygoing kind of fellow, I'm forgive and forget. I like to think that way. But I'm a little shy of these people. I'm not interested in finding out any more about any film.

Did you like *Don't Look Back?*

I'd like it a lot more if I got paid for it [laughter].

**What is the nature of your acquaintance
with John Lennon?**

Oh, I always love to see John. Always. He's a wonderful fellow and I always like to see him.

**He said that the first time that you met, in New York,
it was a very uptight situation.**

It probably was, yes. You know how it used to be for them. They couldn't go out of their room. They used to tell me you could hardly get in to see them. There used to be people surrounding them, not only in the streets, but in the corridors in the hotel. I should say it was uptight.

Do you keep up with current music?

Well, I try to keep up-to-date. I realize I don't do a very good job in keeping up-to-date, but I try to. I don't know half the groups that are playing around now. I don't know half of what I should. See, I never saw Traffic...I never even saw Cream. I feel bad about those things, but what can I do?

I'm going to see this new group called Blind Faith. I'm going to make it my duty to go see them because they'll probably be gone [laughter] in another year or so. So I'd better get up there quick and see them. Stevie Winwood, he came to see us in Manchester. That was 1966. Or was it Birmingham?

There was a series recently in the *Village Voice* about your growing up, living, and going to high school. Was it accurate?

Well, it was accurate as far as this fellow who was writing it, was using me to write his story. So I feel a little unusual in this case, because I can see through this writer's aims. But as far as liking it or disliking it, I didn't do neither of those things. It's just publicity from where I am. So if they want to spend six or seven issues writing about me [laughs], as long as they get it right, you know, as long as they get it in there, I can't complain.

The one thing I don't like is the way this writer talked about my father who has passed away. I didn't dig him talking about my father and using his name. Now that's the only thing about the article I didn't dig. That boy has got some lessons to learn.

What did he say?

He didn't have no right to speak about my father, who has passed away. If he wants to do a story on me, that's fine. I don't care what he wants to say about me. But I got the feeling that he was taking advantage of some good people that I used to know and he was making fun of a lot of things. I got the feeling he was making fun of quite a few things, this fellow, Toby. You know what I mean, Jann? Soooo...we'll just let that stand as it is. For now.

I've gone through all the collected articles that have appeared, all the early ones and Columbia Records' biographies — that's got the story about running away from home at eleven and twelve and thirteen and a half... Why did you put out that story?

I didn't put out any of those stories!

Well, it's the standard Bob Dylan biography...

Well, you know how it is, Jann. If you're sittin' in a room, and you have to have something done... I remember once, I was playing at Town Hall, and the producer of it came over with that biography... You know, I'm a songwriter, I'm not a biography writer, and I need a little help with these things.

So if I'm sitting in a room with some people, and I say, "Come on, now, I need some help; gimme a biography," so there might be three or four people there, and out of those three or four people maybe they'll come up with something, come up with a biography. So we put it down, it reads well, and the producer of the concert is satisfied. In fact, he even gets a kick out of it. You dig what I mean?

But in actuality, this thing wasn't written for hundreds of thousands of people. It was just a little game for whoever was going in there and getting a ticket, they get one of these things, too. That's just show business. So you do that, and pretty soon you've got a million people who get it on the side. They start thinkin' that it's written all for them. And it's not written for them, it was written for someone who bought the ticket to the concert. You got all these other people taking it too seriously. Do you know what I mean? So a lot of things have been blown out of proportion.

Are there any artists around today that you'd like to produce?

Well, there was some talk about producing Burt Lancaster doing the hymn "I Saw St. Augustine"...

Why didn't you publish *Tarantula?*

Well…it's a long story. It begins with when I suddenly began to sell quite a few records, and a certain amount of publicity began to be carried in all the major news magazines about this "rising young star." Well, this industry being what it is, book companies began sending me contracts, because I was doing interviews before and after concerts, and reporters would say things like, "What else do you write?" And I would say, "Well, I don't write much of anything else." And they would say, "Oh, come on. You must write other things. Tell us something else. Do you write books?" And I'd say, "Sure, I write books."

After the publishers saw that I wrote books, they began to send me contracts. Doubleday, Macmillan, Hill & Range [laughter]. We took the biggest one and then owed them a book. You follow me? But there was no book. We just took the biggest contract. Why? I don't know. Why I was told to do it, I don't know. Anyway, I owed them a book.

I said, "Wow, I've done many things before, it's not so hard to write a book." So I sat down and wrote them a book in the hotel rooms and different places, plus I got a lot of other papers laying around that other people had written, so I threw it all together in a week and sent it to them.

Well, it wasn't long after that when I got it back to proofread it. I got it back and I said, "My gosh, did I write this? I'm not going to have this out." Do you know what I mean? "I'm not going to put this out. The folks back home just aren't going to understand this at all." I said, "Well, I have to do some corrections on this," I told them, and set about correcting it. I told them I was improving it.

Boy, they were hungry for this book. They didn't care what it was. People up there were saying, "Boy, that's the second James Joyce," and "Jack Kerouac again," and they were saying, "Homer revisited"…and they were all just talking through their heads.

They just wanted to sell books, that's all they wanted to do. It wasn't about anything. I figured they had to know that, they were in the business of it. I knew that, and I was just nobody. If I knew it, where were they at? They were just playing with me. My book.

So I wrote a new book. I figured I was satisfied with it and I sent that in. Wow, they looked at that and said, "Well, that's another book." And I said, "Well, but it's better." And they said, "Okay, we'll print this." So they printed that up and sent that back to proofread it. I proofread it — I just looked at the first paragraph — and knew I just couldn't let that stand. So I took the whole thing with me on tour. I was going to rewrite it all. Carried a typewriter around the world, trying to meet this deadline which they'd given me to put this book out. They just backed me into a corner. A lot of invisible people. So finally, I had a deadline on it, and was working on it before my motorcycle accident. And I was studying all kinds of different books and how I wanted them to print the book by this time. I also was studying at lot of other poets at this time. I had books which I figured could lead me somewhere and I was using a little bit from everything.

But still, it wasn't any book; it was just to satisfy the publishers who wanted to print something that we had a contract for. Follow me? So eventually, I had my motorcycle accident and that just got me out of the whole thing, because I didn't care anymore. As it stands now, Jann, I could write a book. But I'm going to write it first, and then give it to them. You know what I mean?

**Do you have any particular subject
in mind, or plan, for a book?**

Do you?

For yours or mine?

[Laughs] For any of them.

**What writers today do you dig? Like, who would you read
if you were writing a book? Mailer?**

All of them. There's something to be learned from them all.

**What about the poets? You once said something
about Smokey Robinson...**

I didn't mean Smokey Robinson, I meant Arthur Rimbaud. I don't know how I could've gotten Smokey Robinson mixed up with Arthur Rimbaud [laughter]. But I did.

Do you see Allen Ginsberg much?

Not at all. Not at all.

Do you think he had any influence on your songwriting at all?

I think he did at a certain period. That period of... "Desolation Row," that kind of New York–type period, when all the songs were just "city songs." His poetry is city poetry. Sounds like the city.

**How much of your songwriting has connected to the drug
experience? Not in the sense of them being "psychedelic music"
or drug songs, but having come out of the drug experience.**

How so?

**In terms of a level of perceptions... the kind of awareness
in the songs...**

Awareness of the minute. You mean that?

An awareness of the mind.

I would say so.

Did taking drugs influence the songs?

No, not the writing of them, but it did keep me up there to pump them out.

Many people — writers, college students, college writers — all feel tremendously affected by your music and what you're saying in the lyrics.

Did they?

Sure. They felt it had a particular relevance to their lives. You must be aware of the way that people come on to you.

Not entirely. Why don't you explain to me?

I guess if you reduce it to its simplest terms, the expectation of your audience — the portion of your audience that I'm familiar with — feels that you have the answer.

What answer?

Like from the film *Don't Look Back*, people asking you, "Why? What is it? Where is it at?" People are tremendously hung up on what you write and what you say. Do you react to that at all? Do you feel responsible to those people?

I don't want to make anybody worry about it. But boy, if I could ease someone's mind, I'd be the first one to do it. I want to lighten every load. Straighten out every burden. I don't want any-body to be hung up... [laughs]... especially over me, or anything I do. That's not the point at all.

> Let me put it another way... What I'm getting at is that
> you're an extremely important figure in music
> and an extremely important figure in the experience
> of growing up today. Whether you put yourself in that
> position or not, you're in that position. And you must have
> thought about it... and I'm curious to know
> what you think about that...

What would I think about it? What can I do?

> You wonder if you're really that person.

What person?

> A great "youth leader"...

If I thought I was that person, wouldn't I be out there doing it? Wouldn't I be, if I thought I was meant to do that, wouldn't I be doing it? I don't have to hold back. This Maharishi, he thinks that, right? He's out there doing it. If I thought that, I'd be out there doing it. Don't you agree, right? So obviously, I don't think that.

> What do you feel about unwillingly
> occupying that position?

I can see that position filled by someone else... not by... the position you're speaking of... I play music, man. I write songs. I have a certain balance about things, and I believe there should be an order to everything. Underneath it all, I believe, also, that there are people trained for this job that you're talking about, the "youth leader" type of thing, you know? There must be people trained to do this type of work. And I'm just one person, doing what I do. Trying to get along...staying out of people's hair, that's all.

You've also been a tremendous influence on a lot of musicians and writers. They're very obviously affected by your style, the way you do things...

Who?

Do you see any influence in the Motown? All those things that the Motown records are doing now? Like "Runaway Child" and those kind of things.

Motown wasn't doing those kind of records a few years ago, were they? I have always liked the Motown records. Always. But because I like them so much, I see that change. What do you think they're doing, Jann? Are they really sincere and all that kind of thing?

Have you got anything to do with that change?

Have I? Not that I know of.

Do you think that you've played any role in the change of popular music in the last four years?

I hope not [laughs].

Well, a lot of people say you have.

[Laughs] Well, you know, I'm not one to argue [laughs].

There's a lot of talk about your relationship
with Albert Grossman, and whether he's going
to continue to manage you.

Well, as far as I know, things will remain the same, until the length of our contract. And if we don't sign another contract, or if he does not have a hand in producing my next concerts or have a hand in any of my next work, it's only because he's too busy. Because he's got so many acts now, it's so hard for him to be in all places all the time. It's the old story: you can't be in two places at once. That old story. You know what I mean?

When does your contract with him expire?

Sometime this year.

You were supposed to leave Columbia and sign with
MGM? A million dollars...what happened to that?

It...went up in smoke.

Did you want a new label?

I didn't, no.

Who did?

I believe my advisers.

You've been very reluctant to talk to reporters, the press,
and so on... Why is that?

Why would you think?

Well, I know why you won't go on those things.

Well, if you know why, you tell them, because I find it hard to talk about. People don't understand how the press works. People don't understand that they just use you to sell papers. And in a certain way, that's not bad, but when they misquote you all the time, and when they just use you to fill in some story ... And when you read it after, it isn't anything like the way you pictured it happening. Well, anyhow, it hurts. It hurts because you think you were just played for a fool. And the more hurts you get, the less you want to do it. Ain't that correct?

Were there any writers that you met that you liked? That you felt did good jobs? Wrote accurate stories.

On what?

On you. For instance, I remember two big pieces — one was in *The New Yorker*, by Nat Hentoff ...

Yeah, I like them all, whether I feel bad about them or not. I seldom get a kick out of them, Jann, but I just can't be spending my time reading what people write [laughter]. I don't know anybody who can, do you?

Let me explain something about this interview. If you give one magazine an interview, then the other magazine wants an interview. If you give one to one, then the other one wants one. So pretty soon, you're in the interview business, you're just giving interviews. Well, as you know, this can really get you down. Doing nothing but giving interviews.

So the only way you can do it is to give press conferences. But you have to have something to give a press conference about. Follow me? So that's why I don't give interviews. There's no mysterious reason to it, there's nothing organized behind it. It's just that if you give an interview to one magazine, then another one'll get mad.

Why have you chosen to do this interview?

Because this is a music paper. Why would I want to give an interview to *Look* magazine? Tell me, why?

I don't know... To sell records.

To sell records, I could do it. Right. But I have a gold record without doing it, do you understand me? Well, if I had to sell records, I'd be out there giving interviews to everybody. Don't you see? Mr. Clive Davis, he was president of Columbia Records, and he said he wouldn't be surprised if this last album sold a million units. Without giving one interview. Now you tell me, Jann, why am I going to go out and give an interview?

To get hassled...

Why would I want to go out and get hassled? If they're going to pay me, I mean, who wants to do that? I don't.

———————

Do you set aside a certain amount of time during the day to write? How much of the day do you think about songwriting?

I try to get it when it comes. I play the guitar wherever I find one. But I try to write the song when it comes. I try to get it all because if you don't get it all, you're not going to get it. So the best kinds of songs you can write are in motel rooms and cars, places which are all temporary. Because you're forced to do it. Rather, it lets you go into it.

You go into your kitchen and try to write a song, and you can't write a song. I know people who do this, I know some songwriters who go to work every day at eight thirty and come home at five. And usually bring something back. I mean, that's legal, too. It just depends on how you do it. Me, I don't have those kind of things known to me yet, so I just get them when they come. And when they don't come, I don't try for it.

**Have you written any songs lately specifically
for any other artists to do? Or any
of your old songs.**

I wrote "To Be Alone with You" — that's on *Nashville Skyline* — I wrote it for Jerry Lee Lewis. He was down there when we were listening to the playbacks, and he came in. He was recording an album next door. He listened to it. I think we sent him a dub. "Peggy Day" — I kind of had the Mills Brothers in mind when I did that one [laughter].

Have you approached them yet? [Laughter]

No, unfortunately, I haven't.

**What do you look for when you make a record?
What qualities do you judge it
by when you hear it played back?**

The spirit. I like to hear a good lick once in a while. Maybe it's the spirit…Don't you think so? If the spirit's not there, it don't matter how good a song it is.

What was the origin of that collection of songs, now called
The Basement Tapes?

The origin of it? What do you mean? That was done out in somebody's basement. Just a basement tape. They weren't demos for myself, they were demos of the songs. I was being pushed again into coming up with some songs. You know how those things go. They were just fun to do. That's all. They were a kick to do. Fact, I'd do it all again. That's really the way to do a recording, in a peaceful, relaxed setting in somebody's basement. With the windows open... and a dog lying on the floor.

Do you have any idea how much money your publishing
has brought in over the last five years?

Well, now, that's difficult to answer because my songs are divided up into three — no, four companies. So there you have it. There you have it right there.

Which companies?

Well, I've got songs with Leeds Music. I've got songs with Witmark Music. I've got a bunch of songs with Dwarf Music. I've got songs in Big Sky Music. My songs are divided up.

Do you own Big Sky Music wholly yourself?

It's my company. I chose to start this company.

You put all the estimated income from those four
companies together, or estimated gross income from
publishing from those, it must be a considerable...

Not as much as the Beatles.

Yeah, but other than the Beatles?

Not as much as those writers from Motown. You know there are many more musical organizations than me. They've got staffs of writers bringing in more money than you can dream of.

Any soul singers you particularly dig?

You mean rhythm and blues pop? Well, you know I've always liked Mavis Staples ever since she was a little girl. She's always been my favorite, she's always had my favorite voice.

Have you heard their new Stax album?

I heard one of the ones they're doing with other people. Yeah, I heard that, that one that Pops Staples did [laughs]. It's ridiculous. Oh, Steve Cropper did do a nice song on that album that he wrote, called "Water." I've always dug Steve Cropper's guitar playing. Ever since the first Booker T. record. I heard that back in the Midwest. Yeah, everybody was playing like him.

What is your day-to-day life like?

Hmmmm...there's no way I could explain that to you, Jann. Every day is different. Depends on what I'm doing. Well, I may be fiddling around with the car or I may be painting a boat, or possibly washing the windows. I just do what has to be done. I play a lot of music. I'm always trying to put shows together, which never come about. I don't know what it is, but sometimes we get together and I say, "Okay, let's take six songs and do them up." So we do six songs, we got them in, let's say, forty minutes. We got a stopwatch timing them. But nothing happens to it. We could do anything with it, but I mean...

Boy, I hurried, I hurried for a long time. I'm sorry I did. All the time you're hurrying, you're not really as aware as you should be. You're trying to make things happen instead of just letting it happen. You follow me?

You said in one of your songs on *Highway 61*, "I need a dump truck, Mama, to unload my head." Do you still need a dump truck or something? Asking you something like that is awkward.

Well, I don't find anything awkward about it. I think it's going real great.

The purpose of any interview is to let the person who's being interviewed unload his head.

Well, that's what I'm doing.

And trying to draw that out is...

Boy, that's good. That'd be a great title for a song. "Unload my head. Going down to the store...going down to the corner to unload my head." I'm going to write that up when I get back: [laughter] "Going to Tallahassee to unload my head."

What do you think can happen with your career as a singer?

What are the possibilities?

Go on the road, continue to make records. For instance, do you foresee continuing to make records?

If they're enjoyable. I'm going to have to receive a certain amount of enjoyment out of my work pretty soon. I'd like to keep a little closer to the studios than I am now. It's awful hard for me to make records when I've got to go four thousand miles away, you know?

Can you see a time when you would stop making records?

Well, let's put it this way: making a record isn't any more than just recording a song, for me. So, if I was to stop writing songs, I would stop recording. Or let's say if I was to stop singing, I guess I would stop recording. But I don't foresee that. I'll be recording, because that's a way for me to unload my head.

What are the changes that have gone on between the time you did *Highway 61* and *Nashville Skyline* or *John Wesley Harding?*

The changes. I don't think I know exactly what you mean.

How has life changed for you? Your view of what you do...

Not much. I'm still the same person. I'm still going at it in the same old way. Doing the same old thing.

Do you think you've settled down, and slowed down?

I hope so. I was going at a tremendous speed...At the time of my *Blonde on Blonde* album, I was going at a tremendous speed.

How did you make the change? The motorcycle accident?

I just took what came. That's how I made the changes. I took what came.

What do they come from?

They come from the same sources that everybody else's do. I don't know if it comes from within oneself any more than it comes from without oneself. Or outside of oneself. Don't you see what I mean? Maybe the inside and the outside are both the same. I don't know. But I feel it just like everyone else. What's that old line — there's a line from one of those old songs — "I can recognize it in others, I can feel it in myself." You can't say that's from the inside or the outside; it's like both.

What influenced the change from *Highway 61* to *Nashville Skyline*?

I'm not probably as aware of that change as you are, because I haven't listened to that album *Highway 61* for a while. I'd probably do myself a lot of good going back and listening to it. I'm not aware of that change. I probably could pinpoint it right down if I heard that album, but I haven't heard it for quite a while.

Are there any old albums that you do listen to?

Well, I don't sit around and listen to my records, if that's what you mean.

Like picking up a high school yearbook, and just...

Oh, I love to do that... every once in a while. That's the way I listen to my records: every once in a while. Every once in a while I say, "Well, I'd like to see that fellow again."

Are there any albums or tracks from the albums that you think now were particularly good?

Oh yeah, quite a few.

Which ones?

Well, if I was performing now...if I was making personal appearances, you would know which ones, because I would play them. But I don't know which ones I'd play now. I'd have to pick and choose. Certainly couldn't play them all.

Thinking about the titles on *Bringing It All Back Home*.

I like "Maggie's Farm." I always liked "Highway 61 Revisited." I always liked that song. "Mr. Tambourine Man" and "Blowin' in the Wind" and "Girl from the North Country" and "Boots of Spanish Leather" and "Times They Are a-Changin'"...I liked "Ramona"...

Where did you write "Desolation Row"? Where were you when you wrote that?

I was in the back of a taxicab.

In New York?

Yeah.

During the period where you were recording songs with a full-scale band, of those rock and roll songs that you did, which do you like?

The best rock and roll songs? Which ones are there?

"Like a Rolling Stone"...

Yeah, I probably liked that the best. I can hear it now, now that you've mentioned it. I like that sound.

On *Nashville Skyline,* you use lots of echo,
and a lot of limiting. What made you decide to alter your
voice technically and use those kind of studio effects?
Rather than doing it more or less flat.

Well, how would you have liked it better? Would you have
liked it flat?

I dig the echo.

I do, too. I dig the echo myself. That's why we did it that way.
The old records do sound flat. There's just a flatness to them,
they're like two-dimensional. Isn't that right? Well, in this day and
age, there's no reason to make records like that.

There's a cat named Alan Weberman who writes
in the *East Village Other.* He calls himself the world's
leading Dylanologist. You know him?

Is this the guy who tears up all my songs? Well, he oughta
take a rest. He's way off. I saw something he wrote about "All
Along the Watchtower," and boy, let me tell you, this boy's off. Not
only did he create some type of fantasy — he had Allen Ginsberg
in there — he couldn't even hear the words to the song right. He
didn't hear the song right. Can you believe that? I bet he's a hard-
working fellow, though. I bet he really does a good job if he could
find something to do but it's too bad it's just my songs, because I
don't really know if there's enough material in my songs to sustain
someone who is really out to do a big job. You understand what I
mean?
I mean a fellow like that would be much better off writing
about Tolstoy, or Dostoyevsky, or Freud, doing a really big analysis

of somebody who has countless volumes of writings. But here's me, just a few records out. Somebody devoting so much time to those few records, when there's such a wealth of material that hasn't even been touched yet, or hasn't even been heard or read...that escapes me. Does it escape you?

He's to some degree representative of thousands of people who do take it seriously.

Well, that's their own business. Why don't I put it that way? I'm the source of that and I don't know if it's my business or not, but I'm the source of it. You understand? So I see it a little differently than all of them do.

Does the intensity of some of the response annoy you?

No. No, I rather enjoy it.

Did you vote for president?

We got down to the polls too late [laughter].

People are always asking about if a song is based on some real person. Are there any songs that you can relate to particular people, as having inspired the song?

Not now I can't.

What do you tell somebody who says, "What is 'Leopard-Skin Pill-Box Hat' about?"

It's just about that. I think that's something I might have taken out of the newspaper. Might have seen a picture of one in a department store window. There's really no more to it than that. I know it can get blown up into some kind of illusion. But in reality, it's no more than that. Just a leopard-skin pillbox. That's all.

What kind of sound did you hear when you went in to make *John Wesley Harding?*

I heard the sound that Gordon Lightfoot was getting, with Charlie McCoy and Kenny Buttrey. I'd used Charlie and Kenny both before, and I figured if he could get that sound, I could. But we couldn't get it [laughs]. It was an attempt to get it, but it didn't come off. We got a different sound. I don't know what you'd call that. It's a muffled sound.

There used to be a lot of friction in the control booth, on these records I used to make. I didn't know about it, I wasn't aware of them until recently. Somebody would want to put limiters on this and somebody would want to put an echo on that, someone else would have some other idea. And myself, I don't know anything about any of this. So I just have to leave it up in the air. In someone else's hands.

Was the friction between the engineer and the producer...

No, the managers and the advisers and the agents.

Do you usually have sessions at which all these people are there, or do you prefer to have the session closed?

Well, sometimes there's a whole lot of people. Sometimes you can't even move, there's so many people, and other times there's no one. Just the musicians. Well, it's much more comfortable when there's...oh, I don't know, I could have it both ways. Depends what kind of song I'm going to do. I might do a song where I want all those people around. Then I do another song, and have to shut the lights off, you know?

Was "Sad Eyed Lady of the Lowlands" originally planned as a whole side?

It started out as just a little thing, "Sad Eyed Lady of the Lowlands," but I got carried away, somewhere along the line. I just sat down at a table and started writing. At the session itself. And I just got carried away with the whole thing. I just started writing and I couldn't stop. After a period of time, I forgot what it was all about, and I started trying to get back to the beginning [laughs]. Yeah.

Did you plan to go down and make a double-record set?

No. Those things just happen when you have the material.

Do you like that album?

Blonde on Blonde? Yeah. But like I always think that a double set could be made into a single album. But I dug *Blonde on Blonde* and the Beatles' thing. They are like huge collections of songs. But a real great record can usually be compacted down...although the Beatles have that album, and *Blonde on Blonde* — I'm glad that there's two records, that there's that much...

How long did that take to record?

Blonde on Blonde? I was touring and I was doing it whenever I got a chance to get into the studio. So it was in the works for a while. I could only do maybe two or three songs at a time.

How long did *John Wesley Harding* take?

You mean how many sessions? That took three sessions, but we did them in a month. The first two sessions were maybe three weeks to a month apart, and the third one was about two weeks later.

John Wesley Harding — why did you call the album that?

Well, I called it that because I had that song, "John Wesley Harding." It didn't mean anything to me. It started out to be a long ballad, like maybe one of those old cowboy ballads. But in the middle of the second verse, I got tired. I had a tune, and I didn't want to waste the tune, it was a nice little melody, so I just wrote a quick third verse, and I recorded that. But it was a silly little song [laughs], It's not a commercial song in any kind of sense. At least, I don't think it is.

It was the one song on the album which didn't seem to fit in. And I had it placed here and there, and I didn't know what I was going to call the album anyway. No one else had any ideas either. I placed it last and I placed it in the middle somewhere, but it didn't seem to work. So somehow the idea came up to just put it first and get done with it right away, and that way if someone's listening to "All Along the Watchtower" and that comes up, and they won't say, "Wow, what's that?" [laughs].

You knew that cowboy...

I knew people were going to be brought down when they heard that, and say "Wow, what's that?" A lot of people said that to me, but I knew it in front. I knew people were going to listen to that song and say that they didn't understand what was going on, but they would've singled that song out later, if we hadn't called the album *John Wesley Harding* and placed so much importance on that, for people to start wondering about it. If that hadn't been done, that song would've come up and people would have said it was a throwaway song. It would have probably got in the way of some other songs. See, I try very hard to keep my songs from interfering with each other. That's all I'm trying to do. Place them all out on the disc.

Why did you choose the name of the outlaw John Wesley Harding?

Well, it fits in tempo. Fits right in tempo. Just what I had at hand.

What about *Blonde on Blonde*?

Well, that title came up when... I don't even recall how exactly it came up, but I do know it was all in good faith. It has to do with just the word. I don't know who thought of that. I certainly didn't.

Of all the albums as albums, excluding your recent ones, which one do you think was the most successful in what it was trying to do? Which was the most fully realized, for you?

I think the second one [*The Freewheelin' Bob Dylan*]. I felt real good about doing an album with my own material. My own material and I picked a little on it, picked the guitar, and it was a big Gibson — I felt real accomplished on that. "Don't Think Twice." Got a chance to do some of that. Got a chance to play in open tuning... "Oxford Town," I believe that's on that album. That's open tuning. I got a chance to do talking blues. I got a chance to do ballads, like "Girl from the North Country." It's just because it had more variety. I felt good at that.

Of the electric ones, which do you prefer?

Well, sound-wise, I prefer this last one, because it's got the sound. See, I'm listening for sound now.

As a collection of songs?

Songs? Well, this last album maybe means more to me, because I did undertake something and in a certain sense there's a certain pride in that.

Where did the name *Nashville Skyline*...

Well, I always like to tie the name of the album in with some song. Or if not some song, some kind of general feeling. I think that just about fit because it was less in the way, and less specific than any of the other ones on there. Certainly couldn't call the album *Lay Lady Lay*. I wouldn't have wanted to call it that, although that name was brought up. It didn't get my vote, but it was brought up. *Peggy Day — Lay Peggy Day*, that was brought up. A lot of things were brought up. *Tonight I'll Be Staying Here with Peggy Day*. That's another one. Some of the names just didn't seem to fit. *Girl from the North Country*. That was another title which didn't really seem to fit. Picture me on the front holding a guitar and *Girl from the North Country* printed on top. [Laughs] *Tell Me That It Isn't Peggy Day*. I don't know who thought of that one.

What do you see yourself as? A poet, a singer, a rock and roll star, married man...

All of those. I see myself as it all. Married man, poet, singer, songwriter, custodian, gatekeeper...all of it. I'll be it all. I feel "confined" when I have to choose one or the other. Don't you?

JOHN LENNON

[1970]

I HAD BEEN on a long and winding path up a mountain whose summit couldn't be seen through the cloud layer. I was in search of the music and the mysteries of the gods who lived there.

The Beatles were the gods; they could send their music to hundreds of millions across the planet through the miracle of television, radio, and records.

We followed their lives, their trials and travels, as if they were the operatic Hindu deities or the sometimes cruel Olympians of Greek mythology. These were beneficent gods, gods of joy who came from Pepperland, where they all lived in a Yellow Submarine. Their message was joy ("Come on, it's such a joy / Come on and take it easy"), fun ("With a little help from my friends"), love ("Say the word and you'll be free"), play ("Dear Prudence, won't you come out to play?"), togetherness ("I am he as you are he as you are me and we are all together"), and peace ("Give peace a chance").

When I finally got to the mountaintop, there were no

blue skies, no strawberry fields, no newspaper taxis, and no Lucy in the Sky with Diamonds. John and Paul were breaking up, the sky was raining, and John was wielding lightning and thunder. Of all my interviews, this one was like catching the whirlwind.

My pilgrimage had begun with *A Hard Day's Night*, when I was seventeen. I created *Rolling Stone* in the year of *Sgt. Pepper's Lonely Hearts Club Band*. In a twist of fate, John Lennon was on the cover of our first issue. One year later, on our first anniversary, he was on the cover again, this time standing naked with Yoko Ono as if they were Adam and Eve. We got on board for their honeymoon "bed-in" in Amsterdam on their crusade for peace, and once again they were on the cover, this time holding the dove of peace. We often talked on the phone and were thus always able to report on the latest news from John and Yoko land.

Out of the blue, without notice, one day they walked into our offices in San Francisco in the summer of 1970. We spent the weekend together, riding cable cars, hanging out, and watching movies, including *Let It Be*, which melted them, myself, and my wife all to tears when it ended. He was in intensive psychotherapy in Los Angeles and agreed to give me the "big interview" later that year when he was done with coming to terms with the buried anger of his childhood.

John had started to write and record his first solo record, in parts a musical equivalent to Edvard Munch's painting *The Scream*. "God," he sang, "is a concept by which we measure our pain." The tracks are simple, stripped of ornament, just melody and the rock basics. The honesty is brutal and fairly upsetting. It is a far cry from the characteristic British credo of "Keep calm and carry on." He wanted to write about his truth, and he intended to take it to the unforgiving limit. He was haunted by being deserted by his father and mother as a child, and he was going to face it, and face us with it.

That record, *John Lennon/Plastic Ono Band,* is the soundtrack for this interview, and the interview can be seen as the liner notes for the record. They are primary source documents. John had decided to leave the Beatles, to sever the ties that bound him to Paul. In that process he had many memories to expunge, scores to settle, records to set straight. This is John's side of the Beatles story. This process was rough, often bitter, and painful to hear. It's all here.

There is a lot more than the breakup in the interview, which I titled *Lennon Remembers.* These are his personal and revelatory discussions about the Beatles, their early days, Brian Epstein, the songwriting partnership with Paul, their orgiastic and painful life on tour, their first acid trips, and their slow dissolution. It is the most vivid description of what Beatle life was like.

What John says about Paul is particularly tough to read. John's bitterness overshadows too much of his epilogue to the Beatles. He gave an honest appraisal of Paul's remarkable talents. His grievances were no less real than those between so many other great songwriting partnerships, from Gilbert and Sullivan to Jagger and Richards.

John was a commanding figure of the twentieth century. His life was tumultuous, often tortured. He contained multitudes: a jealous guy, a loving guy, foolish and playful, courageous and vulnerable, peaceful and angry, enlightened. He could not sit still nor stop talking. You may say he was a dreamer.

The finale on *Plastic Ono Band* is "God," in which Lennon renounces his belief in all forms of religion and fads — I Ching and the Bible, Jesus and Kennedy, Elvis and Bob Dylan, and...the Beatles. "The dream is over. What can I say?" he sang. "I was the walrus, but now I'm John. And so dear friends, you'll just have to carry on."

It's as sad — and majestic — a song as you could imagine. And just like that, the Beatles disappeared. Perhaps this is when the Sixties ended. The dream was over.

These four men appeared on earth at the same time and in the same provincial city. It could be just random chance. John Lennon and Paul McCartney each came with the gifts of words and voice, of melody and harmony that were unprecedented in modern times. Some say never before in history. Some say they were sent to save us. John Lennon said to save ourselves.

Do you think your singing is better on your new album, your first solo one?

Well, it's probably better because I've got the whole time to meself. I'm pretty good at home with me tapes [laughs]. But this time it was my album. It used to get a bit embarrassing in front of George and Paul because we know each other so well: "Oh, he's trying to be Elvis, oh, he's doing this now." We're a bit supercritical of each other. So we inhibited each other a lot. Now I had Yoko there and Phil [Spector] there, alternatively and together, who sort of love me, okay, so I can perform better. And I relaxed.

It says on the album that Yoko does "wind."

Yeah. Well, she plays wind. She played the atmosphere.
YOKO: I was around.
JOHN: No, she wasn't around, she has a musical ear and she can produce rock and roll. She can produce me, which she did for some of the tracks when Phil couldn't come at first. She knows when a bass sounds right and when the guy's playing out of rhythm.

What do you think of the album overall?

I think it's the best thing I've ever done. I think it's realistic and it's true to the me that has been developing over the years from "In My Life," "I'm a Loser," "Help!," "Strawberry Fields." They were all personal records. I always wrote about me and didn't really enjoy writing third-person songs about people who lived in concrete flats and things.

I like first-person music. But because of hang-ups and many other things, I would only now and then specifically write about me. And now I wrote all about me, and that's why I like it. It's me, and nobody else. I like it.

The only true songs I ever wrote were "Help!" and "Strawberry Fields." And I can name a few others, I can't think of them offhand, that I always considered my best songs. They were the ones that I really wrote from experience and not projecting myself into a situation and writing a nice story about it, which I always found phony. But I'd find occasion to do it because I've had to produce so much work or because I'd be so hung up I couldn't even think about myself.

On this album there's practically no imagery at all.
There's no "newspaper taxi"...

There was none in my head. There were no hallucinations. I was writing poetry then, and that's self-conscious poetry. But the poetry on this album is superior to anything I've done because it's not self-conscious in that way. I had the least trouble ever writing the songs.

The music is very simple and very sparse...

I always liked simple rock and nothing else. I was influenced by acid and got psychedelic, like the whole generation, but really, I like rock and roll. I express myself best in rock, and I had a few ideas to do *this* with "Mother" and *that* with "Mother," but the piano does it all for you. Your mind can do the rest of it. I think the backings are as complicated as the backings on any record you've ever heard. If you've got an ear, you can hear. Any musician will tell you, just play a note on a piano, it's got a lot of harmonics in it. So it got to that. What the hell, it didn't need anything else.

How did you put together that litany in "God"?

Well, like a lot of the words, they just came out of me mouth. It started off like that. "God" was stuck together from three songs almost. I had the idea, "God is the concept by which we measure our pain." So when you have a phrase like that, you just sit down and sing the first tune that comes into your head. And the tune is the simple [sings] "God is the concept — *bomp-bomp-bomp-bomp*" because I like that kind of music. And then I just rolled into it. [Sings] "I don't believe in magic" — and it was just going on in me head. And "I Ching" and "the Bible," the first three or four just came out, whatever came out.

When did you know that you were going to be working toward the line "I don't believe in Beatles"?

I don't know when I realized I was putting down all these things I didn't believe in. I could have gone on, it was like a Christmas card list — where do I end? Churchill, and who have I missed out? It got like that and I thought I had to stop...I was going to leave a gap and say, "Just fill in your own, for whoever you don't believe in." It just got out of hand. But Beatles was the final thing because it's like I no longer believe in myth, and Beatles is another myth. I don't believe in it. The dream's over. I'm not just talking about the Beatles is over, I'm talking about the generation thing. The dream's over, and I have personally got to get down to so-called reality.

What do your personal tastes run to?

"Wop bop a loo bop." You know? I like rock and roll, man, I — I don't like much else.

Why rock and roll?

That's the music that inspired me to play music. There's nothing conceptually better than rock and roll. No group, be it Beatles, Dylan, or Stones, has ever improved on "Whole Lotta Shakin' [Goin' On]" for my money. Maybe I'm like our parents, that's my period. I dig it and I'll never leave it.

Do you get any pleasure out of the top ten? Do you listen to the top ten?

No, I never listen, only when I'm recording or about to bring something out. And I'll listen, just before I record, to a few albums to see what people are doing, if they improved any or if anything has happened. And nothing's really happened. There's a lot of great guitarists and musicians around, but nothing's happening. I don't like the Blood, Sweat and Tears shit — I think all that is bullshit. Rock and roll is doing like jazz, as far as I can see. And the bullshitters are going off into that "excellentness," which I never believed in.

The Beatles were talked about as being four parts of the same person. What's happened to those four parts?

They remembered that they were four individuals. You see, we believed the Beatles myth, too. I don't know whether the others still believe it, but we were four guys that — I met Paul and said, "Do you want to join me band?," and then George joined and then

Ringo joined. We were just a band who made it very, very big—that's all. Our best work was never recorded.

Why?

Because we were performers in spite of what Mick [Jagger] says about us, in Liverpool, Hamburg, and around the dance halls. What we generated was fantastic when we played straight rock, and there was nobody to touch us in Britain. But as soon as we made it, the edges were knocked off. Brian Epstein put us in suits and all that, and we made it very, very big. We sold out. The music was dead before we even went on the theater tour of Britain. We were feeling shit already, because we had to reduce an hour or two hours' play—and which we were glad to do in one way—to twenty minutes, and go on and repeat the same twenty minutes every night. The Beatles' music died then, as musicians. That's why we never improved as musicians. We killed ourselves then to make it—and that was the end of it. George and I are more inclined to say that. We always missed the club dates because that's when we were playing music. Then later on we became technically efficient recording artists, which was another thing. Because we were competent people. Whatever media you put us in, we can produce something worthwhile.

How do you rate yourself as a guitarist? As a musician?

Well, it depends what kind of guitarist...

Rock and roll.

I'm okay. I'm not technically very good, but I can make it fucking howl and move. I was rhythm guitarist, and it's an important job. I can make a band drive.

How do you rate George?

He's pretty good. I prefer meself — I have to be honest. I'm really very embarrassed about my guitar playing in one way because it's very poor. I can never move. But I can make a guitar speak. I think there's a guy called Ritchie Valens — no, Richie Havens. Did he play very strange guitar? He's a black guy that was on at the Isle of Wight concert, sang "Strawberry Fields" or something. He plays one chord all the time — pretty funky guitar. He doesn't seem to be able to play in the real sense. I'm like that. But Yoko's made me get cocky about me guitar. One part of me says, "Yes, of course I can play because I can make a rock move." But the other part of me says, "Well, I wish I could just do it like B.B. King." If you put me with B.B., I'll feel silly. But I'm an artist and if you give me a tuba, I'll bring you something out of it.

You said that you can make the guitar speak. In which songs do you feel you've done that?

"I Found Out," I think it's nice. It drives along. I don't know, ask Eric Clapton, he thinks I can play [laughs]. A lot of you people want the technical thing, then you think, oh, well, that's like wanting technical films. Most critics of rock and roll and guitarists are in the stage of the Fifties where they wanted a technically perfect film finished for them and then they would feel happy. I'm a cinema verité guitarist-musician. You have to break down your barriers to be able to hear what I'm playing. There's a nice little bit I played on *Abbey Road*. Paul gave us each a piece, a little break where Paul plays, George plays, and I play. When you listen to it you know.

Which is that?

There's one bit, one of those where it stops, on "Carry That Weight," then suddenly it goes *boom-boom-boom* on the drums and we all take it in turns to play. I'm the third one on it. I have a definite style of playing, always had. But I was overshadowed. They call George the "invisible" singer; I'm the "invisible" guitarist.

You said you played the obbligato on "Get Back"?

I played the solo on that. When Paul was feeling kind, he'd give me a solo. Maybe if he was feeling guilty that he'd had most of the A sides or something, he'd give me a solo. And I played the solo on that. I think George produces some beautiful guitar playing, but I think he's too hung up to really let go. But so is Eric, really. Maybe he's changed. They're all so hung up. Well, we all are, that's the problem. But I really like B.B. King.

We saw *Let It Be* together in San Francisco. What were your feelings about that?

I felt sad. That film was set up by Paul, for Paul. That's one of the main reasons the Beatles ended, because...I can't speak for George, but I pretty damn well know, we got fed up with being sidemen for Paul. After Brian died, that's what began to happen to us. And the camerawork was set up to show Paul and not to show anybody else. That's how I felt about it. And on top of that, the people that cut it, cut it as "Paul is God" and we're just lying around there. And that's what I felt.

I knew there was some shots of Yoko and me that had been just chopped out of the film for no other reason than the people were oriented towards Engelbert Humperdinck. I felt sick.

How would you trace the breakup of the Beatles?

After Brian died, we collapsed. Paul took over and suppos-edly led us, you know. But what is leading us when we went round in circles? We broke up then. That was the disintegration.

When did you first feel that the Beatles had broken up?

I don't remember. I was in my own pain. I wasn't noticing, really. I just did it like a job. The Beatles broke up after Brian died. We made the double album, the set. It's like if you took each track off and put all mine and all George's. It's just like I told you many times, me and a backing group, Paul and a backing group. And I enjoyed it. But we broke up then.

**So Brian died and then what happened is
Paul started to take over?**

I don't know how much of this I want to put out, I'll tell you. I think Paul had an impression — he has it now, like a parent, that we should be thankful for what he did, for keeping the Beatles going. But when you look upon it objectively, he kept it going for his own sake. Not for my sake did Paul struggle. But Paul made an attempt to carry on as if Brian hadn't died. By saying, "Now, now, boys, we're going to make a record." And being the kind of person I am, I thought, "Well, you know, we're going to make a record, all right." So I went along, we went and made a record. And I suppose we made *Pepper*, I'm not sure.

That was before.

That was before Brian died. Oh, I see. Well, we made the double album then. But it was like that. Was *Magical Mystery Tour* after Brian? Paul had a tendency to just come along and say, "Well,

[I've] written ten songs, let's record now." And I said, "Give us a few days and I'll knock a few off." He came and showed me what his idea was for *Magical Mystery Tour* and how it went, the story and production, and he said, "Here's the segment, you write a little piece for that." And I thought, "Fuckin' hell, I've never made a film, what's he mean?" He said, "Write a script." So I ran off and wrote the dream sequence for the fat woman and all the things — the spaghetti and all that. So it was like that. George and I were sort of grumbling, "Fuckin' movie, well, we better do it." A feeling that we owed the public to do these things. So we made it.

When did your songwriting partnership with Paul end?

That ended, I don't know, around 1962 or something. If you give me the albums, I can tell you exactly who wrote what, and which line. We sometimes wrote together and sometimes didn't. But all our best work — apart from the early days, like "I Want to Hold Your Hand," which we wrote together and things like that — we always wrote apart. Even "One After 909," on the whatsit LP, is one I wrote when I was seventeen or eighteen in Liverpool separately from Paul. "The Sun Is Fading Away" ["I'll Be on My Way"] and things like that Paul wrote. We always wrote separately. But we also wrote together because we enjoyed it a lot sometimes and also because they'd say, "You're going to make an album." We'd get together and knock off a few songs. Just like a job.

You said you quit the Beatles first. How?

Well, I said to Paul, "I'm leaving." We were in the Apple offices. I knew before I went to Toronto. I told Allen [Klein, their new manager] I was leaving. I told Eric Clapton and Klaus [Voormann] that I was leaving and I'd like to probably use them as a group. I hadn't decided how to do it, to have a permanent new group or what. And then later on I thought, "Fuck it, I'm not going to get stuck with another set of people, whoever they are." So I announced it to myself and to the people around me the few days before going on the way to Toronto. When I got back [to London], there were a few meetings and Allen said, "Cool it," because there was a lot to do business-wise, and it wouldn't have been suitable at the time. Then we were discussing something in the office with Paul and Paul was saying to do something, and I kept saying "No, no, no" to everything he said.

So it came to a point that I had to say something. So I said, "The group's over, I'm leaving." Allen was there, and he was saying, "Don't tell." He didn't want me to tell Paul, even. But I couldn't help it, I couldn't stop it, it came out. And Paul and Allen said they were glad that I wasn't going to announce it, like I was going to make an event out of it. I don't know whether Paul said, "Don't tell anybody," but he was damn pleased that I wasn't. He said, "Oh well, that means nothing really happened if you're not going to say anything." So that's what happened.

How did Paul react when you said you were quitting?

Well, like when you say "divorce," the face goes all sorts of colors. It's like he knew *really* that this was the final thing. And then six months later Paul comes out with whatever, that he was leaving. A lot of people knew I'd left, but I was a fool not to do what Paul did, which is use it to sell a record.

You were really angry with Paul.

No, I wasn't angry.

Well, when he came out with his "I'm leaving."

I wasn't angry, I was just, "Shit!" He's a good PR man, Paul.

He's about the best in the world, probably. He really does a job. I wasn't angry. We were all hurt that he didn't tell us what he was going to do. I think he claims that he didn't mean that to happen, but that's bullshit. He called me in the afternoon of that day and said, "I'm doing what you and Yoko were doing." And I said, "Good." Because that time last year, they were all looking at us as if it was strange trying to make a life together and doing all the things and being fab, fat myths. So he rang me up on that day and said, "I'm doing what you and Yoko are doing and putting out an album. And *I'm* leaving the group, too," he said. I said "Good." I was feeling a little strange, because *he* was saying it this time — a year later. I said "Good," because he was the one that wanted the Beatles most. And then the midnight papers came out.

How did you feel then?

I was cursing because I hadn't done it.

Do you think you're a genius?

Yes. If there's such a thing as one, I am one.

When did you first realize it?

When I was about twelve. I used to think, "I must be a genius, but nobody's noticed. Either I'm a genius or I'm mad, which is it?" I said, "I can't be mad because nobody's put me away; therefore, I'm a genius." Genius is a form of madness and we're all that way. But I used to be a bit coy about it, like me guitar playing. If there's such a thing as genius — which is just *what?* What the fuck is it? — I am one. And if there isn't, I don't care. But I used to think, when I was a kid, writing me poetry and doing me paintings — I didn't become something when the Beatles made it or when you heard about me, I've been like this all me life. Genius is pain, too. It's just pain.

How did you meet Yoko?

I'm sure I've told you this many times. There was a sort of underground clique in London: John Dunbar, who was married to Marianne Faithfull, had an art gallery in London called Indica and I'd been going around to galleries a bit on my off days in between records. I'd been to see a Takis exhibition — I don't know if you know what that means; he does multiple electromagnetic sculptures — and a few exhibitions in different galleries who showed these sort of unknown artists or underground artists.

I got the word that this amazing woman was putting on a show and there was going to be something about people in bags, in black bags, and it was going to be a bit of a happening and all that. So I went down to a preview of the show. I got there the night before it opened. She didn't know who I was or anything. I was wandering around, there was a couple of artsy-type students that had been helping lying around in the gallery. I was astounded. There was an apple on sale there for two hundred quid. I thought it was fantastic — I got the humor in her work immediately. I didn't have to have much knowledge about avant-garde or underground art, but the humor got me straightaway. There was a fresh apple on a stand — this was before Apple — and it was two hundred quid to watch the apple decompose. But there was another piece which really decided me for-or-against the artist: a ladder which led to a painting which was hung on the ceiling. It looked like a black canvas with a chain with a spyglass hanging on the end of it. This was near the door when you went in. I climbed the ladder, you look through the spyglass, and in tiny little letters it says "Yes." So it was positive. I felt relieved. It's a great relief when you get up the ladder and you look through the spyglass and it doesn't say "No" or "Fuck you" or something, it said "Yes."

I was very impressed and John Dunbar introduced us — neither of us knew who the hell we were, she didn't know who I was, she'd only heard of Ringo, which I think means "apple" in Japanese. And John Dunbar had been sort of hustling her, saying, "That's a good patron, you must go and talk to him or do something," because I was looking for action, I was expecting a happening and things like that. John Dunbar insisted she say hello to the millionaire. And she came up and handed me a card which said "Breathe" on it, one of her instructions, so I just went [pants]. This was our meeting.

Then I went away, and the second time I met her at a gallery opening of Claes Oldenburg in London. We were very shy, we nodded at each other and we didn't know. She was standing behind me but I looked away because I'm very shy with people, especially chicks. We just smiled and stood frozen together in this cocktail party thing.

The next thing she came to me to get some backing — like the bastard underground do — for a show she was doing. She gave me her *Grapefruit* book. I used to read it and sometimes I'd get very annoyed by it; it would say things like "Paint until you drop dead" or "Bleed" and then sometimes I'd be very enlightened by it and I went through all the changes that people go through with her work — sometimes I'd have it by the bed and I'd open it and it would say something nice and it would be all right and then it would say something heavy and I wouldn't like it. I gave her the money. It was *Half-A-Wind* show. The show was in Lisson Gallery, another one of those underground places. For this whole show everything was in half: there was half a bed, half a room, half of everything, all beautifully cut in half and all painted white. And I said to her, "Why don't you sell the other half in bottles?," having caught on by then what the game was, and she did that — this is still before we'd had any nuptials — and we still have the bottles from the show, it's my first. It was presented as *Yoko Plus Me* — that was our first public appearance. I didn't even go to see the show, I was too uptight.

When did you realize that you were in love with her?

I would start looking at her book, but I wasn't quite aware what was happening to me, and then she did a thing called *Dance Event*, where different cards kept coming through the door every day saying "Breathe" and "Dance" and "Watch all the lights until dawn," and they upset me or made me happy depending on how I felt.

I'd get very upset about it being intellectual or all fucking avant-garde, then I'd like it and then I wouldn't. Then I went to India with the Maharishi and we were corresponding. The letters were still formal, but they just had a little side to them. I nearly took her to India as I said, but I still wasn't sure for what reason, I was still sort of kidding myself, with sort of artistic reasons, and all that.

When I got back from India, we were talking to each other on the phone. I called her over, it was the middle of the night and Cyn was away, and I thought, "Well, now's the time if I'm going to get to know her any more." She came to the house and I didn't know what to do, so we went upstairs to my studio and I played her all the tapes that I'd made, all this far-out stuff, some comedy stuff, and some electronic music. There were very few people I could play those tapes to. She was suitably impressed, and then she said, "Well, let's make one ourselves," so we made *Two Virgins*. It was midnight when we started *Two Virgins*; it was dawn when we finished, and then we made love. It was very beautiful.

**Your marriage and honeymoon was your first reexposure
to the public. You used the occasion to start your
campaign for peace. What was that like?**

It was a nice high. We were on the seventh floor of the Hilton looking over Amsterdam. It was very crazy, the press came expecting to see us fucking in bed. They all heard John and Yoko were going to fuck in front of the press for peace. So when they all walked in — about fifty or sixty reporters flew over from London all sort of very edgy, and we were just sitting in pajamas saying, "Peace, brother," and that was it.

Did you feel satisfied with the *Bed Peace*...?

That was beautiful. It was like the wedding album, and it was a move for peace. It's no question about it. On the peace thing there's lots of heavy discussion with intellectuals about how you should do it and how you shouldn't. The bed-ins were great events when you think that the world newspaper headlines were the fact that we were a married couple in bed talking about peace. It was one of our greater episodes. It was like being on tour without moving, sort of a big promotional thing. I think we did a good job for what we were doing, which was trying to get people to own up.

You chose the word "peace" and not "love," or another word that carries a similar weight. What did you like about the word "peace"?

Yoko and I were discussing our different lives and careers when we first got together. What we had in common in a way was that she'd done things for peace like standing in Trafalgar Square in a black bag and things like that. We were just trying to work out what we could do. The Beatles had been singing about "love" and things. So we pooled our resources and came out with the *Bed Peace* — it was some way of doing something together that wouldn't involve me standing in Trafalgar Square in a black bag because I was too nervous to do that. Yoko didn't want to do anything that wasn't for peace.

What were the Beatles' reactions when you first brought Yoko by?

They despised her.

From the very beginning?

They insulted her and they still do. They don't even know I can see it. And even when it's written down, it'll look like I'm just paranoid or she's paranoid. But I know just by the way the publicity on us was handled by Apple, all of the two years we were together, and the attitude of people to us and the bits we hear from the office girls. So they can go stuff themselves.

YOKO: In the beginning we were too much in love to notice anything else.

JOHN: We were in our own dream. They're the kind of idiots that really think that Yoko split the Beatles, or Allen [Klein], it's the same joke. They're that insane about Allen, too.

How would you characterize George, Paul, and Ringo's reaction to her?

It's the same. You can quote Paul, you can look it up in the papers. He's said many times, at first he hated Yoko and then he got to like her. It's too late for me. And for Yoko. Why should she take that kind of shit from those people? They're writing about her looking miserable in *Let It Be*. You sit through sixty sessions with the most bigheaded, uptight people on earth and see what it's fuckin' like. And be insulted just because you love someone. George insulted her right to her face in the Apple office at the beginning, just being straightforward, that game of, "Well, I'm going to be up front because this is what I've heard and Dylan and a few people said you've got a lousy name in New York and you give off bad vibes." That's what George said to her, and we both sat through it. And I didn't hit him, I don't know why. But I was always hoping that they'd come round. I couldn't believe it! They all sat there with their wives like a fucking jury and judged us. The only thing I did was write that piece about "some of our beast friends" — in my usual way, because I was never honest. I always had to write in that gobbledygook. And that's what they did to us. Ringo was all right. So was Maureen.

But the other two really gave it to us. I'll never forgive them. I don't care what fuckin' shit about Hare Krishna and God and Paul — well, I've changed me mind. I don't forgive them.

Did Yoko's avant-garde music background clash with the music the Beatles made?

Yoko played me tapes that I understood. I know it was very strange, and avant-garde music is a tough thing to assimilate and all that. But I've heard the Beatles playing avant-garde music when nobody was looking for years. But they're artists, and all artists have fuckin' big egos. Whether they like to admit it or not. And when a new artist came into the group, they were never allowed. Sometimes George and I would like to bring someone in, like Billy Preston. We would have had him in the group. We were fed up with the same old shit. But it wasn't wanted. I would have expanded the Beatles, gotten their pants off, stopped being God. But it didn't work.

It didn't work and Yoko was naïve, she came in and would expect to perform with them, like you would with any group. She was jammin'. But they'd [have] a sort of coldness about it. When I decided to leave the group, I decided that I could no longer artistically get anything out of the Beatles. And here was somebody that could turn me on to a million things.

You always said the Beatles wanted to be bigger than Elvis. Why?

Because Elvis was the biggest. We wanted to be the biggest. Doesn't everybody?

When did you decide that?

Well, first of all, Paul and I wanted to be the Goffin and King [songwriting team Gerry Goffin and Carole King] of England. This is an old story. Then we decided, well, we're better than them, so we want to be this, we want to be the next thing, we want to be president or whatever. It goes on and on and on. But we always wanted to be bigger than Elvis, because Elvis was the thing. Whatever we say, he was it.

At what moment did you realize that you were bigger than Elvis?

I don't know. It's different when it happens, you've forgotten about it. It's like when you actually get the number one or whatever it is, it's different. It's the going for it which is the fun.

When did you first start getting the spiritual reactions from people who had listened to Beatles records?

There's a guy in England called William Mann who writes in *The Times* who wrote the first intellectual review of the Beatles, which got people talking about us in that intellectual way. He wrote about Aeolian cadences and all sort of musical terms. He's a bullshitter, and he wrote about Paul's album as if it was written by Beethoven. He's just voted it the album of the year and all that shit. He's still writing the same shit. But it did us a lot of good in that way, because people — all the middle classes and intellectuals — are going, "Ooh, aren't they clever."

YOKO: When did they start the message thing?

JOHN: The message thing? About love and that?

When did somebody first come up to you with "John Lennon is God"?

"What to do" and all that? Like, "You tell us, guru." That bit?

Yeah.

Probably after acid.

Rubber Soul?

I can't remember it exactly happening. We just took that position. We started putting out messages — like "The word" and "The word is love" and things like that. I like messages.

How did you first get involved with LSD?

A dentist in London. He laid it on George, me, and our wives without telling us at a dinner party at his house. He was a friend of George's, and our dentist at the time. He just put it in our coffee or something. He didn't know what it was, it was just, "It's all the thing" with the middle-class London swingers. They had all heard about it and didn't know it was different from pot or pills. And they gave it to us, and he was saying, "I advise you not to leave," and we thought he was trying to keep us for an orgy in his house and we didn't want to know.

We went out to the Ad Lib [nightclub] and these discotheques and there was incredible things going on. This guy came with us, he was nervous, he didn't know what was going on. We were going crackers. It was insane going around London on it. When we entered the club, we thought it was on fire. And then we thought it was a premiere, but it was just an ordinary street light outside. We thought, "Shit, what's going on here?" We were cackling in the street, and then people were shouting, "Let's break a window." We were just insane. We were just out of our heads. We finally got in the lift and we all thought there was a fire in the lift. It was just a little red light, and we were all screaming — it was hysterical. We all arrived on the floor, because this was a discotheque that was up a building. The lift stops and the door opens and we're all going, "Aaahhhhh" [loud scream], and we just see that it's the club, and then we walk in, sit down, and the table's elongating. I think we went to eat before that, where the table went this long, just like I'd read somebody — who is it; Blake, is it? — somebody describing the effects of the opium in the old days. And I thought, "Fuck, it's happening." And then we went to the Ad Lib and all that. And then some singer came up to me and said, "Can I sit next to you?" And I was going, [loudly] *"Only if you don't talk"* [laughs], because I just couldn't think.

When you came down, what did you think?

I was pretty stunned for a month or two.

Where did you go after that?

It seemed to go on all night. I can't remember the details, it just went on like that. George somehow or another managed to drive us home in his mini. We were going about ten miles an hour, but it seemed like a thousand. And Pattie was saying, "Let's jump out and play football, there's these big rugby poles," and things like that. I was getting all these hysterical jokes coming out, like with speed, because I was always on that, too. George was going, "Don't make me laugh." Oh God! It was just terrifying. But it was fantastic. I did some drawings at the time — I've got them somewhere — of four faces and "We all agree with you," things like that. I gave them to Ringo, I've lost the originals. I did a lot of drawing that night. George's house seemed just like a big submarine. I was driving it — they all went to bed and I was carrying on on me own — it seemed to float above his wall, which was eighteen foot, and I was driving it. The second time we had acid was in L.A., which was different.

What happened then?

Well, then we took it deliberately.

Where were you when you took it the second time?

We were on tour, in one of those houses, like Doris Day's house or wherever it was we used to stay. And the three of us took it. Ringo, George, and I. I think maybe Neil [Aspinall]. And a couple of the Byrds, you know, that what's-his-name, the one in the Stills and Nash thing. You know the Byrds? B-y-r-d — [David] Crosby and the other guy, who used to be the leader.

McGuinn.

[Roger] McGuinn. I think they came round, I'm not sure, on a few trips. But there were so many reporters. We were in the garden, it was only the second time. We still didn't know anything about doing it in a nice place and cool it and all that, we just took it. And all of a sudden we saw the reporter and we're thinking, "How do we act normal?" Because we imagined we were acting extraordinary, which we weren't. We thought, "Surely somebody can see." We were terrified waiting for him to go, and he wondered why he couldn't come over, and Neil, who had never had it either, had taken it, and he still had to play road manager. We said, "Go and get rid of Don Short [the reporter]," and he didn't know what to do, he just sort of sat with it. And Peter Fonda came, that was another thing, and he kept on saying, [whispering] "I know what it's like to be dead." We said, "What?" And he kept saying it, and we were saying, "For chrissake, shut up, we don't care. We don't want to know." But he kept going on about it. That's how I wrote "She Said She Said." [Half singing] "I know what it's like to be dead."

So how long did LSD go on?

It went on for years. I must have had a thousand trips.

Literally a thousand or —

Yeah.

A couple hundred?

No, lots. I used to just eat it all the time. I never took it in the studio. Once I did accidentally. I thought I was taking some uppers, and I was not in a state of handling it. I can't remember what album it was, but I took it and then [whispers] I just noticed all of a sudden I got so scared on the mic. I said, "What was it?" I thought I felt ill. I thought I was going cracked. Then I said, "I must get some air." They all took me upstairs on the roof, and George Martin was looking at me funny. And then it dawned on me: I must have taken acid. And I said, "Well, I can't go on, I have to go. You'll have to do it and I'll just stay and watch." They were all being very kind. They said, "Yes, it's all right." And I said, "Are you sure it's all right?" They carried on making the record.

The other Beatles didn't get into LSD as much as you did.

George did...in L.A. Paul felt very out of it because we were all a bit cruel. It's like, "We're taking it and you're not." We couldn't eat our food, I just couldn't manage it. Picking it up with the hands, and there's all these people serving us in the house, and we're just knocking it on the floor. It was a long time before Paul took it. And then there was the big announcement. I think George was pretty heavy on it. We were probably both the most cracked. I think Paul's a bit more stable than George and I.

He's more straight.

I don't know about straight. Stable. I think LSD profoundly shocked him.

Did you ever start getting bad trips?

Oh yeah, I had many. Jesus Christ. I stopped taking it because of that. I just ... couldn't stand it. I dropped it for I don't know how long. Then I started taking it just before I met Yoko. I got a message on acid that you should destroy your ego, and I did. I was reading that stupid book of Leary's and all that shit. We were going through a whole game that everybody went through. And I destroyed meself. I was slowly putting meself together after Maharishi, bit by bit, over a two-year period. And then I destroyed me ego and I didn't believe I could do anything.

I let Paul do what he wanted and let them all just do what they wanted. And I just was nothing, I was shit. And then Derek [Taylor] tripped me out at his house after he'd got back from L.A. He said, "You're all right." And he pointed out which songs I'd written, and said, "You wrote this, and you said this, and you are intelligent, don't be frightened." The next week I went down with Yoko and we tripped out again, and she freed me completely to realize that I was me and it's all right. And that was it. I started fighting again and being a loudmouth again and saying, "Well, I can do this," and "Fuck you, and this is what I want," and "Don't put me down. I did this." So that's where I am now.

**How do you think acid affected
your conception of music in general?**

It was only another mirror, it wasn't another miracle. It was more of a visual thing, and the therapy, that "looking at yourself" bit, it did all that. I don't quite remember. You hear the music, but *it* didn't *write* the music. *I* write the music in the circumstances in which I'm in, whether it's on acid or in the water.

What did you think when you saw *Hard Day's Night?*

I thought it wasn't bad. It could have been better. There's another illusion that we were just puppets and that these great people like Brian Epstein and Dick Lester created this whole fuckin' thing, precisely because we were what we were and realistic. We didn't want to make a fuckin' shitty pop movie. We didn't even want to make a movie that was going to be bad.

We insisted on having a real writer and Brian came up with Alun Owen, from Liverpool, who'd written a play for TV called *No Trams to Lime Street*, which I knew and maybe they all knew. Lime Street's a famous street in Liverpool where the whores used to be in the old days. And he was famous for writing Liverpool dialogue. We knew his work, and we said, "All right." But then he had to come round with us to see what we were like. He was a phony, like a professional Liverpool man, or like professional Americans. And he stayed with us two days and wrote the whole thing based on our characters: me, witty; Ringo, dumb, cute; George, this; Paul, that. We were a bit infuriated by the glibness of it, and the shittiness of the dialogue. We were always trying to get it more realistic, even with Dick [Lester] and all that, and make the camerawork more realistic. But they wouldn't have it. They made that movie and so that's how it happened. And the next one was just bullshit.

I just hate this illusion about George Martin, Brian Epstein, Dick Lester, and all these people making something out of us. We're the ones that are still creating.

**My impression from the movie was that it was you
and it wasn't anybody else.**

It was a good projection of one facade of us, which was on tour, once in London and once in Dublin, of us in that situation together. In a hotel having to perform before people. We were like that. Alun Owen saw the press conferences. He re-created it pretty well, but we thought it was phony then even. It wasn't realistic enough.

**At some point, right in there between *Help!*
and Hard Day's *Night*, you got into drugs?**

Yeah, but in *Hard Day's Night*, I was on pills. That's drugs, you know, that's bigger drugs than pot. I've been on pills since I was fifteen — no, since I was seventeen. Since I became a musician. The only way to survive in Hamburg, to play eight hours a night, was to take pills. The waiters gave you the pills and drink. I was fuckin' drop-down drunk in art school. I was a pill addict until *Help!*, just before *Help!* where we were turned on to pot and we dropped drink. Simple as that. I've always needed a drug to survive. The others, too, but I always had more, I always took more pills and more of everything, because I'm more crazy.

**Rubber Soul seemed like the first attempt at a serious
album, a more mature feeling work.**

No, we just were getting better technically and musically, that's all. We finally took over the studio. In the early days we had to take what we were given. We had to make it in two hours or whatever it was. And three takes was enough, and we didn't know about "You can get more bass," and we were learning the technique. With *Rubber Soul*, we were more precise about making the album — that's all. We took over the cover and everything.

Shall we stop for a while?

I don't mind. No, we better go on, because Yoko's got your pal, Jonathan Cott, to do the same trick with her next, how she formed the Beatles in 1929. And we like to be together, because it's nicer.

Why can't you be alone without Yoko?

I can be, but I don't wish to be. There is no reason on earth why I should be without her. There is nothing more important than our relationship, nothing. We dig being together all the time. Both of us could survive apart, but what for? I'm not going to sacrifice love, real love, for any fuckin' whore or any friend, or any business, because in the end you're alone at night. Neither of us want to be and you can't fill the bed with groupies, that doesn't work. I don't want to be a swinger. Like I said in the song, I've been through it all and nothing works better than to have somebody you love hold you.

**Why did Derek [Taylor, their publicist]
and Brian [Epstein, their manager] fall out?**

Because Derek is another egomaniac and Brian was very hard to live with, to take. He had a lot of tantrums and things like that. Like most fags do. They're very insecure. Something happened, which I don't remember, maybe Paul or somebody would, but you'd have to ask them. They had many arguments and Derek would walk off because he was too proud to do certain jobs. It's the same now. And I don't blame him, but don't get paid for it. Heh heh. So that's what happened, they had a big row. Derek was hired by Brian, so was Peter Brown. They really were not hired by us. We hired Neil in Liverpool and Mal [Evans] in Liverpool. Those were the only people we ever hired.

Did you like the Hunter Davies book, the authorized Beatles biography?

Well, it was really bullshit. It was written in the sort of *Sunday Times* style, "the Fab Four." No truth was written, and my auntie knocked all the truth bits about my childhood and me mother and I allowed her, which is my cop-out, et cetera, et cetera. There was nothing about the orgies and the shit that happened on tour and all that. And I wanted a real book to come out, but we all had wives and didn't want to hurt their feelings. End of that one, because they still have feelings. The Beatles' tours were like Fellini's *Satyricon*. We had that image, but man, our tours were like something else; if you could get on our tours you were *in*. Just think of *Satyricon*, with four musicians going through it.

Wherever we went, there was always a whole scene going. We had our four bedrooms separate, we tried to keep them out of our room. Derek and Neil's rooms were always full of junk and whores and fuck knows what. And policemen, everything. *Satyricon*. We really...well, we had to do *something*. And what do you do if the pill doesn't wear off—when it's time to go? You just go. I used to be up all night with Derek, whether there was anybody there or not. I just could never sleep. Such a heavy scene it was. They didn't call them groupies.

You never had an affair with Brian?

No, not an affair.

What were the pressures from Brian?

Cyn was having a baby and the holiday was planned, but I wasn't going to break the holiday for a baby and that's what a *bastard* I was. And I just went on holiday. I watched Brian picking up the boys. I like playing a big faggy, all that. It was enjoyable, but there were big rumors in Liverpool, it was terrible. Very embarrassing.

Rumors about you and Brian?

Oh, fuck knows — yes, yes. I was pretty close to Brian because if somebody's going to manage me, I want to know them inside out. And there was a period when he told me he was a fag and all that. I introduced him to pills, which gives me a guilt association for his death. They go that way anyway. And to make him talk — to find out what he's like. And I remember him saying, "Don't ever throw it back in me face, that I'm a fag." Which I didn't. But his mother's still hiding that. Brian was a nice guy, but he knew what he was doing, he robbed us. He fucking took all the money and looked after himself and his family, and all that. And it's just a myth. I hate the way that Allen [Klein] is attacked and Brian is made like an angel, just because he's dead. He wasn't, he was just a guy. Allen will go berserk when he hears all this.

What else about that Hunter Davies book?

Well, that . . . I don't know, I can't remember it. *Love Me Do!* was a better book, by Michael Braun. That was a true book. He wrote how we were, which was bastards. You can't be anything else in a situation so pressurized. We took it out on people like Neil, Derek, and Mal. That's why underneath the facade they resent us but could never show it. And they won't believe it when they read it if it's in print. But they took a lot of shit from us because we were in such a shitty position. It was hard work and somebody had to take it. Those things are left out, about what bastards we were. Fuckin' big bastards, that's what the Beatles were. You have to be a bastard to make it, man. That's a fact, and the Beatles were the biggest bastards on earth. Like Allen's Christmas card says, "Yea, though I walk through the valley of the shadow of death, I will fear no evil, because I'm the biggest bastard in the valley," or something. There's no kidding, if you make it, you're a bastard.

**How did you manage to keep that clean image?
It's amazing.**

Because everybody wants the image to carry on. The press around you want to carry it on because they want the free drinks and the free whores and the fun. Everybody wants to keep on the bandwagon, it's *Satyricon*. We were the Caesar. Who was going to knock us when there's a million pounds to be made, all the hand-outs, the briberies, the police, all the fucking hype, you know? Everybody wanted in. That's why some of them are still trying to cling on to this. "Don't take it away from us. Don't take Rome from us, not a portable Rome. We all have our houses and our cars and our lovers and our wives and office girls and parties and drink and drugs, don't take it from us." Otherwise, "You're mad, John, you're crazy, silly John wants to take all this away."

What do you think of the Stones today?

I think it's a lot of hype. I like "Honky Tonk Women," and I think Mick's a *joke*, with all that fag dancing. I always did. I enjoy him. I'm going to see his films and all that, like everybody else. But, really, I think it's a joke.

Do you see him much now?

No, I never do see him. We saw a bit of each other round when Allen was first coming in. I think Mick got jealous. I always was very respectful about Mick and the Stones, but he said a lot of sort of tarty things about the Beatles, which I am hurt by, because I can knock the Beatles, but don't let Mick Jagger knock them. Because I'd like to just list what we did and what the Stones did two months after, on every fuckin' album and every fuckin' thing we did, Mick does exactly the same. He imitates us. And I'd like one of you fuckin' underground people to point it out.

Satanic Majesties is *Pepper.* "She's a Rainbow" — it's the most fuckin' bullshit — that's "All You Need Is Love." I resent the implication that the Stones are like revolutionaries and that the Beatles weren't, you know? If the Stones were, or are, then the Beatles *really* were. They're not in the same class, music-wise or power-wise. Never were. And Mick always resented it. I never said anything, I always admired them because I like their funky music and I like their style.

I like rock and roll, and I like the direction they took, after they got over trying to imitate us. But [Mick] is even going to do Apple now. He's going to do the same thing. If it happens, he'll do exactly what we did and lose all his money. He's obviously so upset by how big the Beatles are compared to him, and he never got over it. He's now in his old age, and he's beginning to knock us.* And he keeps knocking, like everybody jumped in on the bandwagon to knock Beatles when we split. I resent it, because even his first — second fuckin' record, we wrote for him [laughs].

When *Sgt. Pepper* came out did you know after you had put it together that it was a great album? Did you feel that while you were making it?

Yeah, yeah. And *Rubber Soul*, too. And *Revolver.* Yeah.

What did you think of the reviews?

I don't remember. Those days, reviews weren't that important because we had it made, whatever happened. Nowadays, I'm sensitive as shit, and every review counts. But those days, we were too

---

* Editor's note: Mick Jagger was then twenty-seven years old.

big to touch. I don't remember the reviews at all. I never read them, and we were so blasé we never even read the news clippings. I didn't bother with them or read anything about us. It was a bore to read about us. Maybe Brian told us or somebody told us about it, that it was great or lousy. They have been trying to knock us down since we began, including the British press.

The big joke with us was, "What are you going to do when the bubble bursts?" And we told them, privately, that we'd go when we decided, not when some fickle public decides.

We're not a manufactured group. That we are what we are is because we know what we're doing. Of course we made many mistakes and et cetera, et cetera. But we knew instinctively that it would end when we decided and not when the ATV decides to take off our series, or anything like that. There were very few things that happened to Beatles that weren't really well thought out by us: whether to do it or not, what reaction, and would it last forever. We had an instinct for it.

You say on your new record, *Plastic Ono Band*, that "freaks on the phone won't leave me alone." And "don't gimme that brother, brother."

I'm sick of all these aggressive hippies or whatever they are — the now generation — sort of being very uptight with me. Just either on the street or anywhere, on the phone or demanding my attention, as if I owe them something. I'm not their fucking parents. That's what it is. They come to the door with a fucking peace symbol and expect to march round the house or something, like an old Beatle fan. They're under a delusion of awareness by having long hair. And that's what I'm sick of. They frighten me. There's a lot of uptight maniacs going round wearing fuckin' peace symbols.

**What were your feelings when Charles Manson quoted
"Helter Skelter"?**

Well, he's barmy. He's like any other Beatle kind of fan who
reads mysticism into it. I mean we used to have a laugh — put in
this, that, or the other in a lighthearted way — that some intellectual would read as some symbolic youth generation whatsit. But
we also took seriously some parts of the role. But I don't know
what's "Helter Skelter" got to do with knifin' somebody? I've never
listened to the words properly.

What do you think the future of rock and roll is?

Whatever we make it. If we want to go bullshitting off into
intellectualism with rock and roll, we're going to get bullshitting
rock intellectualism. If we want *real* rock and roll, it's up to all of us
to create it. And stop being hyped by revolutionary image and long
hair. We've got to get over *that* bit. That's what cutting hair's about.
Let's own up now and see who's who and who's doing something
about what. And who's making music and who's laying down bullshit. Rock and roll will be whatever we make it.

Why do you think it means so much to people?

Rock and roll? Because it's primitive enough and it has no
bullshit — the best stuff. And it gets *through* to you. It's beat. Go to
the jungle and they have the rhythm, throughout the world. It's as
simple as that. You get the rhythm going, everybody gets into it. I
read that Malcolm X or Eldridge Cleaver or somebody said that,
with rock, the blacks gave the middle-class whites back their bodies, put their minds and bodies to it. It's something like that. It gets

through. To me it got through. It was the only thing that could get through to me out of all the things that were happening when I was fifteen. Rock and roll was real. Everything else was unreal. And the thing about rock and roll, good rock and roll, whatever good means, et cetera, ha ha, and all *that* shit, is that it's *real*. And realism gets through to you, despite yourself. You recognize something in it which is true, like all true art. *Whatever* art is, readers. Okay? It's that. If it's real, it's simple, usually. And if it's simple, it's true. Something like that.

**And you feel the same way about rock and roll now
at thirty as you did at fifteen?**

Well, it'll never be as new. It's never going to do what it did to me then. But "Tutti Frutti" or "Long Tall Sally" is pretty avant-garde. I met an old avant-garde friend of Yoko's in the Village the other day who was talking about "one note," and "Didn't Dylan sing one note?" — like he's just discovered that. That's about as far-out as you can get, because it's real. It's not a concept. It is a chair, not a design for a chair or a better chair or a bigger chair or a chair with leather or with design. It is the first chair, it's chairs for sitting on, not chairs for looking at or being appreciated. You *sit* on that music.

How would you describe Beatles music?

Well, it means a lot of things to me. There's not *one* thing that's Beatle music, because I'm part of it. What is Beatle music: "Walrus" or "Penny Lane"? Which? It's that diverse. Or "I Want to Hold Your Hand" or "Revolution 9"?

What do you think it was about "Love Me Do"…

"Love Me Do" was rock and roll. Pretty funky.

**What was it about the sound, not just
"Love Me Do" but anything from that period,
that caught everybody?**

Because we didn't sound like everybody else, that's all.
We didn't sound like the black musicians because we weren't black
and because we were brought up on a different kind of music and
atmosphere. And so "Please Please Me" and "From Me to You"
and all those were our version of the chair. We were building our
own chairs, that's all, and they were sort of local chairs. I don't
know.

What were the first devices and tricks that you used?

The first gimmick was the harmonica. There'd been a few
songs: "Hey! Baby," and there was a terrible thing called "I
Remember You" in England. And I played a lot of harmonica,
mouth organ, really, when I was a child. We started using it on
"Love Me Do," just for arrangement, because we used to work
out arrangements. And then we stuck it on "Please Please Me"
and then we stuck it on "From Me to You," like that. It went on
and on, it got to be a gimmick, and we dropped it. It got
embarrassing.

Have you ever thought if there's a live album?

Yeah, Hollywood Bowl — it was pretty tatty. It's nice to hear.
It'll probably go out one day, I suppose. But we were so nervous.
Dean Martin was in the audience and all their children. It wasn't
like people anymore. It was like that. And we were always nervous.
There's also Shea Stadium somewhere. There's one in Italy apparently that somebody recorded there. But you always did everything
twenty times faster than normal.

**What do you think of those concerts,
like the Hollywood Bowl?**

It was awful. Hated it. Some of them were good, some weren't. I didn't like Hollywood Bowl. If we knew we were being recorded, it was *death*, we were so frightened. You knew it was always terrible: you could never hear yourself and you knew that they were fucking it up on the tape anyway. There was no bass, and they never recorded the drums, you can never hear them. The places were built for fuckin' orchestras, not groups. Some of those big gigs were good but not many of them.

**What part did you ever play in the songs that are heavily
identified with Paul, like "Yesterday" and "Eleanor Rigby"?**

"Yesterday" I had nothing to do with. "Eleanor Rigby" I wrote a good half of the lyrics or more.

**Did you hear Ike and Tina Turner doing
"Come Together"?**

Yeah, I think they did too much of a job on it. I think they could have done it better. They did a better "Honky Tonk Women."

Ray Charles doing "Yesterday"?

That was quite nice.

**And you had Otis doing "Day Tripper";
what did you think of that?**

I don't think he did a very good job on "Day Tripper." I never went much for the covers. It doesn't interest me, really. I like people doing them — I've heard some nice versions of "In My Life"; I don't know who it was, though. José Feliciano did "Help!" quite nice once. I like people doing it, I get a kick out of it. I think it was interesting that Nina Simone did a sort of answer to "Revolution." That was very good — it was sort of like "Revolution," but not quite. That I sort of enjoyed, somebody who reacted immediately to what I had said.

Who wrote "Nowhere Man"?

Me, me.

Did you write that about anybody in particular?

Probably about myself. I remember I was just going through this paranoia trying to write something and nothing would come out, so I just lay down and tried to not write and then this came out, the whole thing came out in one gulp.

**What songs really stick in your mind
as being Lennon-McCartney songs?**

"I Want to Hold Your Hand," "From Me to You," "She Loves You" — I'd have to have the list, there's so many, trillions of them. Those are the ones. In a rock band you have to make singles, you have to keep writing them. Plenty more. We both had our fingers in each other's pies.

I remember that the simplicity on the new album was evident on the Beatles' double album. It was evident on "She's So Heavy." In fact, a reviewer wrote of "She's So Heavy": "He seems to have lost his talent for lyrics, it's so simple and boring." "She's So Heavy" was about Yoko. When it gets down to it, like she said, when you're drowning you don't say, "I would be incredibly pleased if someone would have the foresight to notice me drowning and come and help me"; you just scream. And in "She's So Heavy" I just sang, "I want you, I want you so bad, she's so heavy, I want you," like that. I started simplifying my lyrics then, on the double album.

A song from the *Help!* album, like "You've Got to Hide Your Love Away," how did you write that? What were the circumstances? Where were you?

I was in Kenwood and I would just be songwriting. The period would be for songwriting and so every day I would attempt to write a song, and it's one of those that you sort of sing a bit sadly to yourself: "Here I stand, head in hand..."

I started thinking about my own emotions — I don't know when exactly it started, like "I'm a Loser" or "Hide Your Love Away" or those kind of things. Instead of projecting myself into a situation, I would try to express what I felt about myself which I'd done in me books. I think it was Dylan helped me realize that — not by any discussion or anything but just by hearing his work. I had a sort of professional songwriter's attitude to writing pop songs; he would turn out a certain style of song for a single and we would do a certain style of thing for this and the other thing. I was already a stylized songwriter on the first album. But to express myself I would write *Spaniard in the Works* or *In His Own Write*, the personal stories which were expressive of my personal emotions. I'd have a separate songwriting John Lennon who wrote songs for the sort of meat market, and I didn't consider them — the lyrics or anything — to have any depth at all. They were just a joke. Then I started being me about the songs, not writing them objectively, but subjectively.

What about "Norwegian Wood"?

I was trying to write about an affair without letting me wife know I was writing about an affair, so it was very gobbledygook. I was sort of writing from my experiences, girls' flats, things like that.

When did you decide to put a sitar on it?

I think it was at the studio. George had just got the sitar and I said, "Could you play this piece?" We went through many different sort of versions of the song, it was never right and I was getting very angry about it, it wasn't coming out like I said. They said, "Just do it how you want to do it," and I said, "I just want to do it like this." They let me go and I did the guitar very loudly into the mic and sang it at the same time, and then George had the sitar and I asked him could he play the piece that I'd written — dee diddley dee diddley dee, that bit — and he was not sure whether he could play it yet because he hadn't done much on the sitar but he was willing to have a go, as is his wont, and he learned the bit and dubbed it on after. I think we did it in sections.

**You also have a song on that album, "In My Life."
When did you write that?**

I wrote that in Kenwood. I used to write upstairs where I had about ten Brenell tape recorders all linked up — I still have them. I'd mastered them over the period of a year or two. I could never make a rock and roll record, but I could make some far-out stuff on it. I wrote it upstairs, that was one where I wrote the lyrics first and then sang it. That was usually the case with things like "In My Life" and "Universe" and some of the ones that stand out a bit.

Would you just record yourself and a guitar on a tape and then bring it into the studio?

I would do that just to get an impression of what it sounded like sung and to hear it back for judging it — you never know till you hear the song yourself. I would double-track the guitar or the voice or something on the tape. I think on "Norwegian Wood" and "In My Life" Paul helped with the middle eight, to give credit where it's due. From the same period, same time, I never liked "Run for Your Life," because it was a song I just knocked off. It was inspired— this is a very vague connection—from "Baby Let's Play House." There was a line on it—I used to like specific lines from songs—"I'd rather see you dead, little girl, than to be with another man"—so I wrote it around that, but I didn't think it was that important. "Girl" I liked because I was, in a way, trying to say something or other about Christianity, which I was opposed to at the time.

Why Christianity in that song?

Because I was brought up in the church. One of the reviews of *In His Own Write* was that they tried to put me in this satire boom with Peter Cook and those people that came out to Cambridge, saying, "He's just satirizing the normal things like the church and the state," which is what I did in *In His Own Write*. Those are the things that you keep satirizing because they're the only things. I was pretty heavy on the church in both books, but it was never picked up, although it was obviously there, I was just talking about Christianity in that...a thing like you *have* to be tortured to attain heaven. I'm only saying that I was talking about "pain will lead to pleasure" in "Girl" and that was the Catholic Christian concept—to be tortured and then it'll be all right, which seems to be a bit true but not in their concept of it. But I didn't believe in that, that you have to be tortured to attain anything, it just so happens that you were.

On "Glass Onion" you set out to write a little message to the audience.

Yeah, I was having a laugh because there'd been so much gobbledygook about *Pepper*, play it backwards and you stand on your head and all that. Even now, I just saw Mel Tormé on TV the other day saying that "Lucy" was written to promote drugs and so was "A Little Help from My Friends," and none of them were at all. "A Little Help from My Friends" only says "get high" in it. It's really about a little help from my friends, it's a sincere message. Paul had the line about "little help from my friends." I'm not sure, he had some kind of structure for it and — we wrote it pretty well fifty-fifty but it was based on his original idea.

> **You say in "Glass Onion": "Here's another**
> **clue for you all…"**

Ray Coleman [the British music journalist] asked me about it. At that time, still in my love cloud with Yoko, I felt, "I'll just say something nice to Paul," that it's all right, and "You did a good job over these few years holding us together." He was trying to organize the group and do the music and be an individual artist and all that stuff. I wanted to say something to him. And I did it for that reason. I thought, "Well, you can *have* it, I've got Yoko, and thank you, you can have the credit."

"The walrus" is Paul.

> **And now you've decided…**

I decided I'm sick of reading things about Paul is the musician and George is the philosopher and I wonder where I fit in. What was my contribution? I get hurt. I'm sick of it. I'd sooner be like [Frank] Zappa and say, "Listen, you fuckers, this is what I did. And I don't care whether you like my attitude saying it, but that's what I am, I'm a fuckin' artist, man." And I'm not a fuckin' PR agent or the product of some other person's imagination, whether you're the public or whatever.

I'm standing by my work, whereas before I would not stand by it. So that's what I'm saying. *I* was the walrus, whatever that means.

We saw the movie in L.A. and the walrus was a big capitalist that ate all the fucking oysters [laughs], if you must know. That's what he was. I always had this image of "The Walrus and the Carpenter" and I never checked what the walrus was. I've been going around and saying, "I'm the walrus," that it's something, but he's a fucking bastard [laughs]. That's what it turns out to be. The way it's written everybody presumes that it *means* something. Even I did, so we all just presumed, just because I said "I am the walrus," that it must mean I am *God* or something, but it's just poetry. But it became symbolic with me.

What did you think of *Abbey Road*?

I liked the A side. I never liked that sort of pop opera on the other side, I think it's *junk*. Yeah, because it was just bits of song thrown together. And I can't remember what some of it is. "Come Together" is all right. And some things on it. Yeah, that was my song. That's all I remember. Did I do anything else on *Abbey Road*? [Sings "Come Together."] It couldn't be an album with just one track on it. It was a competent album, like *Rubber Soul*, in a way, it was together in that way, but it had no life, really.

How did you come to write "Come Together"?

I can't say this, we're being sued, you see. See, the Learys [Tim and his wife, Rosemary] wanted me to write — this is not the suing bit — them a campaign song. And their slogan was "Come together." I wrote it, I've still got it, it's actually very like the Kinks — [sings] "Dra-a-a-a-g," you know, some song of theirs. But before I wrote their song, I was writing in the office, just sort of... I can't say this because we're going to get sued; it's silly. I was writing this like, "You Can't Catch Me," the same rhythm and I'm using the old words. I often do it, if I'm trying to write one like "Long Tall Sally" or I'm just singing, I'm going, [sings] "Oh, going to tell Mary," and just make up—parodize the words; I was doing that. And then when I stopped and I said—just came out—"Come together," because "Come together" was rolling around in me head. "Right now, over me." Now, "over me" was meant to be like a joke—but "oh-oh-ver me," like Elvis used to "o-o-o-ver you." And then I never put the other [one out]—the other one went, [sings] "Come together, and [claps in rhythm] join the party, co-o-ome together and join the party." For Leary—like "Give Peace a Chance," a chant-along thing.

And they're suing me because it's like "You Can't Catch Me," for the first half a line or something, because Chuck Berry's words went something like that. But anyway, it's not him that's suing me, it's his people. So you have to not put that in because they'll say, "Oh there, he admitted it." And I think it's a *compliment* to Chuck Berry. I mean, we resurrected him.

Many songs are similar, and I always like to say where the source was. I say, "Well, that was 'You Can't Catch Me.'" But if I never said it, nobody'd ever know. Just one guy spotted it.

What was it like recording "Instant Karma!," your first record with Phil [Spector]?

It was great. I wrote it in the morning on the piano, like I said many times, and I went to the office and I sang it. I thought, "Hell, let's do it," and we booked the studio. And Phil came in, he said, "How do you want it?" I said, "You know, 1950 but now." And he said "Right," and *boom*, I did it in just about three goes. He played it back, and there it was. I said, "A bit more bass," that's all. And off we went. Phil doesn't fuss about with fuckin' stereo or all the bullshit. Just "Did it sound all right? Let's have it." It doesn't matter whether some sound is prominent or not prominent. If it sounds good to you as a layman or as a human, *take* it. Don't bother whether this is like that or the quality of this. That suits me fine.

What did you think of "Give Peace a Chance"?

I thought it was beautiful.

Did you see Moratorium Day in Washington?

That's what it was for. That was a very big moment for me. That's what the song was about, because I'm shy and aggressive. I have great hopes for what I do, my work. And I also have great despair that it's all pointless and shit — how can you top Beethoven or Shakespeare or whatever? And in me secret heart I wanted to write something that would take over "We Shall Overcome." I don't know why, that's the one they always sang. I thought, "Why isn't somebody writing one for the people now?" That's what my job is. Our job is to write for the people now. So the songs that they go and sing on their buses are not just love songs.

I have the same kind of hope for "Working Class Hero," but I know it's a different concept. I think it's a revolutionary song. I just think its concept is revolutionary. I hope it's for workers and not for tarts and fags. I hope it's about what "Give Peace a Chance" was about. But on the other hand, it might just be ignored. I think it's for the people like me who are working class, who are supposed to be processed into the middle classes, or into the machinery. It's my experience, and I hope it's just a warning to people. I don't want praise, I'm just saying I think it's a revolutionary song. Not the song itself; it's a song for the revolution.

What's your thinking about the new album?
What's the single to release?

People aren't going to buy my album just because *Rolling Stone* liked it. People have got to be *hyped* in a way, they've got to have it presented to them in all the best ways possible. And if "Love" can...I like the song, the melody and the words and everything, I think it's beautiful. I'm more of a rocker, that's all. I originally conceived of "Mother" and "Love" as being a single, but I want to put one out with Yoko. I think "Love" will do me more good.

I'm opening a door for John Lennon, not for music or for the Beatles or for a movement or anything. I'm presenting myself to as broad a scope as I can. I mean to sell as many albums as I can, because I'm an artist who wants everybody to love me and everybody to buy my stuff. And I'll go for that. Without selling out anymore.

"Love" will attract more people because of the message. Many, many people will not like "Mother." It hurts them. The first thing that happens to you when you get the album is you can't take it. Everybody's reacted exactly the same. They think, *"Fuck!"* That's how everybody is. And the second time, they start saying, "Oh, well, there's a little..." So I can't lay "Mother" on them. It confirms the suspicions that something nasty's going on with that John Lennon and his broad again. People aren't that hip. Students aren't that aware and all that bullshit. They're just like anybody else. "Oh, oh misery, is that what it's... Don't tell me I'm... It is really awful."

"Love" I wrote in a spirit of love. In all that shit, I wrote it in a spirit of love. It's for Yoko, it has all that connotation for me. It's a beautiful melody and I'm not even known for writing melody.

What do you think are your best songs?

Ever? Ever? The one best song?

Have you thought of that?

I don't know, you see, somebody asked me what's my favorite song, is it "Stardust" or something like that. That kind of decision-making I can't make. I always like "Walrus," "Strawberry Fields," "Help!," "In My Life." Those are some favorites.

Why "Help!"?

Because I *mean* it. It's real. The lyric is as good now as it was then. It's not different. It makes me feel secure to know that I was that sensible or whatever — not sensible but aware of myself then. That's with no acid, no nothing — well, pot, or whatever. It was just me singing "Help!" and I meant it. I don't like the *recording* that much. The song I like. We did it too fast to try to be commercial and all that. I like "I Want to Hold Your Hand." We wrote that together — it's a beautiful melody. I might do "I Want to Hold Your Hand" and "Help!" again, because I like them. I sing them, they're the kind of songs I sing.

Why "Strawberry Fields"? Again, because that was real?

Because it's real, yeah. It was real for then, and it's like talking. "I sometimes think no but I — then again I mean, you know," like that. It's like that Elton John one where he talks to himself, sort of singing, which I thought was nice. It reminded me of that.

Songs like "Girl"?

Yeah, I like that one.

"Run for Your Life"?

"Run for Your Life" I always hated.

Why?

I don't know. Because it was one of those I knocked off just to write a song. It was phony, but "Girl" is real. There's no such thing as the girl, she was a dream. But the words are all right. It's about, well, "Was she taught when she was young that pain would lead to pleasure, did she understand it," all that. They're sort of philosophy quotes. It was reasonable. I was thinking about it when I wrote it. It wasn't just *a* song. It was about that girl that happened to turn out to be Yoko in the end, but the one that a lot of us were looking for. There are many songs I forget like that, that I do like. I like "Across the Universe," too.

Why?

It's one of the best lyrics I've written. In fact, it could be the best. It's one of the best. It's good poetry, or whatever you call it. Without tune, it stands. The ones I like are ones that stand as words, without melody. They don't have to have any melody. It's a poem, you could read them.

———————

So what happened with Let It Be?

Well, it was another one like *Magical Mystery Tour* that . . . [sigh] well, sort of — this is — it's hard to say. In a nutshell, it was time for another Beatle movie or something, and Paul wanted us to go on the road or do something. As usual, George and I were going, "Oh, we don't want to do it, fuck," and all that. He set it up and there were discussions about where to go and all that. I would just tag along and I had Yoko by then, I didn't even give a shit about anything. I was stoned all the time, too, on H, et cetera. And I just didn't give a shit. And nobody did, you know. Anyway, it's like in the movie when I go to do "Across the Universe," Paul yawns and plays boogie, and I merely say, "Oh, anybody want to do a fast one?" That's how I am. Year after year, that begins to wear you down.

How long did those sessions last?

Oh, fucking — God knows how long. Paul had this idea that

we were going to rehearse or . . . See, it all was more like Simon and Garfunkel [laughs], looking for perfection all the time. And so he has these ideas that we'll rehearse and then make the album. And of course we're lazy fuckers and we've been playing for twenty years, for fuck's sake, we're grown men, we're not going to sit around rehearsing. I'm not, anyway. And we couldn't get into it. And we put down a few tracks and nobody was in it at all. It was a dreadful, dreadful feeling in Twickenham Studio, and being filmed all the time. I just wanted them to go away, and we'd be there, eight in the morning. You couldn't make music at eight in the morning or ten or whatever it was, in a strange place with people filming you and colored lights.

How did it end?

So the tape ended up like the bootleg version. We let Glyn Johns remix it and we didn't want to know, we just left it to him and said, "Here, do it." It's the first time since the first album we didn't have anything to do with mixing it. We just said, "Do it." Glyn Johns did it, none of us could be bothered going in. Nobody called anybody about it. The tapes were left there, and we got an acetate each, and we'd call each other and say, "Well, what do you think? Oh, let it out." We were going to let it out in a really shitty condition, disgusted. I didn't care, I thought it was good to go out to show people what had happened to us. Like this is where we're at now, we can't get it together and don't play together anymore. Leave us alone [laughs]. Glyn Johns did a terrible job on it, because he's got no idea. Never mind. But he hasn't, really. And so the bootleg version is what it was like. Paul was probably thinking, "Well, I'm not going to fucking work on it." It was twenty-nine hours of tape, it was like a movie. I mean just so much tape. Ten, twenty takes of everything, because we're rehearsing and taking everything. Nobody could face looking at it.

So when Spector came around, it was like, "Well, all right, if you want to work with us [laughs], go and do your audition, man." And he worked like a pig on it. He'd always wanted to work with the Beatles and he was given the shittiest load of badly recorded shit and with a lousy feeling to it. And he made something out of it. It wasn't fantastic, but I heard it, I didn't puke. I was so relieved after six months of this black cloud hanging over, that this was going to go out. I thought it would be good to go out, the shitty version, because it would break the Beatles, it would break the myth. That's us with no trousers on and no glossy paint over the cover and no sort of hype. "This is what we're like with our trousers off. So would you please end the game now?" But that didn't happen, and we ended up doing *Abbey Road* quickly and putting out something slick to preserve the myth.

Why?

To preserve the myth. I wasn't going to fight for *Let It Be*. Because I really couldn't stand it.

When *Let It Be* was finally going to be released,
Paul at that point wanted to release his solo album?

I think he wanted to show he was the Beatles. I think so.

Were you surprised when you heard it?
At what he had done?

Yeah, I was surprised it was so poor. I expected just a little more, because if Paul and I are sort of disagreeing and I feel weak, I think he must feel strong. That's in an argument. Not that we've had much physical argument, I mean when we're talking. So I was just surprised. And I was glad, too [laughs]. I suddenly got it all in perspective.

What do you think Paul will think of your new album?

I think it'll probably scare him into doing something decent, and then he'll scare me into doing something decent, and I'll scare him like that. I think he's capable of great work. I think he *will* do it. I wish he wouldn't. I wish nobody would, Dylan or anybody. In me heart of hearts I wish I was the only one in the world — or whatever it is. But I can't see him doing it twice.

**I read something Derek wrote about handicapped
and other afflicted people coming up to you to be cured.
What was that like?**

Well, that was our version of what was happening. People were sort of touching us as we walked past, that kind of thing. Wherever we went we were supposed to be not normal and we were supposed to put up with all sorts of shit from lord mayors and their wives and be touched and pawed like *Hard Day's Night* only a million more times. At the American embassy, the British embassy in Washington, or wherever it was, some bloody animal cut Ringo's hair. I walked out of that, swearing at all of them. I just left in the middle of it.

And wherever we went on tour, like in Britain or wherever we went, there's always a few seats laid aside for people in wheelchairs. Because we were famous, we were supposed to have people — sort of epileptics and whatever — in our dressing room all the time. We're supposed to be good. But you wanted to be alone, and you don't know what to say. They're usually saying, "I've got your record," or they can't speak or something. And they just want to touch...

It's always the mother or the nurse pushing them on you. They're pushing them at you like you're Christ or something, or as if there's some aura about you which will rub off on them. It got to be like that. We got very callous about it. It was just dreadful. You'd open up every night, and instead of seeing kids there you'd just see a row full of wheelchairs in the front. It seemed like we were just surrounded by crippled and blind people all the time. And when we'd go through corridors, everybody, they'd be all touching us. It got *horrifying.*

Didn't it astound you at that point to see that you were supposed to be able to cure people, perform miracles?

That was a glib way of saying what was going on. It was sort of the "in" joke that we were supposed to cure them, the kind of thing that Derek would say. It's a cruel thing to say. We felt sorry for them. *Anybody* would. There's a kind of embarrassment when you're surrounded by blind, deaf, and crippled people. There's only so much we could say, with the pressure on us to perform and things like that. But it just built up, it built up, the bigger we got, the more unreality we had to face, the more we were expected to do, until when you didn't shake hands with the mayor's wife, she starts abusing you and screaming or saying, "How dare they?"

There's one of Derek's stories where we were asleep after the session, in the hotel somewhere in America, and this mayor's wife comes and says, "Get them up! I want to meet them." And Derek said, "I'm not going to wake them up." And she starts saying, "You get them up or I'll tell the press!" It was always that, always threatening what they would tell the press about us, the bad publicity if we didn't see their bloody daughter with braces on her teeth. And it was always the police chief's daughter and the lord mayor's, all the most *obnoxious* kids. Because they got the most obnoxious parents. We had these people *thrust* on us. And those were the most humiliating experiences for me. Like sitting with the governor of the Bahamas because we were making *Help!* and being insulted by these fucking jumped-up middle-class bitches and bastards, who would be commenting on our work and our manners. And I was always *drunk*, like the typical — whatever it is — insulting them.

I couldn't take it. It hurt me so, I would go insane, swearing at them and whatever. I'd always do something. It was awful. All that business was awful. It was a fuckin' humiliation. One has to completely humiliate oneself to be what the Beatles were, and *that's* what I resent. I did it, but I didn't know, I didn't foresee that and it just happened bit by bit till this complete craziness is surrounding you. And you're doing exactly what you don't want to do with people you can't *stand* — the people you hated when you were ten. And that's what I'm saying in this album, I'm saying, "I *remember* what it's all about now, you fuckers, *fuck you all*." That's what I'm saying. "*Fuck you all. You don't get me twice!*"

Would you take it all back?

What?

Being a Beatle?

If I could be a fuckin' *fisherman*, I would! If I had the capabilities of being something other than I am, I would. It's no fun being an artist. You know what it's like writing, it isn't fun, it's torture. I read about van Gogh or Beethoven, any of the fuckers. I read an article the other day which said, "If they'd had psychiatrists, we wouldn't have had Gauguin's great pictures." And these fuckin' bastards, they're just sucking us to death.

About all we can do is do it like fuckin' circus animals. I resent being an artist in that respect. I resent performing for fuckin' idiots who won't know — who don't know — anything, because they can't feel; I'm the one that's feeling, because I'm the one expressing what they are trying to. They live vicariously through me and other artists. Even with the boxers. When Oscar [Bonavena] comes in the ring, they're booing the shit out of him. He only hit [Cassius]

Clay once, they're all cheering him. That's what I resent. I'd sooner be in the audience, really, but I'm not *capable* of it. One of my big things is that I wish I was a fuckin' fisherman! I know it sounds silly, and I'd sooner be rich than poor and all the rest of that shit. But the pain, I'd sooner not be. Ignorance is bliss or something. If you don't know, man, there's no pain. Oh, probably there is, but that's how I express it. It's *shit*!

**What do you think the effect of the Beatles was
on the history of Britain?**

The people who are in control and in power and the class system and the whole bullshit bourgeois scene are exactly the same, except that there's a lot of fag fuckin' middle-class kids with long hair walking around London in trendy clothes. And Kenneth Tynan's making a fortune out of the word "fuck." But apart from that, nothing happened. But we all dressed up. The same bastards are in control, the same people are running everything. It's exactly the same! They hyped the kids. We've grown up a little, all of us, and there has been a change and we are a bit freer and all that, but it's the same game. Nothing's really changed. It's the same! They're doing exactly the same things, selling arms to South Africa, killing blacks on the street, people are living in fuckin' poverty with fuckin' rats crawling over them. It just makes you puke, and I woke up to that, too. That dream is over, it's just the same, only I'm thirty and a lot of people have got long hair, that's all.

**Why do you think the impact of the Beatles was
so much bigger in America than it was in England?**

Grass is greener. And we really were professional by the time we got here. We learned the whole game. We knew how to handle press. The British press are the toughest in the world so we could handle anything. We were all right. I know on the plane over I was thinking, "Oh, we won't make it," or I said it on a film somewhere. But we knew. We would wipe them out if we could just get a grip on you. We were new. When we got here you were all walking around in fucking Bermuda shorts with Boston crew cuts and stuff on your teeth. The chicks looked like fuckin' 1940s horses. There was no conception of dress or any of that jazz. We just thought, "What an ugly race." It looked just disgustin'.

And we thought how hip we were, but, of course, we weren't. It was just the five of us — us and Mick — were really the hip ones; the rest of England is just the same as it ever was. But you tend to get nationalistic. We used to really laugh at America, except for its music. It was the black music we dug. Over here, even the blacks were laughing at people like Chuck Berry and the blues singers. The blacks thought it wasn't sharp to dig the really funky black music. The whites only listened to Jan and Dean and all that. We felt like we had the message: "Listen to this music." It was the same in Liverpool. We felt very exclusive and underground in Liverpool listening to Ritchie Valens and Barrett Strong and all those old-time records that nobody was listening to anywhere, except for Eric Burdon in Newcastle and Mick Jagger in London. It was that lonely. It was fantastic. When we came over here it was the same. Nobody was listening to rock and roll or to black music in America. We thought we were coming to the land of its origin. But nobody wanted to know about it.

Why did you make "Revolution"?

Which one? Three of them. There's three.

Starting with the single.

When George and Paul and all them were on holiday, I made

"Revolution," which is on the LP, and "Revolution 9"; I wanted to put it out as a single. I had it all prepared and they came back and said it wasn't good enough and we put out "Hello, Goodbye" or some *shit*. No, we put out "Hey Jude," sorry, which was worthy. But we could have had both.

I wanted to put out what I felt about revolution, I thought it was about time we fuckin' spoke about it, the same as I thought it was about time we stopped not answering about the Vietnamese war, on tour with Brian. We had to tell him, "We're going to talk about the war this time, we're not going to just waffle." I wanted to say what I thought about revolution. I'd been thinking about it up in the hills in India. I still had this "God will save us" feeling about it. "It's going to be all right." But even now I'm saying, "Hold on, John, it's going to be all right." Otherwise, I won't hold on. I wanted to say my piece about revolution. I wanted to tell you or whoever listens and communicate and say, "What do you say? This is what I say." And that's why I say on one version, about violence, "In or out?" Because I wasn't sure. But the version we put out said, "Count me out," I don't fancy a violent revolution happening all over. I don't want to die. But I'm beginning to ask what else can happen. It seems inevitable.

The violent revolution?

Yeah. And the "Revolution 9" was an unconscious picture of what I actually think will happen when it happens. That was just like a drawing of revolution. I was arbitrarily making the thing with loops. I had about thirty loops going, I fed them onto one basic track. I was getting like Beethoven and I'd go upstairs, chopping it up and making it backwards and things like that to get sound effects. And one thing was an engineer's testing tape, where they'd come on talking and say, "This is EMI test series number nine." So I just cut up whatever he said, and I had "number nine." "Nine" turned out to be my birthday and me lucky number and everything, but I didn't realize it. It was just so funny; the voice went, "Number nine." It was like a joke, bringing "number nine" in all the time. That's all it was.

The Chairman Mao bit I always feel a bit strange about, because I thought that if they're going to get hurt, the idea was don't aggravate the pig by waving the red flag in his face. I really thought that — that love would save us all, but now I'm wearing a Chairman Mao badge, so that's where it's at. I'm just beginning to think he's doing a good job.

Did you put in "fucking" deliberately on "Working Class Hero"?

No, I put it in because it does fit. I didn't even realize there was two in till somebody pointed it out. And actually when I sang it, I missed a bloody verse. I had to edit it in. But you do say "fucking crazy," don't you? That's how I speak. I was very near to it many times in the past, but I would deliberately not put it in, which is the real hypocrisy, the real stupidity. I would deliberately not say things, because it might upset somebody, or whatever I was frightened of.

"Happiness Is a Warm Gun" is a nice song.

I like that. One of me best, I forgot about that. I think it's a beautiful song. I just like all the different things that are happening in it. That was like "God." I put together three sections of different songs. But it was meant to be like — I don't know, it seemed to run through all the different kinds of rock music. It wasn't about H [heroin] at all.

It wasn't. It was never. Like LSD and "Lucy in the Sky," which I swear to God or swear to Mao, or anybody you like, I'd no intention. "Happiness Is a Warm Gun" is the same. George Martin had a fuckin' book on guns, or he told me about it — I can't remember — I think he showed me a cover of a magazine that said, "Happiness Is a Warm Gun." It was a gun magazine. I just thought it was a fantastic, insane thing to say. A warm gun means you just shot something [laughs].

**On "Lucy in the Sky," when did you realize
that the initials spelled "LSD"?**

Only after I read it — or somebody told me, like you coming up. I didn't even see it on the label, I didn't look at the initials. I never play things backwards, I just listened to it as I made it. There will be things on this one, if you fiddle about with it, but I don't know what they are. Every time after, I would look at titles, see what it said, but it never said anything.

**You said to me, *Sgt. Pepper's* was the one,
that was the album.**

It was a peak, and Paul and I definitely were working together, especially on "A Day in the Life." The way we wrote a lot of the time was he'd write the good bit that was easy, like "I read the news today, oh boy" — or whatever it was, or "Day Tripper," anything like that. And then when you got stuck, instead of carrying on, whenever it got hard, you'd just drop in and meet each other and I'd sing half and he'd be inspired to write the next bit and vice versa. He was a bit shy about it, because I think he thought, "Well, it's a good song." And sometimes we wouldn't let each other interfere with a song either. You tend to be a bit lax with somebody else's stuff — you experiment a bit. We were doing it in his room with the piano, and he's saying, "Would you — should we do this?" I said, "Yeah, let's do that." And that's how it happened.

I always kept saying I prefer the double album [*The White Album*], because *my* music is better on the double album. I don't care about the whole concept of *Pepper*. It might be better, but the *music* is better for me on the double album, because I'm being meself on it. I'm doing it how I like it. It's as simple as Plastic Ono Band. My stuff on the double album, like "I'm So Tired" and all that, it's just the guitar. I felt more at ease with *that* than the production. I don't like productions so much, but *Pepper* was a peak, all right.

YOKO: In a way, the thing is, people...

JOHN: Hello.

YOKO: Yes. People say something like, "Oh, that's the peak," but this new album of John's is a real peak that's higher than any other thing that he has done.

JOHN: Thank you, dear.

Do you think it is?

Yeah, sure. I think it's, you know, *Sgt. Lennon.* I don't really know how it'll sink in, or where it'll lie, in the spectrum of rock and roll and the generation and all the rest of it. But I know what it is. It's something else, and it's another door... We didn't know really what *Pepper* was going to do or what anything was going to do. I have a feeling, but I don't know whether it's going to settle down in a minority. It could do that, because in one way it's terribly uncommercial. It's so miserable in a way and heavy, but it's reality. I'm not going to veer away from it for anything.

What was the state of the Beatles business at that point?

Chaos. Exactly what I said in *Rolling Stone,* wasn't it? It all happens in the *Rolling Stone!* This accountant whom we fired because we couldn't stand him, a young guy, sent me a letter one day saying, "You're in chaos. You're losing—this is so much a week going out of Apple." People are always saying, "You sold out the dream of Apple." People were robbing us and living on us for the tune of fuckin' eighteen or twenty thousand pounds a week that was rolling out of Apple like that, and nobody was doing anything about it. All our buddies that worked for us for fifty years, all just living and drinking and eating like fucking Rome, man! And I suddenly realized it. And I said it to you: "We're losing money at such a rate that we would have been broke, really broke."

We didn't have anything in the bank, really, none of us did. Paul and I could have probably floated, but we were sinking fast. It was just hell. It had to stop! When Allen heard me say that — he read it in *Stone* — he came over right away, he said as soon as he realized that I knew what was going on, then he said, "Now I can get through." Until somebody knows they're in Shit Street, how can somebody come and get in? It's just like somebody coming up to me now and saying, "I want to help you with the business." I would say, "I've *got* somebody" or "I'm doing all right, Jack." But soon as Allen Klein realized that I *realized* what was going on, he came over.

Brian Epstein was not a good businessman. He had a flair for presenting things, he was more theatrical than good at the actual substance of business. And he was hyped a lot. He was advised by the gang of crooks, really. That's what's going on, and the battle's still going on to the Beatles' rights. We put in a bill to Lew Grade [entertainment mogul] for five million pounds. They've been underpaying us for fucking years: Dick James [the publisher of the Beatles songs], the whole lot of them, sold us out. And they still think we're like Tommy Steele or some fuckin' product just simply because of *Hard Day's Night*. We got to wake up one day. And we're not the same as the last generation of stars or whatever they were fucking called.

Do you think you all will ever record again?

No. Not a chance. I wouldn't record with anyone again. I record with Yoko, but I'm not going to record with another egomaniac. There's only room for one on an album nowadays, and so there's no point. There's just no point at all. At one time there was a reason to do it, but there's no reason to do it anymore. I had a *group*, I was the *singer* and the *leader*. I met Paul, and I made a decision whether to — and he made a decision, too — whether to have him in the group or not. Was it better to have a guy who was obviously better than the people I had or not? To make the group stronger or to let me be stronger? That decision was to let Paul in to make the group stronger.

Then from that, Paul introduced me to George, and Paul and I had to make the decision — or I had to make the decision — whether to let George in. And I listened to him play and said, "Play 'Raunchy,'" or whatever the old story is, and I let him in. I said okay, "You come in," and that was the three of us then. And then the rest of the group was thrown out gradually. It just happened like that. Instead of going for an individual thing, we went for the strongest format. And for equals.

George is ten years younger than me, or some shit like that. I couldn't be bothered with him when he first came round. He used to follow me around like a bloody kid, hanging around all the time. It took me years to start considering him as an equal or anything. He was a kid who played guitar. And he was a friend of Paul's and that made it all easier. Then we had all sorts of different drummers over time. People who owned drum kits were far and few between. It was an expensive item. And they were usually idiots. And then we ended up — we got Pete Best just because we needed a drummer the next day to go to Hamburg. We'd passed the audition on our own with a stray drummer. And there's other myths about Pete Best was the Beatles or Stuart Sutcliffe was the Beatles. His mother's writing that in England.

You're the Beatles.

No, I'm not the Beatles, I'm me. But nobody's the Beatles. Paul isn't the Beatles. And Brian Epstein isn't the Beatles, neither is Dick James. The Beatles are the Beatles and separately they're separate. Nobody's the Beatles. How could they be? We all had our roles to play. George was a separate individual singer with his own group as well before he came in with us. He had the Rebels.

What were the Beatles?

I don't believe in the Beatles myth. I don't believe in the Beatles — there's no other way of saying it, is there? I don't believe in them, whatever they were supposed to be in everybody's head, and including our own for a period. It was a dream. That's all. I don't believe in the dream anymore. But I made me mind up not to talk about all that shit. I'm sick of it. I'd like to talk about the album, which I was going to do and say to you, "Look, Jann, I don't want to talk about all that Beatles splitting up," because it not only hurts me, but it always ends up looking like I'm blabbing off and just attacking people. I don't want it!

How would you assess George's talents?

I don't want to assess him. George has not done his best work yet. His talents have developed over the years, and he was working with two fucking brilliant songwriters and he learned a lot from us. And I wouldn't have minded being George, the invisible man, and learning what he learned. And maybe it was hard sometimes for him, because Paul and I are such egomaniacs, but that's the game. So is George — just give him a chance, and he'll be the same. The best thing he's done is "Within You Without You," still for me. I can't assess his talents. He's not the kind of person I would buy the records of. But I don't want to say this about him. It will hurt him. I don't want to hurt his feelings. But just personally, I think it's nothing. "Something" was a nice tune, but it doesn't mean anything to me. I'm talking about not just rock and roll, just the *universe* or whatever. I don't consider my talents fantastic compared with the fuckin' universe, but I consider George's less. As an artist I can only consider myself.

If you ask me what music I listen to, I'm really interested in concepts and philosophies and not wallpaper, which most music is.

What music do you listen to today?

I don't. If you want the record bit, since I've been listening to the radio here I like something or whatever it is called by Neil Young — [half singing] "Something special" — and something by Elton John. A song by him. And a few things I've heard. But I couldn't — didn't find out who they were. On FM. Some really good sound, but then there's no — there's no follow-through. There'll be a section of fantastic sound come over the radio and then you wait for the conclusion or the concept or something to finish it off, and then nothing happens, it just goes on. A jam session or whatever.

You've had a chance to listen to FM radio in New York. What have you heard?

"My Sweet Lord." Every time I put the radio on it's "Oh my Lord" — I'm beginning to think there must be a God! I knew there wasn't when "Hare Krishna" never made it on the polls with their own record; that really got me suspicious. We used to say to them, "You might get number one," and they'd say, "Higher than that."

It's interesting to hear Van Morrison. He seems to be doing nice stuff — sort of 1960s black music — he is one of them that became an American like Eric Burdon. I just never have time for a whole album. I only heard Neil Young twice — you can pick him out a mile away, the whole style. He writes some nice songs. I'm not stuck on Sweet Baby [James Taylor] — I'm getting to like him more hearing him on the radio, but I was never struck by his stuff.

I like Creedence Clearwater. They make beautiful Clearwater music — they make good rock and roll music. There's lots of stuff I've heard that I think is fantastic on the radio here, but I haven't caught who they are half the time. I'm interested in what's it called, something that means something for *everyone*, not just for a few *kids* listening to wallpaper. I'm just as interested in poetry or whatever or art or anything. And always have been. That's been my hang-up, continually trying to be Shakespeare or whatever it is. That's what I'm doing, I'm not pissing about. I consider I'm up against them; I'm not competing meself against Elvis.

I'm in the game of *all* those things. Of *concept* and *philosophy* and *ways of life* and *whole movements* in history. I'm not interested in good guitarists. Just like van Gogh was or any other of those fucking people, they're no more nor less than I am or Yoko is. They're no more, no less, they were just living those days. I'm interested in expressing myself, like they expressed it, that will mean something to people in any country, in any language, and at any time in history. And rock just happens to be the media which I was born into, that's all. It was the one. It's like those people picked up paintbrushes, van Gogh probably wanted to be Renoir or whoever went before him. And I wanted to be Elvis or whatever the shit it is. But to me it's art.

**When did you realize that what you were doing really
transcended the ordinary?**

Listen, people like me are aware of their genius so-called at ten, eight, nine. I always thought I was. Why has nobody discovered me? In school, can't they see that I'm cleverer than anybody in this school? That the teachers are stupid, too? That all they had was information, which I didn't need, to give me? I didn't become aware of it in the Beatle thing. I got fuckin' lost in being at high school or something. I used to say to my auntie, "You've thrown my fuckin' poetry out and you'll regret it when I'm famous!" And she threw the bastard stuff out.

I never forgave her, for not treating me like a fuckin' genius or whatever I was when I was a child! It was *obvious* to me! Why didn't they put me in art school? Why didn't they train me? Why would they keep forcing me to be a fuckin' cowboy like the rest of them? I was different, I was *always different*. Why didn't anybody notice me? A couple of teachers would notice me, encourage me to be something or other, to draw or to paint, express meself. But most of the time they were trying to *beat* me into being a *fuckin'* dentist or a teacher! And then the fuckin' *fans* tried to beat me into being a fuckin' Beatle or an Engelbert Humperdinck, and the critics tried to beat me into being Paul McCartney!

But that's what makes me what I am! It comes out that people like me have to save themselves, because we get fucking kicked! Nobody says it! Zappa's there screaming, "Look at me, I'm a genius, for fuck's sake, what do I have to do to prove to you son of a bitches what I can do and who I am, and don't dare fuckin' criticize my work like that! You who don't know anything about it!" Fucking bullshit! I know what Zappa's going through! And a half! I'm just coming out of it now, just fuckin' hell, I've been in school again, I've had teachers ticking me off and marking my work! Fuck you all! If nobody can recognize what I am, fuck them! And Yoko, too, fuckin' hell!

YOKO: That's why it's an amazing thing, after somebody who's done something like the Beatles, you'd think that he's sort of satisfied, but actually...

JOHN: The Beatles was nothing, it was like...

YOKO: ...the Beatles situation was cutting him down into a smaller size than what he is.

JOHN: And I learned *lots* from Paul and George in many ways. But they learned a *damn sight* lot from me! They learned a *fuckin'* lot from me! And it's like George Martin or anything, just come back in twenty years' time and see what we're doing and see who's doing what. And don't mark my papers like I'm top of the math class or did I come number one in English language, because I never did. But just assess me on what I *am* and what comes out of my mouth and what my work is, don't mark me in classrooms. It's like I've just left school again! I just *graduated* from the school of showbiz or whatever it was called.

Who do you think is good today?

Sigh.

In any art.

You see, the unfortunate thing about egomaniacs is they don't take much attention of other people's work. I only assess people on whether they're a danger to my work or not. Yoko is as important to me as Paul and Dylan rolled into one. I don't think the poor bastard will get recognition till she's dead. There's me and maybe I could count the people on one hand that can have any conception of what she is or what her mind's like or what her work means to this fuckin' idiotic fuckin' generation. She has the hope that she might be recognized, but...If I can't get recognized, and I'm doing it in a fuckin' clown's costume, man. I'm doing it on the streets.

I admire Yoko's work. I admire Andy Warhol. I admire Zappa a bit, but I think he's a fucking intellectual. I can't think of anybody else. I admire people from the past. I admire Fellini. I admire Fluxus. I really think what they do is beautiful and important. Yoko has educated me into things that I didn't know about before, just because of the scene I was in. So I'm getting to know some other great work that's been going on in the past and now. But I still love Little Richard. And I love Jerry Lee Lewis. They're like primitive painters.

Chuck Berry is one of the all-time great poets, a rock poet, you could call him. He was well advanced of his time lyric-wise. We all owe a lot to him, including Dylan. I've loved everything he's done, ever. He was in a different class from the other performers, he was in the tradition of the great blues artists but he really wrote his own stuff — I know Richard did, but Berry *really* wrote stuff, just the lyrics were fantastic, even though we didn't know what he was saying half the time.

All I ever learned in art school was about fuckin' van Gogh and stuff. They didn't teach me anything about anybody that was alive now. They never taught me about Marcel Duchamp, which I despise them for, and Yoko has taught me about Duchamp and what he did, which is just fantastic. He got a fuckin' bike wheel and said, "This is art, you cunts!" He wasn't Dalí. Dalí's all right, but he's like *Mick*. Dalí is like Mick and Duchamp is like me or Yoko. I love Dalí, but fuckin' Duchamp was spot-on.

What do you think of America?

I love it, you know, and I hate it. America is where it's at. I should have been born in New York, man, I should have been born in the Village. That's where I belong! Why wasn't I born there? Like Paris was in the eighteenth century or whatever it was. London I don't think has ever been it. It might have been it literary-wise when Wilde and Shaw and all them were there. New York was *it*. I regret *profoundly* not being *American* and not being born in Greenwich Village. That's where I should have been. But it never works that way. Everybody heads towards the center, that's why I'm here now. I'm here just to breathe it. It might be dying, or there might be a lot of dirt in the air, but this is where it's happening. And you go to Europe to rest, like in the country.

But it's so overpowering, America, for me, and I'm such a fuckin' cripple that I can't take much of it, it's too much for me. I'm too frightened of it. People are so aggressive. I can't take all that. I need to go home, I need to look at the grass. I'm always writing about English garden and that lot. I need that, the trees and the grass. I need to go into the country. Because I can't stand too much...

What did being from Liverpool have to do with your art?

Because it was a port, it was less hick than somewhere in the Midlands, like the Midwest or whatever you call it. We were a port, the second biggest port in England. The north was where all the money was made in the 1800s, that was where all the brass and the heavy people were. And that's where the despised people were. We were the ones that were looked *down* upon by the southerners as *animals*. Like the South, you, all you Easterners think that people are pigs down south, and the people in New York think West Coast's hick and all that. We were hicksville, and also we were a great amount of Irish descent and blacks and Chinamen, all sorts there.

Liverpool was like that, but there was nothing big, it wasn't American, it was going poor. It was a very poor city and tough. But people had a sense of humor because they're in so much pain. So they're always cracking jokes, they're very witty. And it's an Irish place. It's where the Irish came when they ran out of potatoes. And it's where black people were left or worked as slaves or whatever and the trader communities. It's cosmopolitan, and it's where the sailors would come home with the blues records from America on the ships. And the biggest country and western following in England is in Liverpool, besides London — always besides London, because there's more of it there. I remember the first guitar I ever saw was a guy in a cowboy suit in a province of Liverpool, with the stars and the cowboy hat. And a big Dobro. They're real cowboys there, they take it seriously. There've been cowboys long before there was rock and roll.

Right after *Sgt. Pepper*, George came to San Francisco.

George went over, in the end. I was all for going there and living in the Haight. In my head I thought, "Well, hell, acid's it and this is the answer, I'll go there." I was going to go there. But I'm too nervous to do anything, actually. I thought, "Haight, I'll go there now and we'll live like that, and I'll make music and all that." But of course it didn't come true. But it happened in San Francisco, it *happened* all right, didn't it? It goes down in history. And in London we created something there, with Mick and us and all of them. We didn't know what we were doing, but we were all talking and blabbing over coffee like they must have done in Paris talking about painting. We — [Eric] Burdon and Brian Jones would be up night and day talking about music and playing records and blabbing and arguing and getting drunk. It's beautiful history. It happened in all these different places.

I just missed New York. They have their own cool clique. Yoko came out of that. This is the first time I'm really seeing it because I was always too nervous or I was a famous Beatle. Dylan showed it to me once on a sort of guided tour around the Village, but I never got any feel of it. I just knew Dylan was New York, and I always sort of wished I'd been there for the experience that Bob got, from living around it.

What's the nature of your relationship with Dylan?

It's sort of acquaintance, because we're so nervous. Whenever we used to meet, it was always under the most nerve-racking circumstances. I know I was always uptight and I know Bobby was. People like [journalist] Al Aronowitz would try and bring us together. And we were together and we'd spend some time, but I'd always be too paranoid or I'd be aggressive or something and vice versa. We didn't really speak, but we spent a lot of time together, and he came to me house, which was Kenwood, can you imagine it? And I didn't know where to put him in this sort of bourgeois homelife I was living, I didn't know what to do and things like that. It was all strange. I used to go to his hotel. And I loved him, because he wrote some beautiful stuff. I used to love his so-called protest things. But I like the sound of him. I didn't have to listen to his words. He used to come with his acetate and say, [imitates Dylan] "Listen to this, John." And "Did you hear the words?" And I said, "That doesn't matter, just the sound is what counts. The overall thing." You didn't have to hear what Bob Dylan's saying, you just have to hear the way he says it, like medium is the message. Dylan was like that. I respected him, I respect him a lot. I know *Paul* didn't. I think Paul was jealous. Paul didn't like any other artist. But that's valid. Paul didn't get hyped by me. I had too many father figures.

Do you see him as the great artist?

No, I see him as another poet, or as competition. You just read my books, which are written before I'd heard of Dylan or read Dylan or even heard of anybody, it's the same. I didn't come after Elvis and Dylan, I've been around always. But if I see or meet a great artist, I love them. I just love them, I go fanatical about them for a short period, and then I get over it. And if they wear green socks, I'm liable to wear green socks for a period, too.

When was the last time you saw Bob?

He came to our house with George when I'd written "Cold Turkey," and his wife — I was just trying again to put him on piano for "Cold Turkey" to make a rough take, but his wife was pregnant or something and they left. But he's calmed down a lot now more than he was. I just remember we were both in shades and both on fucking junk. And all these freaks around us, and Ginsberg and all those people. I was nervous as shit.

You were in *Don't Look Back* with him.

I've never seen it. I was so frightened. I was always so paranoid that when Bob said, "I want you to be in this film," I thought, "*Why? What?* He's going to put me down!" I went through this terrible thing. So in the film, I'm just blabbing off, I'm commenting all the time, like you do when you're very high and stoned. I'd been up all night. Yeah. We were being smart alecks. But it was *his* scene. That was the problem for me. It was *his* movie and I was on his territory. That's why I was so nervous. I was on *his* session.

What's a rough picture of your immediate future — say, the next three months?

I'd like to just vanish a bit. It wore me out, New York. I love it. I'm just sort of fascinated by it, like a fucking monster. Doing the films was a nice way of meeting a lot of people. I think we've both said and done enough for a few months, especially with this article. I'd like to get out of the way and wait till they all…

Do you have a rough picture of the next few years?

Oh no, I couldn't think of the next few years; it's abysmal thinking of how many years there are to go, millions of them. I just play it by the week. I don't think much ahead of a week.

I have no more to ask.

Well, fancy that.

Do you have anything to add?

No, I can't think of anything positive and heartwarming to win your readers over.

Do you have a picture of "When I'm Sixty-Four"?

I hope we're a nice old couple living off the coast of Ireland or something like that, looking at our scrapbook of madness.

JERRY GARCIA

[1972]

L IVING IN San Francisco, I fell into the gravitational force field of the Grateful Dead well before I started *Rolling Stone*. There were dance concerts every Friday and Saturday night at the Fillmore Auditorium, which had originally been a skating rink, or the smaller Avalon Ballroom, a dance academy from the 1920s that now accommodated five hundred quite stoned hippies. No seats, just lay on the floor or dance your heart out. In addition to the Dead, the Jefferson Airplane, Quicksilver Messenger Service, the Charlatans, and Big Brother and the Holding Company with Janis Joplin were the local talent. Lying in front of a ten-foot-high stack of Voice of the Theatre speakers, adrift in swirling light show projections, flying on Jerry Garcia's golden and silvery reverb-drenched riffs and runs — this was a cosmic connection like no other, and it has stayed with me forever.

I wasn't an intimate of Jerry's but saw him often. My best friend was a high school buddy of the band's drummer, Bill Kreutzmann, and for a while helped "manage" the group. Once I started *Rolling Stone*, Jerry volunteered that his favorite articles were the interviews and that we needed more of them, and he earnestly advised me to keep the staff to no more than fifty people and to never go beyond the point where I couldn't remember everyone's names. He saw the humor in everything, had an inner mirth born from empathy and compassion. People thought of him as a Buddha or a guru because he was gentle and seemed so wise. He had an aura of contentment and was as close to an enlightened man as I had ever known. Jerry didn't have a million fans; he had a million friends.

When I interviewed Jerry, he had become the central figure of an international touring and recording band. We set up a tape machine on a sunny afternoon, sitting picnic-style on the front lawn of his modest house looking out over the Pacific Ocean. He and everyone in the band were no longer communards in the Haight-Ashbury but suburban-ites in beautiful Marin County.

Jerry was scheduled to be on the cover of our hundredth issue. I brought with me Charles A. Reich, a popular Yale Law School professor then at the top of the best-seller lists with *The Greening of America*, a vision of an enlightened new society. Reich wanted to explore arcane New Age theory, so I wandered off into the rose gardens when it was his turn to interrogate Captain Trips.*

That afternoon, my interest was philosophical and cultural. And of course we talked about drugs. The music of America has, at least in the twentieth century, been imbued with drugs. They seemed to be handmaidens to musicians.

Living near Stanford University, Jerry came up at a place and time when government research into LSD spread out into the local community. I wanted to ask him all about

---

* Reich's part of the interview is not included here but is in a book we coauthored, *Garcia: A Signpost to New Space*.

that. Was the role of LSD as powerful as I thought? How did it change him, his music, his band, and his audience? This was, after all, my own story, too. The regular use of LSD bound so many together. It is also a true tale of a magical time in San Francisco. Jerry's story is often overlooked but is as central as any to the social and cultural history of the times.

In 1994, twenty-two years further down the road of that long strange trip, I inducted the Grateful Dead into the Rock and Roll Hall of Fame in a formal black-tie ceremony at the Waldorf Astoria in New York. The members of the Dead stood next to me as I declared, "I am a proud Deadhead," and presented them with their statuettes. The band had brought onstage with them a life-size cardboard cutout of Jerry, who couldn't be there, weakened with another bout of uncontrolled diabetes and weariness, which soon felled him.

The last song Jerry ever sang, "Black Muddy River," had lyrics written by Robert Hunter, his lyricist and dear friend from years earlier when they lived together in two broken-down cars parked next to each other just south of San Francisco.

> When the strings of my heart start to sever
> And stones fall from my eyes instead of tears
> I will walk alone by the black muddy river
> And dream me a dream of my own
> I will walk alone by the black muddy river
> And sing me a song of my own

You'll be on the cover of our hundredth issue.

Far out. We were in the first one, too: "Grateful Dead Busted."

I wrote that story.

I loved it. It's got some stunning pictures.

**In one picture you can see Phil [Lesh]
in dark glasses, holding a gun.**

And there's a picture of Bobby [Weir] handcuffed to Florence [Nathan, Lesh's girlfriend], coming down the stairs with a victorious grin. It was incredible.

Start us at the beginning.

Which beginning?

Your beginning, the day you were born.

My father was a musician. He played in jazz bands in the places that I play in San Francisco, the same ballrooms. I never knew too much about my father. He played clarinet, saxophone, reeds, woodwinds. He was an immigrant, moved out in the Twenties or the Teens from Spain with his whole family. My mother was born in San Francisco. Her mother is a Swedish lady and her father is Irish, gold rush days people who came to San Francisco then. My mother met my father somewhere back there in the Thirties, something like that, he a musician, she a nurse.

Then the Depression came along and my father couldn't get work as a musician. I understand there was some hassle. He was blackballed by the union or something because he was working two jobs or something like that, some musician's union trip, so he wasn't able to remain a professional musician and he became a bartender, bought a bar, a little bar like a lot of guys do. He died when I was real young and my mother took over that business. All through this time there was always instruments around the house because of my father. My mother played piano a little and I had lots and lots of abortive piano lessons. I couldn't learn how to read music, but I could play by ear. My family was a singing family, on the Spanish side, and every time there was a party everybody sang. My brother and my cousin and I, when we were pretty young, did a lot of street corner harmonizing rock and roll, good old rhythm and blues, pop songs, all that. It was radio days, *Lucky Lager Dance Time*. And then my mother remarried when I was about ten or eleven or so and she decided to get the kids out of the city, that thing, go down to the Peninsula, and we moved down to Menlo Park for about three years and I went to school there.

Somewhere before that, when I was in the third grade in San Francisco, I had a lady teacher who was a bohemian; she was colorful and pretty, energetic and vivacious. She wasn't like one of those dust-covered crones that characterize old-time public school people. She was really lively. She had everybody in the class, all the kids in this homogenous school, making things out of ceramics and papier-mâché. It was an art thing and that was more or less my guiding interest from that time on. I was going to be a painter and I really was taken with it. I got into art history. It was finally something for me to do.

When we went down to the Peninsula, I fell in with a teacher who turned me on to the intellectual world. He said, "Here, read this." It was *Nineteen Eighty-Four*, when I was eleven or twelve. And all of a sudden I became aware of a whole other world that was other than the thing you got in school, than you got in the movies. And so right away I went a long way because of this teacher, who ultimately got fired that same year because he got the kids stirred up, all the classic things.

We moved back to the city when I was about thirteen or so and I became a hoodlum, a survival thing. You had to be a hoodlum otherwise you walk down the street and somebody beat you up. I had my friends, and we were hoodlums and we went out on the weekends and did a lot of drinking. Meanwhile I was still reading and buying books and going to San Francisco Art Institute on the weekends and leading this whole secret life.

I was fifteen when I got turned on to marijuana. Finally there was marijuana: wow! Marijuana! Me and a friend of mine went up into the hills with two joints, the San Francisco foothills, and smoked these joints and just got so high and laughed and roared and went skipping down the streets doing funny things and just having a helluva time. It was great, it was just what I wanted, it was perfect.

**What's happening with your music
and talent all this time?**

Nothing much, I'm goofing around, I'm trying to play rock and roll piano, I'm sort of living with my grandmother and I don't really have any instruments. I want a guitar during this time so bad it hurts. I go down to the pawnshops on Market and Third Street and wander around the music stores and look at the electric guitars and my mouth's watering. God, I want that so bad! And on my fifteenth birthday my mother gave me an accordion. I said, "God, I don't want this accordion, I want an electric guitar." So we took it down to a pawnshop and I got this little Danelectro, an electric guitar with a tiny little amplifier, and man, I was just in heaven. I stopped everything I was doing at the time. I tuned it to an open tuning that sort of sounded right to me and I started picking at it and playing at it. I spent about six or eight months on it, just working things out. It was unknown at the time, there were no guitar players around. And I was getting pretty good and finally I ran into somebody at school that played guitar.

Can I ask for the year?

August first, let's see, I was born in '42 — Christ, man, arithmetic, school, I was fifteen, '57. Yeah, '57, there you go, it was a good year, Chuck Berry, all that stuff. Somebody showed me some chords on the guitar and that was the end of everything that I'd been doing until that time. We moved out of town, up to Cazadero, which is up by the Russian River, and I went to high school for about a year, did really badly, finally quit. I decided I was going to get away from everything.

At seventeen I joined the army, smuggled my guitar in. I wanted to just be someplace completely different. Home wasn't really working out for me and school was ridiculous, and I just wasn't working out. I broke off all my communication with family. I just wanted to be goofing off. I didn't want to get a job or go to college or do any of that stuff. So now, there was nobody after me to do it. I would hear from people who had heard from my family. They knew I was okay. I lasted nine months in the army. I was at Fort Ord for basic training and then they transferred me to the Presidio in San Francisco, Fort Winfield Scott, a beautiful, lovely spot in San Francisco, overlooking the water and the Golden Gate Bridge and all that, and these neat old barracks and almost nothing to do.

I was stuck because I just didn't know anybody that played guitar and that was probably the greatest hindrance of all to learning the guitar. I just didn't know anybody. I used to do things like look at pictures of guitar players and look at their hands and try to make the chords they were doing, anything, any little thing. I couldn't take lessons — I knew I couldn't take lessons for the piano — so I had to learn it by myself and I just worked with my ear.

When I got out of the army, I went down to Palo Alto and rejoined some of my old friends who were living off the fat of the land, so to speak, a hand-to-mouth existence. Some were living off their parents, most of them. People were living off people who were living off their parents. We were living in East Palo Alto, which is the ghetto down there, and there were a few, like, kindly households that we could hang out at and get a little something to eat. I met Robert Hunter immediately after I got out of the army. Stanford being a university town, we were hanging out at the coffeehouse and ran into each other. We had our two cars parked next to each other in an empty lot in East Palo Alto. Neither of them ran anymore but we were living in them. Hunter had these big tins of crushed pineapple that he'd gotten from the army, like five or six big tins, and I had this glove compartment full of plastic spoons, and we had this little cooperative scene eating crushed pineapple day after day.

He played a little guitar, we started singin' and playin' together just for something to do. And then we played our first professional gig. We got five bucks apiece. Stanford was a rich place to hang out, there was all this stuff goin' on there. You could always hustle the girls to get you something from the dining room . . . We played around, mostly at Kepler's bookstore. We played at Peninsula schools and we played all these arty scenes and intellectual scenes down there. That coffeehouse beatnik consciousness was what was happening.

I kept going farther and farther into music and Hunter was farther and farther into writing and so finally we just stopped playing together. But we hung out together. He's a poet, essentially. And the direction I went into music was Folkways Records field recordings, that sort of thing, old-time blues and old-time country music, got very serious about it for a long time, although I was still essentially on the street, going around from place to place.

Who are some of the people you met on the coffeehouse circuit?

Still up in San Francisco at the Fox and Hounds, Nick Gravenites was around, Nick the Greek, they called him. Pete Stampfel from the Holy Modal Rounders. A real nice San Francisco guitar player named Tom Hobson that nobody knows about, one of those guys that was sort of lost in the folk shuffle. Let's see…in Berkeley there was Jorma Kaukonen of Jefferson Airplane playing coffeehouses about the same time that I was, and Janis [Joplin]. In fact, Jorma and Janis and I met at the same time. They played at the place in Palo Alto I played at a lot called the Tangent. They came in one night and I just flipped out. Janis was fantastic, she sounded like old Bessie Smith records. And Paul Kantner was playing around; David Freiberg was playing around. David and Nikelah, they called themselves. Him and his chick played left-handed guitar. They did these rowdy Israeli folk songs.

Were you making enough money to support yourself?

Nah…I was either not making money and mostly living off my wits, which was pretty easy to do in Palo Alto — things are very well-fed — or else I was teaching guitar lessons in record stores.

What did you turn the kids on to who came for lessons?

I tried to teach them how to hear. My whole trip with teaching kids was teaching them how to play by ear, teaching them how to learn stuff off records, because kids were always coming in saying, "Here's this record, I'd love to be able to learn to play this guitar part on it." I couldn't follow the notes myself; it would've been really ridiculous of me to try to get them to follow the notes. In a guitar store you get people who don't know anything about music, let alone anything about the guitar. I could relate stuff by making a tape of a whole bunch of kinds of music that would include the guitar that would all be technically pretty easy but attractive to the ear. The Carter Family, for example, is a real good thing to learn because it's all first position, simple chords, rhythmically very easy, technically it's easy and at the same time your ear can dig it, you can get into it.

How did you put the band together?

My fellow freaks. The old Palo Alto Peace Center was a great place for social trips, the place where the sons and daughters of the Stanford professors would hang out. And we, the opportunist wolf pack, the beatnik hordes, would be there preying on their young minds and their refrigerators. And there would be all of these various people turning up in these scenes and it just got to be very good, really high.

Phil Lesh was from Berkeley and his reason for being anywhere on the Peninsula was that he had done some time at San Mateo Junior College playing in their jazz band. Now, Phil, whom I met at the Peace Center, was at that time composing twelve-tone and serial things. He'd also been a jazz trumpet player. We were in two totally different worlds, musically. He was studying music seriously...you'd go over to his house and find orchestra charting paper and incredible symphonies, all meticulously Rapidographed. Phil has absolute pitch and this vast store of musical knowledge, just the complete classical music education. He'd been a trumpet player. Phil and I got together at a party, and he put together a tape of me playing in the kitchen and it sounded pretty good to us. And when in Palo Alto, he'd hang out at Saint Michael's Alley, which was where Hunter and I were hanging out. And we met like we always met, in the course of some apocalyptic conversation from those old days.

Phil and I had always gotten along together real good. So that's me and Phil, one stream as part of the Grateful Dead — the oldest, probably.

Whose idea was it to have a band?

I got into old-time country music, old-time string band music, and in order to play string band music you have to have a band. And Bobby Weir was really a young kid at that time, learning how to play the guitar. He used to hang around in the music store and he used to hang around at the coffeehouse. Bob came from Atherton — he's from that really upper-class trip, his folks are really wealthy. He was the Atherton kid who was just too weird for anybody. He didn't make it in school and people were beating up on him and he was getting kicked out of schools all over the place. His trip was he wanted to learn to play the guitar and have a good old time. He was one of the kingpin pickers — on the town.

At that time he was like fifteen or something, really young. He's the kid guitar player. I would be out recruiting musicians. Bluegrass bands are hard to put together because you have to have good bluegrass musicians to play and in Palo Alto there weren't really very many of them — not enough to keep a band going all the time.

Bill Kreutzmann was working at the music store at the same time I was. My first encounter with Kreutzmann was when I bought a banjo from him way back in '61 or '62. He was just a kid then playing rock and roll. He was in high school. I may have even played a gig with him once when I was playing electric bass in a rock and roll band on weekends.

Since I always liked playing whether it was bluegrass music or not, I decided to put together a jug band, because you could have a jug band with guys that could hardly play anything like that. So we put together the jug band and Weir finally had his chance to play because Weir had this uncanny ability to really play the jug and play it really well, and he was the only guy around and so he of course was the natural candidate.

And Pigpen, who was mostly into playing Lightnin' Hopkins stuff and harmonica. He was another one of the kids from around there, he was the Elvis Presley soul and hoodlum kid. His father was a disc jockey and he heard the blues. He wanted to play the blues and I was like the guitar player in town who could play the blues, so he used to hang around. He took up harmonica and got pretty good at it for those days when nobody could play any of that stuff. So we had the jug band with Pigpen and Weir.

And you ran around and played . . .

Played anyplace that would hire a jug band, which was almost no place, and that's the whole reason we finally got into electric stuff.

Whose idea was that?

Well, Pigpen, as a matter of fact. He'd been pestering me for a while, he wanted me to start up an electric blues band. That was his trip. In the jug band scene we used to do blues numbers, like Jimmy Reed tunes, and even played a couple of rock and roll tunes, and it was just the next step . . . and all of a sudden there were the Beatles and that, wow, the Beatles! *Hard Day's Night*, the movie and everything. Hey great, that really looks like fun. Well, good times is the key to all this.

**And the Beatles were good times,
that's what was in the movie.**

Right, exactly.

So Pigpen fronts the blues band . . .

Theoretically it's a blues band, but the minute we get electric instruments it's a rock and roll band. Because, wow, playing rock and roll, it's fun. Pigpen, because he could play some blues piano and stuff like that, we put him on organ immediately and the harmonica was a natural and he was doin' most of the lead vocals at the time. We had a really rough sound and the bass player was the guy who owned this music store that I had been workin' in, which was convenient because he gave us all the equipment; we didn't have to go out and hassle to raise money to buy equipment. We were playing at this pizza parlor, this is like our first gig, we were the Warlocks, with the music store owner playing bass and Bobby and me and Pigpen...and Bill. And so we went...and played. We played three gigs at that pizza parlor.

What was your repertoire?

At that time, the Kinks, and the Rolling Stones' "King Bee," "Red Rooster," "Walking the Dog," and all that shit. We were just doing hard simple rock and roll stuff...old Chuck Berry stuff, "Promised Land," "Johnny B. Goode," a couple of songs that I sort of adapted from jug band material. "Stealin'" was one of those and that tune called "Don't Ease Me In"...It was our first single, an old ragtime pop Texas song...I don't remember a lot of the other stuff.

Nowhere near Dylan or someone like that?

Oh...yeah, we did "It's All Over Now, Baby Blue." We did that from the very beginning because it was such a pretty song. Weir used to do "She's got everything she needs, she don't look back" ["She Belongs to Me," *Bringing It All Back Home*].

How important were the Beatles to you?

They were important to everybody. They were a model, especially the movies, the movies were a big turn-on. A little model of good times. The Fifties were sure hurting for good times. And the early Sixties were very serious, too — Kennedy and everything. And the Beatles were light, having a good time, and they were good...It was a combination that was very satisfying on the artistic level, it was like saying, "You can be young, you can be far-out, and you can still make it." They were making people happy. That happy thing: that's the stuff that counts — something that we could all see right away.

What about Dylan, who was so unhappy for such a long time?

Dylan was able to tell you the truth about that other thing. He was able to talk about the changes that you'd go through, the bummers and stuff like that — and say it, and say it in a good way, the right way. I dug his stuff really from *Bringing It All Back Home*. Back in the folk music days I couldn't really dig his stuff, but on *Bringing It All Back Home* he was saying something that was relevant to what was going on in my life at the time. Whether he intended it that way or not is completely unimportant.

That first gig...

That first night at the pizza place, nobody was there. The next week, when we played there again, it was on a Wednesday night, there was a lot of kids there, and then the third night there was three to four hundred people...all up from the high schools. In there was this rock and roll band...People were freaking out. Phil came down from San Francisco with some friends because he wanted to hear what our rock and roll band was like and it was a flash to see Phil because he had a Beatles haircut, and he'd been working for the post office and living in the Haight-Ashbury. He wasn't playing any music, though, and he wasn't writing or composing, and I said, "Hey, listen, man, why don't you play bass with us because I know how musical you are, I know you've got absolute pitch and it wouldn't take you too long and I could show you some stuff to get you started." He said, "Yeah, well, that'd be far out." So we got him an old guitar to practice on and borrowed a bass for him, and about two weeks later we rehearsed for a week, and we went out and started playing together.

We never decided to be the Grateful Dead. What happened was the Grateful Dead came up as a suggestion because we were at Phil's house one day. He had a big Oxford dictionary. I opened it up and the first thing I saw was "The Grateful Dead." It was so astonishing. It was truly weird, a truly weird moment.

I didn't like the name, really, I just found it to be powerful. Weir didn't like it, Kreutzmann didn't like it, and nobody really wanted to hear about it. But then people started calling us that and it just started, it just got out, Grateful Dead, Grateful Dead...

We became the Grateful Dead because we heard there was another band called Warlocks. We had about two or three months of no name and we were trying things out, different names, and nothing quite fit.

Like what?

Oh, the Emergency Crew, uh... the Mythical Ethical Icicle Tricycle... ha ha... We had a million funny names, man, really, millions of them, huge sheets of them.

Were you interested in anything besides music?

Drugs, of course. I'd been getting high for a long time. Marijuana turned up in the folk music world and there was speed. The thing about speed in those days was that you stayed up and raved all night or were playing. We could not find mescaline, but we could find peyote. That was the only psychedelic around at that time. Well, in my travels around the Bay Area there was, like, Berkeley, San Francisco, Marin County, and down the Peninsula. You'd go to North Beach and there would be sort of the remnants of that beatnik scene, but I'd been into that scene as a young kid. But then along came LSD and that was the end of that whole world. The whole world just went kablooey. We started hearing about it in '63 and started getting it about in '64. The government was running a series of drug tests over at Stanford and Hunter was one of the participants in these. They gave him mescaline and psilocybin and LSD and a whole bunch of others and put him in a little white room and watched him. And there were other people on the scene that were into that. And as soon as those people had had those drugs they were immediately trying to get them, trying to find some way to cop them or anything, but there was no illicit drug market at that time like there is now.

How did it change your life and how did it change your music?

First of all, for me personally, it freed me, because I suddenly realized that my little attempt at having a straight life was really a fiction and just wasn't going to work out. Luckily I wasn't far enough into it for it to be shattering or anything, it was like a realization that just made me feel immensely relieved. I just felt good and it was the same with my wife — at that time it sort of freed us to be able to go ahead and live our lives rather than having to live out an unfortunate social circumstance, which is what the whole thing is about.

In what specific sense did it free you?

In making it all right to have or not have. That is I think the first lesson that LSD taught me in sort of a graphic way, was accepting things the way they are.

Did it teach you a religious idea of acceptance or a philosophical idea of...

No, no, it was the truth; it's the truth just like these flowers are the truth, or the tape recorder there, or us sitting here or that sound we're hearing or the trees. It's the truth so you know it absolutely, you don't have to wonder whether it is. It's not in the form of an idea, it's in the form of a whole complete reality. I'm not saying that it does that for everybody. I'm just saying that that's what the effect was on me. It meant that everything is possible. It meant that everything else just took a step toward becoming more real and for me being able to do it without any reservations.

It was another release, yet another opening. The first one was that hip teacher when I was in the third grade; and the next one was marijuana and the next one was music and the next one was LSD. It was like a series of continually opening doors — that's the way I see that.

You've talked about continually opening doors. Is that like a philosophy you have? In other words, is that the way you want to keep on going? A sense of direction?

Well, I think that what doors have been opened for me now are enough to occupy my time forever. I don't have a personal philosophy. All I have is an ability to perceive cycles, and I think that things happen in a more or less cyclical way, and the thing is being able to maintain your equilibrium while the cycles are in their most disadvantageous places, and that seems a function of time.

What were you doing when you were dropping acid: listening to music or just wandering around?

Wandering around... We were playing around in this house, we had a couple of Super Balls, hard rubber Day-Glo balls, and we bounced them around and we were reading comic books, doodling, strumming guitars, just doing stuff. All of a sudden you remember that you are free to play. Our scene was totally anarchic. We had no plans, we had nothing to prove or anything like that. Kesey, from what we could understand of what was going on up at his place at that time, was like into specific stuff apparently, although we didn't know.

**Kesey seems to have had a definite idea
of where he was headed toward.**

He was a writer, and writers always have the end of the book.
Dig. I've always been a musician and into improvising and it's like
I consider life to be a continuous series of improvisations...I view
it that way.

When was the first time you played music on LSD?

We were, let's see...we...oh, we were the Warlocks and we
were playing in this straight bar in Belmont, and doing five sets a
night, forty-five minutes on and fifteen minutes off. We'd be sneak-
ing out in the cars smoking joints between each set. One of those
days we took it. We got high, and goofed around in the mountains
and ran around and I remembered we had to work that night. We
went to the gig and we were all a little high and it was all a little
strange. It was so weird playing in a bar being high on acid, it was
just too weird, it was not appropriate...definitely wasn't appropriate. The first time that music and LSD interacted in a way that
really came to life for us as a band was one day when we went out
and got extremely high on some of that early dynamite LSD and
we went that night to see the Lovin' Spoonful...Remember that
thing, the Lovin' Spoonful, whatever, the Charlatans, and whoever
else down at the Family Dog, Longshoremen's Hall, it was one of
the first dance concerts, and we went there and we were stoned on
acid watching these bands play.

That day, the Grateful Dead guys — our scene — we went
out, took acid, and came up to Marin County and hung out somewhere around Fairfax or Lagunitas or one of those places up in the
woods and just went crazy. We ended up going into that rock and
roll dance and it was just really fine to see that there was just
nobody there but heads and this strange rock and roll music playing in this weird building. It was just what we wanted to see. It was

just truly fantastic. We began to see that vision. It became clear to us that working in bars was not going to be right for us to be able to expand into this new idea. And about that time the Acid Test was just starting to happen.

How did the music change? You're still playing country music and you're playing blues and...

Well, we got more into wanting to take it farther. In the night-clubs, mostly what they want to hear is short fast stuff, and we were always trying to stretch out a little. So our trip with the Acid Test was to be able to play long and loud. Man, we can play long and loud, as long and loud as we wanted and nobody would stop us.

And you were improvising?

Of course. We were improvising cosmically, too. Because being high, each note is like a whole universe. And each silence. And the quality of the sound and the degree of emotion. When you're playing and you're high on acid in these scenes, playing is the most important thing in the world.

It's truly cosmic. Our consciousness concerning music is opening up more, so the music is becoming, is having more facets than it seemed to, having more dimensions. All of a sudden we find a certain kind of feeling or a certain kind of rhythm and the whole place is like a sea and it goes *boom...boom...boom*. It's like magic and it's like that something you discover on LSD and you discover that another kind of sound will, like, create a whole other, you know... We're just playing what's there, is finally what it comes down to, because we're not in a position to be deciding.

When did you meet Kesey, and how?

The Chateau, where we were all living several years earlier, was situated physically about two or three blocks from Kesey's place and there were people from Kesey's that were over at our scene and so on. We didn't hang out down there too much because at the time it was a college trip, they were college people and it made us self-conscious to be there. We were so...undesirable. They didn't really want us, nobody really wanted us hangin' out. They were all bright and clean and their whole scene was bright and clean. They were colorful, snappy, and quick — college stuff.

But then, years later, here we are a rock and roll band. They were hearin' about us up at Kesey's place from our friends who are stayin' up there and gettin' high and comin' down and gettin' high with us. There was this interaction goin' on. Just like there was interaction between our scene down on the Peninsula and the San Francisco scene...the San Francisco scene, all these little networks of one or two guys that go back and forth, sometimes it's dealers, sometimes it's musicians. That was like the old line of communication.

So, it became obvious: since you guys are a band and we're right up here in La Honda, and we're having these parties, we want to move the parties out into the world a little bit and just see what happens. So they had this first one down in San Jose. We took our stuff down there.

That was the same night, when I was a Berkeley student,
I went down to San Jose to see the Rolling Stones
at the Civic Auditorium, and somehow ended up going to
a house party a few blocks away. It turned out to be the
first Acid Test. It was right after the Stones concert,
the same night.

Shit, our equipment filled the room, damn near, and we were like really loud and people were just, ah ... There were guys freakin' out and stuff and there were hundreds and hundreds of people all around, in this residential neighborhood, swarming out of this guy's house.

What happened at your first real sit-down between you and Kesey?

After that first one we all got together, us and Kesey and everybody, and had a meeting about it, and thought, well, that first one there was all those people there but it was too weird because it was somebody's house, you know, and...it just didn't make it. We just decided to keep on doing it, but move it to a different location each week.

They had film, endless weird tape recorder hookups, and mystery speaker trips...just all sorts of really strange audio tricks. It always seemed as though the equipment was able to respond in its own way, I mean it...There were always magical things happening. Voices coming out of things that weren't plugged in. God, it was just totally mind-boggling to wander around this maze of wires and stuff like that. Sometimes they were like writhing and squirming. Truly amazing.

That was the Acid Test and the Acid Test was the prototype for our whole basic trip. Nothing has ever come up to the level of the way the Acid Test was. It's just never been equaled, really. The basic hit of it never developed out. What happened was light shows and rock and roll came out of it, and that's like the thing that we've seen go out.

But what was it when it was at its greatest?

Well, something much more incredible than just a rock and roll show with a light show; it was just a million more times incredible. The formlessness, the thing of people wandering around wondering what was going on, stuff happening spontaneously and everybody being prepared to accept any kind of a thing that was happening and to add to it — it was like...everybody was creating.

Everybody was doing something.

Everybody was doing everything. That's about the simplest explanation.

And it was magical besides.

Truly, it was magical because there was that willingness for everybody to be constantly on the lookout for something new. It was just the idea of everybody having their various stuff and doing it all at once.

What do you think stopped it?

The fact that LSD became illegal was the thing that really stopped it. That's the thing that stopped it the hardest.

What was accomplished between the Pranksters and the Dead at that time?

We were even looser than they were. They became a sort of semi-fascist organization as soon as Kesey had to go to Mexico. And Ken Babbs was kind of at the helm and he was very much into keeping everything clean and straight and "We don't want any strangers." And security. We had more or less separate kinds of loose scenes that sorta had spillovers. There were people in Kesey's scene. Page, who was an old friend of mine and an old friend of Phil's. At one time our headquarters were very close together so that we would stumble over to their parties and some of them would spill over to our parties. But we really were different scenes because we were much younger. And because we were younger we were basically undesirable to their scene. We were all just dropouts and they were college people. They were serious. This is going way back and Kesey at that stage was not in the old days, Kesey the writer. And that's going way back.

The Grateful Dead, we were real loose. We were definitely not making ends meet, we were living solely off of Owsley's [Augustus Owsley Stanley III, the pioneering underground manufacturer of LSD] good graces at that time. The free park thing started later after the L.A. Acid Tests, when we moved back up to San Francisco. The Pranksters were on their way to Mexico and we were at that time living at a house that Owsley had rented. We had no money, of course, no furniture, no place to sleep, or anything like that. Owsley's trip was he wanted to design equipment for us and we were going to have to be in sort of a lab situation for him to do it. He was really serious about it and so it was like the long wait for components and stuff while he was working on it, he and his partner.

What happened when Owsley's equipment finally came?

It got there piece by piece but it never really worked. We went on for about a year or so with it and we always had to spend five hours dragging it into a gig and five hours dragging it out afterwards. It was really bringing us down. After going through a million weird changes about it and screaming at poor Owsley and getting just crazy behind it, we finally parted company with him. He agreed to turn some of the equipment back into just regular money and bought us some regular standard simpleminded plain old equipment so we could go out and work.

After you stopped collaborating with Kesey and the Acid Tests and got away from Owsley's experiments,

where did you live and who did you live with and what was the scene like?

When we came back from L.A. [we] ended up with a ranch — Rancho Olómpali — which is the site of the only Indian battle ever fought in California. It's up in Novato. It was a great place. It had a swimming pool and barns and that sort of thing.

The parties are well remembered.

We didn't have that place very long, only about eight weeks. But those parties...Novato was completely comfortable, wide open, high as you wanted to get, run around naked if you wanted to, fall in the pool, completely open scenes. Everything was just super groovy. It was a model of how things could really be good. If they really wanted to be.

All that was a firming-up of the whole social world of rock and roll, because all the musicians in the Bay Area, we have known each other for really a long time in one scene or another. And that was shored up, so to speak, at those parties. The guys in Jefferson Airplane would get together with Quicksilver, and all different players would get together and get high and get loose and have some fun.

What other bands were there?

At that time there were some bands that are no longer in existence, like Clover or Wildflower or something like that. Good guys, all good guys. The P.H. Phactor Jug Band, and the Charlatans. That was when we started getting tight with Quicksilver. I'd known David Freiberg from back in folk music days. They came and hung out at our place in Novato when we had our parties. And a lot of people like the various filmmakers, and writers and dope dealers. All the people who were into doing stuff. People who had seen each other at rock and roll shows and all that shit, in that first year. Those parties were like a chance to move the whole thing closer, so to speak. It was good times...unselfconscious and totally free. After that we moved headquarters back into San Francisco.

Then we got another place out in Marin. Camp Lagunitas, it was called. It used to be a summer camp. Our business was done in the city and we were living out at Camp Lagunitas.

Hell, I went there for summer camp when I was nine years old. It was like a village of dorms, cabins, dining halls, and campfires out in the woods.

Finally, we messed that up and got kicked out and we ended up back in San Francisco at 710 Ashbury Street, near the corner of Haight Street, and a whole lot of us moved in. Not everybody. Bobby and I and Pigpen of the band lived there, and Danny Rifkin and Rock Scully, who were our managers at the time. Tangerine, who was Rock's old lady and a really good chick, and just various other assorted people hanging out at various times.

How many people came drifting in off the streets?

Our place got to be a center of energy. The Diggers would hang out there. The people that were trying to start various spiritual movements would be in and out; our friends trying to get various benefits on for various trips would be in and out. It was all real high in those days because at that time the Haight-Ashbury was a community. We had the Psychedelic Shop — the very first one — and other people were starting to open stores and starting to get under way. It was just about that same time that people started to come to town to find out about the hippie scene. And it was a very small neighborhood affair when we were all working for each other's benefit. Most of the people of the Haight-Ashbury scene were people who had been at San Francisco State and gotten into drugs and acid and were living out there experimenting with all the new things that they'd discovered. It was a very high, healthy kind of thing—there were no hard drugs, only pot and LSD.

Then when the big media flash came out—when the *Time* magazine guys came out and interviewed everybody and took photographs and made it news, the feedback from that killed the whole scene. It was ridiculous. We could no longer support the tiny trickle that was really supporting everybody. The whole theory in hip economics is essentially that you can have a small amount of money and move it around very fast and it would work out, but when you have thousands and thousands of people, it's just too unwieldy. And all the attempts at free food and all that, certain people had to work too hard to justify it. At the early stages we were operating completely purely without anybody looking on, through the big window. It was about the time we started playing free in the parks, we were going along really well. And then the crowds came in who were looking for something. Too many people to take care of and not enough people willing to do something. There were a lot of people there looking for a free ride, weirdos from out of town on the weekends to get in on the free love and all the rest. Gray Line tours stopping in front of our house. People driving by behind locked windows and peering out.

You have a reputation that during the Haight-Ashbury time and later, you were the sort of spiritual adviser to the whole rock scene.

That's a crock of shit, quite frankly.

Jefferson Airplane says that on their first or second album.

That's because at that time, they were making their second

record and they thought it would be helpful to have somebody there who could communicate to their producer. I went down there and hung out and was a sort of go-between and helped out with some arrangements and stuff like that — I just hung out.

How did you avoid the music business taking over your lives? Because nobody wanted it?

That's a good part of it. And with us, we've never really been successful in the music business; we've never had a super big hit album or a hit single or anything like that. Grateful Dead freaks are our audience, you know... We're not mass-market or anything like that, which I think is super great. I think that we've been really lucky we haven't had to put up with all the celebrity stuff. At the same time it's been somewhat of a struggle to survive, but we're doing good, we're doing okay... so it worked out okay.

Do you think you could cope with a Crosby, Stills, Nash & Young type of success?

I might be able to cope with it, but I don't think that I could be really that comfortable with it. I'd like to be fair, so I don't like to pull the thing of having somebody at the door that says, "No, fuck you, you can't see Garcia, you know, you're not going in no matter what, no matter how good your rap is." Our backstage scene and all that is real open, we try to let as much stuff as possible come by, and I've gotten into the thing of being able to move around pretty fast so I don't have to get hung up into anything, but I like to let it flow rather than stop it.

That's why I feel pretty good about finishing up our Warner Brothers contract, stopping being part of that mainstream, and just kinda fallin' back so that we can continue to relate to our audience in a groovy, intelligent way without having to be part of that other world of the celebrity that really doesn't seem to want us too badly. All we could hope to do, all we are really interested in doing is being able to keep doing what we do, but be able to have the energy come more directly back to us and be able to keep more of our friends alive, that kind of trip. Essentially that's what we're interested in doin'.

Do you think it'll go on for a long time...the band?

I don't see why not. Barring everybody dying or complete dis-interest or something like that. As long as it's groovy and the music is happening...We don't have any real plans, but we're committed to this thing...We're following it, we're not directing it. Nobody's making any real central decisions or anything. Everything's just kinda hashed out. It stumbles. It stumbles, then it creeps, then it flies with one wing and bumps into trees and shit. We're commit-ted to it by now, after six years. What the fuck? It's still groovy for us. It's kinda like, why break up the thing when it's working, when it seems to be working good and everybody's getting off?

The way it works is it doesn't depend on a leader, and I'm not the leader of the Grateful Dead or anything like that, there isn't any fuckin' leader. Because I can bullshit you guys real easy, but I can't bullshit Phil and Pigpen and them guys watchin' me go through my changes all these years, and we've had so many weird times together. I know in front that the leader thing don't work, because you don't need it. Maybe it used to, but I don't think you need it anymore because everybody is the leader, when it's the time for them to be the leader, you know what I mean: all of a sudden, you're the guy that knows in that situation. I think the Grateful Dead is like one dumb guy, instead of five. It seems like everything that we learn comes in the form of these big dumb, you know..."Take this." The manager, *krecccchhh,* and we get hit over the head: "Oh yeah, manager, manager, yeah." It takes, like, a big one for us to notice it. That's kind of the way I see it.

Yeah, that's all we can do...I can't do anything else, ha ha ha ha, and the Grateful Dead is still a good trip through all of it, and I've dug every minute of it, man, it's just like I really love it, and that's the payoff, ultimately, that's the reason why we're all doing it. Now actually for us everything is just going real good. It's going good enough where we can actually decide what the hell we want to do, which is — aw, fuck, what's that?

MICK JAGGER

[1995]

I THINK THE Rolling Stones were "the greatest rock and roll band in the world." This kind of judgment is generally personal taste and idiosyncratic. There are better guitar players than Keith Richards, better singers than Mick Jagger, musicians who are better individual craftsmen — although Charlie Watts may have been the best rock drummer ever — but as a whole, as a unity, as a band, there was no equal during their long run, and likely still none better.

The level at which they operated and came to be revered was not only due to the musical excellence of their lineup, but also to their enormous, staggering repertoire, their self-contained songwriting and creative process, their rebellious spirit, their social commentary, their undaunted sexuality, and their longevity. They were the template for the modern rock and roll band; ultimately, they invented the giant-stage stadium tour. They were not the lovable Mop Tops. These guys were disrespectful, sexually subversive, and trouble.

At the center of this was an unlikely middle-class British student who dropped out of the London School of

Economics to throw in with a few musicians with whom he had been doing a set of four songs on Saturday nights. The mates were Keith Richards and Brian Jones. The Rolling Stones evolved from a Muddy Waters–style electric blues band into the rock and roll stratosphere when Jagger and Richards discovered the alchemy of their songwriting partnership.

I met Mick in 1968 while he was making *Beggars Banquet,* the album that launched their golden age, along with *Let It Bleed, Sticky Fingers,* and *Exile on Main Street.* I was twenty-two years old and he was twenty-five. He was a rock star, to be sure, but not at all what I would have expected. He was elegant, well-mannered, and he quickly put me at ease. After sitting in the studio while he mixed "Street Fighting Man," we spent the afternoon together at his house, listening to records. Soon we became partners in a British edition of *Rolling Stone.*

Thus began a relationship that has lasted five decades. We ran in-depth and continuous editorial coverage of their records and tours. (Mick has been on *Rolling Stone's* cover more than any artist other than Paul McCartney, who just edges him out.) We became good friends.

In 1994, I suggested that I interview him at length. This would be his first interview in sixteen years. Mick had given Jonathan Cott a fascinating interview that we published in 1978, but other than that he had limited access to the press to twenty-minute quickies when he had an album or tour to promote. He had never given a deep and defining retrospective interview. I told him that we had an obligation to do it.

It was a moveable interview that took over a year. I was in no hurry. It was the *Voodoo Lounge* tour, and I was happy to spend a lot of time on the road with him. In July, I went to their first dress rehearsal in an empty baseball stadium, watching it from the pitcher's mound. In November, I went to San Antonio to be a fly on the wall backstage and onstage so I could understand his performing technique. I also sat down with Keith and Charlie Watts, to talk about Mick and what they thought I should ask him. Mick and I began our interview later that month in Miami, and then in December we resumed in Montreal. Several months later I went to Cologne, Germany, to finish it up. In every hotel room he was staying the windows were sealed off from day or night with tinfoil.

We started with his early childhood. He loved performing at family gatherings, and then in high school he suddenly found the "girl reaction." I tried to cover early days in Swinging London, Brian Jones, their embrace of LSD, "sister morphine," and "sweet cousin cocaine." We discussed their social concerns, their use of gay imagery, and the themes and times that shaped their career and our culture. I talked to Mick about himself as a singer and performer, as a songwriter, his partnership with Keith, how songs were written, what some of them were about, and how their records were made.

Mick is not given to pouring his heart out, to discussing his life at home, or to publicly gossiping. He is a musical critic *par excellence*, and revealed himself to be an objective and acute observer of the Rolling Stones.

If they were the world's greatest rock and roll band, I felt like I was the world's luckiest rock and roll fan.

———————————

When did you first realize you were a performer, that what you did onstage was affecting people?

When I was eighteen or so. The Rolling Stones were just starting to play some clubs around London, and I realized I was getting a lot of girl action when normally I hadn't gotten much. I was very unsophisticated then.

You realize that these girls are going, either quietly or loudly, sort of crazy. And you're going, "Well, this is good. You know, this is something else." At that age you're just so impressed, especially if you've been rather shy before.

There's two parts of all this, at least. There's this great fascination for music and this love of playing blues — not only blues, just rock and roll generally. There's this great love of that.

But there's this other thing that's performing, which is something that children have or they haven't got. In the slightly post-Edwardian, pre-television days, everybody had to do a turn at family gatherings. You might recite poetry, and Uncle Whatever would play the piano and sing, and you all had something to do. And I was just one of those kids who loved it.

I guess you just want some sort of gratification, some sort of approval. But it's also just the love of actually doing it. Fun.

You were going to the London School of Economics and just getting started playing with the Stones. How did you decide which you were going to do?

Well, I started to do both, really. The Stones thing was weekends, and college was in the week. God, the Rolling Stones had so little work — it was like one gig a month. So it wasn't really that difficult — we just couldn't get any work.

How committed to the group were you then?

Well, I wasn't totally committed; it was a good, fun thing to do. But Keith [Richards] and Brian [Jones] didn't have anything else to do, so they wanted to rehearse all the time. I liked to rehearse once a week and do a show Saturday. The show that we did was three or four numbers, so there wasn't a tremendous amount of rehearsal needed.

Were you torn about the decision to drop out of school?

It was very, very difficult because my parents obviously didn't want me to do it. My father was furious with me, absolutely furious. I'm sure he wouldn't have been so mad if I'd have volunteered to join the army. Anything but this. He couldn't believe it. I agree with him: it wasn't a viable career opportunity. It was totally stupid. But I didn't really like being at college. It wasn't like it was Oxford and had been the most wonderful time of my life. It was really a dull, boring course I was stuck on.

I used to play Saturday-night shows with all these different little groups. I used to do mad things, go on my knees and roll on the ground when I was fifteen, sixteen years old. And my parents were extremely disapproving of it all. Because it was just not done. This was for very low-class people, remember. Rock and roll singers weren't educated people.

I didn't have any inhibitions. I saw Elvis and Gene Vincent, and I thought, "Well, I can do this." And I liked doing it. It's a real buzz, even in front of twenty people, to make a complete fool of yourself. But people seemed to like it. If people started throwing tomatoes at me, I wouldn't have gone on with it. But they all liked it, and it always seemed to be a success, and people were shocked. I could see it in their faces.

Shocked by you?

Yeah. They could see it was a bit wild for what was going on at the time in these little places in the suburbs. Parents were not always very tolerant, but Keith's mum was very tolerant of him playing. Keith was an only child, and she didn't have a lot of other distractions, whereas my parents were like, "Get on your homework."

What was it like to be such a success at such a young age?

It was very exciting. The first time we got our picture in the music paper called the *Record Mirror* — to be on the front page of this thing that probably sold about twenty thousand copies — was so exciting, you couldn't believe it. And this glowing review. There we were in this club in Richmond, being written up in these rather nice terms. And then to go from the music-oriented press to national press and national television, and everyone seeing you in the world of two television channels, and then being recognized by everyone from builders and people working in shops and so on. It goes to your head — very champagne feeling.

I recently listened to the early albums, the first four or five you did, and they're all pretty much the same. You were doing blues and covers. The first full album that really kind of jumps out is *Out of Our Heads*.

It had a unity of sound to it. Most of that was recorded in RCA Studios, in Hollywood, and the people working on it, the engineers, were much better. They knew how to get really good sounds. That really affects your performance, because you can hear the nuances, and that inspires you.

And your singing is different here for the first time, like you're singing soul music.

Yeah, well, it is obviously soul-influenced, which was the goal at the time. Otis Redding and Solomon Burke. "Play with Fire" sounds amazing — when I heard it last. It's a very in-your-face kind of sound and very clearly done. You can hear all the vocal stuff on it. And I'm playing the tambourines. The vocal line is very pretty.

That's the first song you wrote that starts to address the lifestyle you were leading in England and, of course, class consciousness.

No one had really done that. The Beatles, to some extent, were doing it, though they weren't really doing it at this period as much as they did later. The Kinks were kind of doing it — Ray Davies and I were in the same boat. One of the first things that, in that very naïve way, you attempted to deal with were the kind of funny, swinging, London-type things that were going on. I didn't even realize I was doing it at the time. But it became an interesting source for material. Songwriting had only dealt in clichés and borrowed stuff, you know, from previous records or ideas. "I want to hold your hand," things like that. But these songs were really more from experience and then embroidered to make them more interesting.

The lyricist who was really good at the time was Bob Dylan. Everyone looked up to him as being a kind of guru of lyrics. It's hard to think of the absolute garbage that pop music really was at the time. And even if you lifted your game by a marginal amount, it really was a lot different from most everything else that had gone before in the ten years previously.

A lot of it was perhaps not as good as we thought, but at the time it was fantastic. "Gates of Eden," "Like a Rolling Stone," "Positively 4th Street," and all these Mexican-type songs, even the nonsense ones: "Everybody Must Get Stoned."

Then you did *December's Children (and Everybody's)*. That record features "Get Off of My Cloud."

That was Keith's melody and my lyrics. It's a stop-bugging-me,

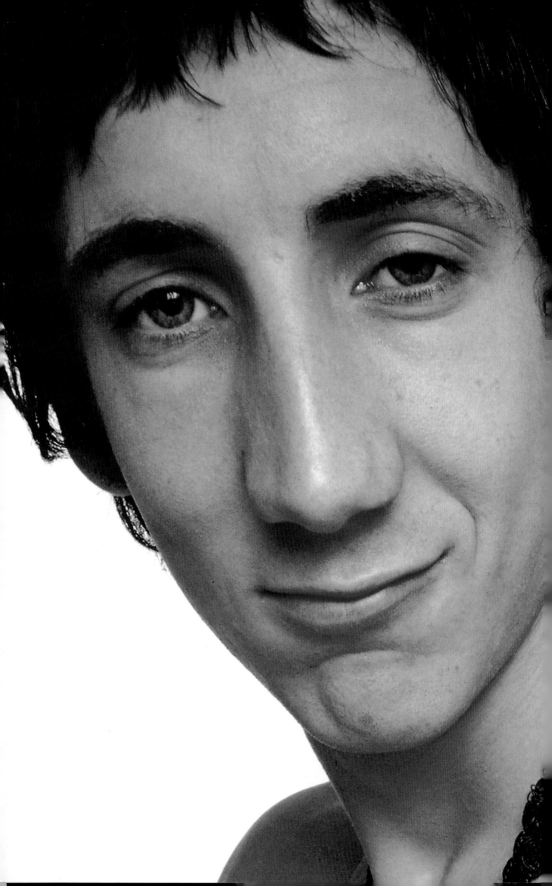

With Bono at the Rollling Stone office on Sixth Avenue in New York, 2015

post-teenage-alienation song. The grown-up world was a very ordered society in the early Sixties, and I was coming out of it. America was even more ordered than anywhere else. I found it was a very restrictive society in thought and behavior and dress.

Based on your coming to the States in '64?

Sixty-four, '65, yeah. And touring outside of New York. New York was wonderful and so on, and L.A. was also kind of interesting. But outside of that we found it the most repressive society, very prejudiced in every way. There was still segregation. Americans shocked me by their behavior and their narrow-mindedness. It's changed fantastically over the last thirty years. But so has everything else.

**Is there anything more to say about
"(I Can't Get No) Satisfaction" than has already been said?**

Keith didn't want it to come out as a single.

**Is there anything special to you about that song,
looking back at it after all these years?**

People get very blasé about their big hit. It was the song that really made the Rolling Stones, changed us from just another band into a huge, monster band. You always need one song. We weren't American, and America was a big thing, and we always wanted to make it here. It was very impressive the way that song and the popularity of the band became a worldwide thing. You know, we went to playing Singapore. The Beatles really opened all that up. But to do that you needed the song; otherwise you were just a picture in the newspaper, and you had these little hits.

Was "Satisfaction" a great, classic piece of work?

Well, it's a signature tune, really, rather than a great, classic painting, because it's only one thing, a kind of signature that everyone knows.

Why? What are the ingredients?

It has a very catchy title. It has a very catchy guitar riff. It has a great guitar sound, which was original at that time. And it captures a spirit of the times, which is very important in those kind of songs. Alienation. Or it's a bit more than that, maybe, but a kind of sexual alienation. Alienation's not quite the right word, but it's one word that would do.

Yeah, it's being in your twenties, isn't it? Teenage guys can't often formulate this stuff — when you're that young.

Who wrote "Satisfaction"?

Well, Keith wrote the lick. I think he had this lyric, "I can't get no satisfaction," which, actually, is a line in a Chuck Berry song called "Thirty Days."

Which is "I can't get no satisfaction"?

"I can't get no satisfaction from the judge."

Did you know that when you wrote it?

No, I didn't know it, but Keith might have heard it back then, because it's not any way an English person would express it. I'm not saying that he purposely nicked anything, but we played those records a lot.

So it just could have stuck in the back of your head.

Yeah, that was just one little line. And then I wrote the rest of it. There was no melody, really.

When you play it today, how do you feel about it?
You've got to play it every night.

Well, I try to do it as well as I can, and I do the verse softer, so I give it some sort of dynamic. I try to make it melodic. Maybe we shouldn't really do it every night; I don't know.

"As Tears Go By" was your first big, classic ballad.
Who wrote that?

I wrote the lyrics, and Keith wrote the melody. But in some rock, you know, there's no melody until the singer starts to sing it. Sometimes there's a definite melody, but quite often it's your job as the singer to invent the melody. I start with one melody, and I make it another melody, over the same chord sequence.

You wrote it when you were twenty-one.
What do you think of it now?

It's a very melancholy song for a twenty-one-year-old to write: "The evening of the day, watching children play…" It's very dumb and naïve, but it's got a very sad sort of thing about it, almost like an older person might write. It's like a metaphor for being old: you're watching children playing and realizing you're not a child. It's a relatively mature song considering the rest of the output at the time. And we didn't think of doing it because the Rolling Stones were a butch blues group. But Marianne Faithfull's version was already a big, proven hit song.

Were you surprised that something of this kind popped
out of you at twenty-one?

It was one of the first things I ever wrote. I see songwriting as having to do with experience, and the more you've experienced, the better it is. But it has to be tempered, and you just must let your imagination run.

You can't just experience something and leave it at that. You've got to try and embroider, like any kind of writing. And that's the fun part of it. You have this one experience looking out of a window, seeing children. Well, you might not have felt anything, but then you just let your mind drift and dream, and you imagine an older person doing that. You put yourself in their point of view, and you start to write other things, and all this is a very subconscious thing. Out of that comes a mature thought, out of a young person.

I was reading Pushkin, and his stories are autobiographical. But not totally, because he was never in Siberia — but his friends were, so he uses it. You use your own experience, and then you spice it up with your friends' observations and your imagination.

The next record was *Aftermath*, which has "Paint It Black," "Under My Thumb," and "Stupid Girl." Does that stand out in your mind?

That was a big landmark record for me. It's the first time we wrote the whole record and finally laid to rest the ghost of having to do these very nice and interesting, no doubt, but, still, cover versions of old R & B songs — which we didn't really feel we were doing justice, to be perfectly honest, particularly because we didn't have the maturity. Plus, everyone was doing it.

Aftermath has a very wide spectrum of music styles: "Paint It Black" was this kind of Turkish song, and there were also very bluesy things like "Goin' Home," and I remember some sort of ballads on there. It had a lot of good songs, it had a lot of different styles, and it was very well recorded. So it was, to my mind, a real marker.

Why does "Under My Thumb" work so well?

It's got Brian playing these marimbas. That riff played on marimbas really makes it. Plus, the groove it gets in the end of the tune. It speeds up, actually. And it becomes this kind of groove tune at the end. It was never a single, but it was always a very well-known album track. And then it became a thing feminists fastened on.

Incorrectly, you think.

It's a bit of a jokey number. It's not really an anti-feminist song any more than any of the others. It's a caricature, and it's in reply to a girl who was a very pushy woman.

Somebody specific?

No, I don't think so.

**Also, on that same album you've got "Stupid Girl,"
which is a really nasty song.**

It's much nastier than "Under My Thumb."

**What was going on in your life when you were writing
songs like "Stupid Girl"?**

Obviously, I was having a bit of trouble. I wasn't in a good relationship. Or I was in too many bad relationships. I had so many girlfriends at that point. None of them seemed to care they weren't pleasing me very much. I was obviously in with the wrong group. [Laughs] The pain I had to go through!

**Then you did *Between the Buttons*. What do you think
of that album?**

Frank Zappa used to say he really liked it. It's a good record, but it was unfortunately rather spoiled. We recorded it in London on four-track machines. We bounced it back to do overdubs so many times we lost the sound of a lot of it.

Does that record mean a lot to you?

No. What's on it?

"Connection."

It's nice. "Connection" is really nice.

"Yesterday's Papers."

Yeah, the first song I ever wrote completely on my own for a Rolling Stones record. "My Obsession," that's a good one. They sounded so great, but then, later on, I was really disappointed with it. Isn't "Ruby Tuesday" on there or something? I don't think the rest of the songs are that brilliant. "Ruby Tuesday" is good. I think that's a wonderful song.

It's just a nice melody, really. And a lovely lyric. Neither of which I wrote, but I always enjoy singing it. But I agree with you about the rest of the songs — I don't think they're there. I don't think I thought they were very good at the time either.

**You then did *Their Satanic Majesties Request*.
What was going on here?**

I probably started to take too many drugs.

What do you think about *Satanic Majesties* now?

Well, it's not very good. It had interesting things on it, but I don't think any of the songs are very good. It's a bit like *Between the Buttons*. It's a sound experience, really, rather than a song experience. There's two good songs on it: "She's a Rainbow" and "2000 Light Years from Home," which we did do. The rest of them are nonsense.

I listened to it recently, and it sounds like Spinal Tap.

Really, I know.

Was it just you trying to be the Beatles?

I think we were just taking too much acid. We were just getting carried away, just thinking anything you did was fun and everyone should listen to it. The whole thing, we were on acid. We were on acid doing the cover picture. I always remember doing that. It was like being at school, you know, sticking on the bits of colored paper and things. It was really silly. But we enjoyed it. [Laughs] Also, we did it to piss Andrew [Loog Oldham, their manager at the time] off, because he was such a pain in the neck. The more we wanted to unload him, we decided to go on this path to alienate him.

Just to force him out?

Yeah. Without actually doing it legally, we forced him out. He wanted out anyway. We were so out of our minds.

After it came out and it was kind of a clunk record, how did you consider it?

A phase. A passing fancy.

You followed up with "Jumpin' Jack Flash."

We did that one as a single, out of all the acid of *Satanic Majesties*.

What's that song about? "Born in a cross fire hurricane..."

It's about having a hard time and getting out. Just a metaphor for getting out of all the acid things.

And it did bring you back. You launch the so-called golden era: *Beggars Banquet, Let It Bleed, Sticky Fingers, Exile on Main Street.* **Let's start with** *Beggars Banquet.* **It had extraordinary power, with songs like "Street Fighting Man," "Salt of the Earth," "Stray Cat Blues," and "Jigsaw Puzzle." What was going on in your life at this time? What were you listening to and reading?**

God, what was I doing? Who was I living with? It was all recorded in London, and I was living in this rented house in Chester Square. I was living with Marianne Faithfull. Was I still? Yeah. And I was just writing a lot, reading a lot. I was educating myself. I was reading a lot of poetry, I was reading a lot of philosophy. I was out and about. I was very social, always hanging out with [art gallery owner] Robert Fraser's group of people.

And I wasn't taking so many drugs that it was messing up my creative processes. It was a very good period, 1968 — there was a good feeling in the air. It was a very creative period for everyone. There was a lot going on in the theater. Marianne was kind of involved with it, so I would go to the theater upstairs, hang out with the young directors of the time and the young filmmakers.

Let's start with "Sympathy for the Devil."

I think that was taken from an old idea of Baudelaire's, I think, but I could be wrong. Sometimes when I look at my

Baudelaire books, I can't see it in there. But it was an idea I got from French writing.* And I just took a couple of lines and expanded on it. I wrote it as sort of like a Bob Dylan song. And you can see it in this movie Godard shot called *Sympathy for the Devil* [originally titled *One Plus One*], which is very fortuitous. Godard wanted to do a film of us in the studio. It would never happen now, to get someone as interesting as Godard. And stuffy.

So that's a wholly Mick Jagger song.

Uh-huh. I mean, Keith suggested that we do it in another rhythm, so that's how bands help you.

Were you trying to put out a specific philosophical idea here? You know, you're singing, "Just as every cop is a criminal and all the sinners saints"...

Yeah, there's all these attractions of opposites and turning things upside down.

When you were writing it, did you conceive of it as this grand work?

I knew it was something good, because I would just keep banging away at it until the fucking band recorded it.

There wasn't any resistance. It was just that I knew that I wanted to do it and get it down. And I hadn't written a lot of songs on my own, so you have to teach it. When you write songs, you have to like them yourself first, but then you have to make everyone else like them, because you can force them to play it, but you can't force them to like it. And if they like it, they'll do a much

---

* Later on, Mick recalled *The Master and Margarita* by Mikhail Bulgakov as another likely influence.

better job than if they're just playing because they feel they're obligated, and then you get inspired, and that's what being in a band's about rather than hiring people.

I knew it was a good song. You just have this feeling. It had its poetic beginning, and then it had historic references and then philosophical jottings and so on. It's all very well to write that in verse, but to make it into a pop song is something different. Especially in England — you're skewered on the altar of pop culture if you become pretentious.

> The song has a very strong opening: "Please allow me
> to introduce myself." And then it's this everyman figure
> in history who keeps appearing from the beginning
> of civilization.

Yeah, it's a very long historical figure — the figures of evil and figures of good — so it is a tremendously long trail he's made as personified in this piece.

> What else makes this song so powerful?

It has a very hypnotic groove, a samba, which has a tremendous hypnotic power, rather like good dance music. It doesn't speed up or slow down. It keeps this constant groove. Plus, the actual samba rhythm is a great one to sing on, but it's also got some other suggestions in it, an undercurrent of being primitive — because it is a primitive African, South American, Afro-whatever-you-call-that rhythm. So to white people, it has a very sinister thing about it.

But forgetting the cultural colors, it is a very good vehicle for producing a powerful piece. It becomes less pretentious because it's a very unpretentious groove. If it had been done as a ballad, it wouldn't have been as good.

Obviously, Altamont gave it a whole other resonance.

Yeah, Altamont is much later than the song, isn't it? I know what you're saying, but I'm just stuck in my periods, because you were asking me what I was doing, and I was in my study in Chester Square.

**After Altamont, did you shy away from performing
that song?**

Yeah, probably, for a bit.

It stigmatized the song in a way?

Yeah. Because it became so involved, sort of journalistically and so on. There were other things going on with it apart from Altamont.

Was it the black magic thing?

Yeah. That's not really what I meant. My whole thing of this song was not black magic and all this silly nonsense — like Megadeth or whatever else came afterward. It was different than that. We had played around with that imagery before — which is *Satanic Majesties* — but it wasn't really put into words.

**After the concert itself, when it became apparent
that somebody got killed, how did you feel?**

Well, awful. Just awful. You feel a responsibility. How could it all have been so silly and wrong? But I didn't think of these things that you guys thought of, you in the press: this great loss of innocence, this cathartic end of the era...I didn't think of any of that.

That particular burden didn't weigh on my mind. It was more how awful it was to have had this experience and how awful it was for someone to get killed and how sad it was for his family and how dreadfully the Hells Angels behaved.

Did it cause you to back off that kind of satanic imagery?

The satanic imagery stuff was very overplayed by journalists. We didn't want to really go down that road. And I felt that song was enough. You didn't want to make a career out of it. But bands did that — Jimmy Page, for instance.

Aleister Crowley...

I knew lots of people that were into Aleister Crowley. What I'm saying is, it wasn't what I meant by the song "Sympathy for the Devil." If you read it, it's not about black magic, per se.

On that same record you did "Street Fighting Man."
Tell me a bit about that.

It was a very strange time in France. But not only in France but also in America, because of the Vietnam War and these endless disruptions.

Did you write that song?

Yeah. I wrote a lot of the melody and all the words, and Keith and I sat around and made this wonderful track, with Dave Mason playing the shehnai on it live.

The shehnai?

It's a kind of Indian reed instrument a bit like a primitive clarinet. It comes in at the end of the tune. It has a very wailing, strange sound.

It's another of the classic songs. Why does it have such resonance today?

I don't know if it does. I don't know whether we should really play it. I was persuaded to put it in this tour because it seemed to fit in, but I'm not sure if it really has any resonance for the present day. I don't really like it that much. I thought it was a very good thing at the time. There was all this violence going on. They almost toppled the government in France; de Gaulle went into this complete funk, as he had in the past, and he went and sort of locked himself in his house in the country. And so the government was almost inactive. It was a direct inspiration, because by contrast, London was very quiet...

Sleepy London town?

Isn't "No Expectations" on that record?

It's got that wonderful steel guitar part.

That's Brian [Jones] playing. We were sitting around in a circle on the floor, singing and playing, recording with open mics.

That was the last time I remember Brian really being totally involved in something that was really worth doing. He was there with everyone else. It's funny how you remember — but that was the last moment I remember him doing that, because he had just lost interest in everything.

Let It Bleed?

Yeah. What's on that? It was all recorded at the same time, these two records.

Some of them were recorded on one and spilled over to the next.

It's got "Midnight Rambler," "Love in Vain," "You Can't Always Get What You Want." This seems to be one of the bleakest records that you made. The songs are very disturbing, and the scenery is grim. The topics are rape, war, murder, addiction. Why this view of the world?

Well, it's a very rough, very violent era. The Vietnam War. Violence on the screens, pillage and burning. And Vietnam was not war as we knew it in the conventional sense. The thing about Vietnam was that it wasn't like World War II, and it wasn't like Korea, and it wasn't like the Gulf War. It was a real nasty war, and people didn't like it. People objected, and people didn't want to fight it.

Are you saying the Vietnam War had a heavy influence on this record?

I think so. Even though I was living in America only part-time, I was influenced. All those images were on television. Plus, the spill out onto campuses.

Who wrote "Midnight Rambler"?

That's a song Keith and I really wrote together. We were on a holiday in Italy. In this very beautiful hill town, Positano, for a few nights. Why we should write such a dark song in this beautiful, sunny place, I really don't know. We wrote everything there — the tempo changes, everything. And I'm playing the harmonica in these little cafés, and there's Keith with the guitar.

"Gimme Shelter"?

That's a kind of end-of-the-world song, really. It's apocalypse; the whole record's like that.

Whose idea was it to do the Robert Johnson song "Love in Vain"?

I don't know. We changed the arrangement quite a lot from Robert Johnson's. We put in extra chords that aren't there on the Robert Johnson version. Made it more country. And that's another strange song, because it's very poignant. Robert Johnson was a wonderful lyric writer, and his songs are quite often about love, but they're desolate.

"You Can't Always Get What You Want"?

It's a good song, even if I say so myself.

Why is that one so popular?

Because it's got a very sing-along chorus. And people can identify with it: no one gets what they always want. It's got a very good melody. It's got very good orchestral touches that Jack Nitzsche helped with. So it's got all the ingredients. I think it's a good record. I'd put it as one of my favorites.

What about your relationship with Keith? Does it bug you, having Keith as your primary musical partner? Does it bug you having a partner at all?

No, I think it's essential. You don't have to have a partner for everything you do. You have good times and bad times with them. It's just the nature of it.

People also like partnerships because they can identify with the drama of two people in partnership. They can feed off a partnership, and that keeps people entertained. If you have a successful partnership, it's self-sustaining.

**Why do you think you and Keith survived,
unlike John Lennon and Paul McCartney?**

That's hard to make even a stab at, because I don't know John and Paul well enough. I know them slightly, same as you, probably, and maybe you knew John better at the end. I can hazard a guess that they were both rather strong personalities, and both felt they were totally independent. They seemed to be very competitive over leadership of the band. The thing in leadership is, you can have times when one person is more at the center than the other, but there can't be too much arguing about it all the time. Because if you're always at loggerheads, you just have to go, "Okay, if I can't have a say in this and this, then fuck it. What am I doing here?" So you sort of agree what your roles are. Whereas John and Paul felt they were too strong, and they wanted to be in charge. If there are ten things, they both wanted to be in charge of nine of them. You're not going to make a relationship like that work, are you?

**How was it when Keith was taking heroin all the time?
How did you handle that?**

I don't find it easy to talk about other people's drug problems. If he wants to talk about it, fine, he can talk about it all he wants. Elton John talks about his bulimia on television. But I don't want to talk about his bulimia, and I don't want to talk about Keith's drug problems.

How did I handle it? Oh, with difficulty. I don't find it easy dealing with people with drug problems. It helps if you're all taking drugs, all the same drugs. But anyone taking heroin is thinking about taking heroin more than they're thinking about anything else. That's the general rule about most drugs. You try and make everything work, but the drug comes first.

How did his drug use affect the band?

I think that people taking drugs occasionally are great. I think there's nothing wrong with it. But if you do it the whole time, you don't produce as good things as you could. It sounds like a puritanical statement, but it's based on experience.

You obviously developed a certain relationship based on him as a drug addict, part of which was you running the band. Drug addicts are basically incompetent to run anything.

Yeah, it's all they can do to turn up. And people have different personalities when they're drunk or take heroin, or whatever drugs. When Keith was taking heroin, it was very difficult to work. He still was creative, but it took a long time. And everyone else was taking drugs and drinking a tremendous amount, too. And it affected everyone in certain ways. But I've never really talked to Keith about this stuff. So I have no idea what he feels. So I'm always second-guessing. When I tell you something, I probably read it in *Rolling Stone*.

What's your relationship with him now?

We have a very good relationship at the moment. But it's a different relationship to what we had when we were fifty and different to what we had when we were thirty. We see each other every day, talk to each other every day, play every day. But it's not the same as when we were twenty and shared rooms.

Can we talk about Brian Jones?

The thing about Brian is that he was an extremely difficult person. You don't really feel like talking bad about someone that's had such a miserable time. But he did give everyone else an extremely miserable ride. There was something very, very disturbed about him. He was very unhappy with life, very frustrated. He was talented, but he was a paranoid personality and not at all suited to be in show business [laughs].

Hmm. Show business killed him?

Yeah. Well, he killed himself, but he should've been playing trad-jazz weekends and teaching in school; he probably would have been better off.

What was Brian's contribution to the band?

Well, he had a huge contribution in the early days. He was very obsessed with it, which you always need. Getting it going and its personality and how it should be. He was obsessed. Too obsessed for me. There's a certain enthusiasm, and after that it becomes obsession. I go back to my thing about collecting: it's nice to collect stamps, but if it becomes obsessive, and you start stealing for your stamps, it becomes too much. He was obsessed about the image of the band, and he was very exclusionary. He saw the Stones as a blues band based on Muddy Waters, Elmore James, and that tradition.

I don't think he really liked playing Chuck Berry songs. He was a purist. He was very middle-class; he came from one of the most middle-class towns in England, Cheltenham, one of the most genteel towns in the most genteel area of England. So his whole outlook and upbringing was even worse in the gentility fashion than mine.

What started causing tensions in the group among Keith, you, and him?

Brian was a very jealous person and didn't read the right books about leadership [laughs]. And you can't be jealous and be a leader. He was obsessed with the idea of being the leader of the band. You have to realize that everyone in a band is all more or less together, and everyone has their own niche, and some people lead in some ways, and some people lead in others. He never could understand that; he never got it, so he alienated people. And as I say, he was very narrow-minded in his view of music, and, really, Keith and I had been very catholic.

But did you take away the leadership of the band from him?

If you're the singer in the band, you always get more attention than anyone else. Brian got very jealous when I got attention. And then the main jealousy was because Keith and I started writing songs, and he wasn't involved in that. To be honest, Brian had no talent for writing songs. None. I've never known a guy with less talent for songwriting.

Did he give the band a sound?

Yes. He played the slide guitar at a time when no one really played it. He played in the style of Elmore James, and he had this very lyrical touch. He evolved into more of an experimental musician, but he lost touch with the guitar, and always as a musician you must have one thing you do well. He dabbled too much.

Can you describe your falling apart?

It happened gradually. He went from [being] an obsessive

about the band to being rather an outsider. He'd turn up late to recording sessions, and he'd miss the odd gig every now and then. He let his health deteriorate because he drank too much and took drugs when they were new, hung out too much, stayed up too late, partied too much, and didn't concentrate on what he was doing. Let his talent slide.

Did you fire him, finally?

Yeah.

How was that?

Not pleasant. It's never pleasant, firing people. But it had to be done because we felt we needed someone, and he wasn't there. He wouldn't come to the studio. He wouldn't do anything. We felt we couldn't go on. In fact, we came to a point where we couldn't play live. We couldn't hold our heads up and play because Brian was a total liability. It was pathetic. Of course, now I suppose we would have had him admitted to rehab clinics and so on, but those things, unfortunately, in those days were not the path. He tried lots of doctors, but they just gave him more pills.

Do you feel guilty somehow about it all?

No, I don't really. I do feel that I behaved in a very childish way, but we were very young, and in some ways we picked on him. Unfortunately, he made himself a target for it; he was very, very jealous, very difficult, very manipulative, and if you do that in this kind of a group of people, you get back as good as you give, to be honest. I wasn't understanding enough about his drug addiction. No one seemed to know much about drug addiction. Things like LSD were all new. No one knew the harm. People thought cocaine was good for you.

Charlie told me: "Brian Jones had a death wish at a young age. Brian's talent wasn't up to it. He wasn't up to leading a band. He was not a pleasant person to be around. And he was never there to help people to write a song. That's when Mick lost his patience. We carried Brian Jones."

That's straight to the point, isn't it? Whether he had a death wish or not, I don't know. He was a very sad, pitiable figure at the end. He was a talented musician, but he let it go and proved to be a rather sad precursor to a lot of other people.

How do you think Brian died?
There's been a lot of speculation.

Drowned in a pool. That other stuff is people trying to make money.

After Brian died, you recorded what has to be considered another classic Stones album, *Sticky Fingers*. Was it strange making an album without Brian?

Oh, yeah. A whole new world, an era away from *Beggars Banquet*. We had Mick Taylor in the band, and we had a new record company. We'd been at Decca, and we'd been rather successful, but we didn't get paid very much, and it was like being with strangers.

The cover of that album is a pair of jeans with a real zipper.

This was Andy Warhol's idea.

There's underwear on the back. Is that you?

No. It's one of Andy's ... "protégés" is the polite word we used to use, I think.

All right. That's the news in this interview.

Why does "Brown Sugar" work like mad?

That's a bit of a mystery, isn't it? I wrote that song in Australia in the middle of a field. They were really odd circumstances. I was doing this movie, *Ned Kelly*, and my hand had got really damaged in this action sequence. So stupid. I was trying to rehabilitate my hand and had this new kind of electric guitar, and I was playing in the middle of the outback and wrote this tune.

But why it works? I mean, it's a good groove and all that. The groove is slightly similar to Freddy Cannon, this rather obscure Fifties rock performer — "Tallahassee Lassie" or something. Do you remember this? "She's down in F-l-a." Anyway, the groove of that — *boom-boom-boom-boom-boom* — is "Going to a go-go," or whatever, but that's the groove.

And you wrote it all?

Yeah.

**This is one of your biggest hits, a great,
classic radio single, except the subject matter is slavery,
interracial sex, eating pussy...**

[Laughs] And drugs. That's a double entendre, just thrown in.

Brown sugar being heroin?

Brown sugar being heroin and —

And pussy?

That makes it...the whole mess thrown in. God knows what I'm on about on that song. It's such a mishmash. All the nasty subjects in one go.

Were you surprised that it was such a success with all that stuff in it?

I didn't think about it at the time. I never would write that song now.

Why?

I would probably censor myself. I'd think, "Oh God, I can't. I've got to stop. I can't just write raw like that."

"Wild Horses." Is that a Keith song?

Yeah, it was his melody. And he wrote the phrase "wild horses," but I wrote the rest of [the lyrics].

It's one of the prettiest.

I like the song. It's an example of a pop song, taking this cliché "wild horses," which is awful, really, but making it work without sounding like a cliché when you're doing it.

What about "Moonlight Mile"? That's a song without Keith — that's you and Mick Taylor.

Yeah, we recorded it in my house in the country, Stargroves. And we recorded a lot of stuff [there]: "Bitch," stuff from *Exile on Main Street*.

**At the same time? And then just divided the songs
between records?**

Yeah. It's a good house to record in. And that's also where the Who made an album. Led Zeppelin recorded one. But anyway, I remember Mick Taylor playing that song. Real dreamy kind of semi–Middle Eastern piece. Yeah, that's a real pretty song—and a nice string arrangement.

**You do "Dead Flowers" on this record. You put on this
kind of loopy country voice.**

I love country music, but I find it very hard to take it seriously. I also think a lot of country music is sung with the tongue in cheek, so I do it tongue in cheek. The harmonic thing is very different from the blues. It doesn't bend notes in the same way, so I suppose it's very English, really. Even though it's been very Americanized, it feels very close to me, to my roots, so to speak.

**Do you have anything to say about "Sister Morphine,"
which is also on this album? Did Marianne
write part of this?**

She wrote a couple of lines; she always says she wrote everything, though. I can't even tell you which ones. She's always complaining she doesn't get enough money from it. Now she says she should have got it all.

What is it about?

It's about a man after an accident, really. It's not about being addicted to morphine so much as that. Ry Cooder plays wonderfully on that. If you listen to the lyrics—that's what I remember, anyway. "Here I lie in my hospital bed."

Cousin cocaine?

Yeah, that's the bit she wrote.

**Critics say your next album, *Exile on Main Street*,
is the best Stones album. What do you think?**

It's a bit overrated, to be honest. Compared to *Let It Bleed* and *Beggars Banquet*, which I think are more of a piece. I don't see it's as thematic as the other two. I'm not saying it's not good. It doesn't contain as many outstanding songs as the previous two records. I think the playing's quite good. It's got a raw quality, but I don't think all around it's as good.

What was the atmosphere recording *Exile*?

Well, *Exile on Main Street* was done in different pieces. There's this part which is recorded at Olympic [Studios], maybe a third. Another part is recorded in my house in the country in England. And half of it's recorded in Keith's basement in the South of France. And it's all mixed in L.A.

What was the band like at that time?

"Stoned" is the word that might describe it. [Laughs] It's the first album Mick Taylor's on, really. So it's different than previous albums, which had Brian on them — or Brian not on them, as the case may be. It was a difficult period, because we had all these lawsuits going with [business manager] Allen Klein. We had to leave England because of tax problems. We had no money and went to live in the South of France — the first album we made where we weren't based in England, thus the title.

Was the band at its drug zenith at that time?

Yeah.

What was the mood? What was the vibe around?

Just winging it. Staying up all night.

Keith was a full-scale junkie at that point?

Totally.

And everybody else?

Stoned on something, one thing or another. So I don't think it was particularly pleasant. I didn't have a very good time. It was this communal thing where you don't know whether you're record-ing or living or having dinner; you don't know when you're going to play, when you're going to sing — very difficult. Too many hangers-on. I went with the flow, and the album got made. These things have a certain energy, and there's a certain flow to it, and it got impossible. Everyone was so out of it. And the engineers, the producers — all the people that were supposed to be organized — were more disorganized than anybody.

So it was a classic of that era, when that was a common approach to things.

Absolutely. But the previous ones were easier to make.

Let It Bleed?

We were still like that, but we were grounded because we were still in England and had this way of doing it. We went to the studio and lived in London. Though it was made in a screwy way, it was organized, structured — a studio rather than a home recording. Those home recordings have a good side to them, but they get floaty; you don't really know what you're doing.

Who wrote "Tumbling Dice"?

[Laughs] Keith and me. I wrote the lyrics.

And he did the groove?

Yeah. It comes back to that thing where I really don't remember who had the melody or not, but it doesn't really matter.

Why does that beat grab you so quick?

I don't really know what people like about it. I don't think it's our best stuff. I don't think it has good lyrics. But people seem to really like it, so good for them.

Do you cringe when you hear some of the old drug songs?

Sometimes. Not only the drugs — I just cringe, period.

Many people would be embarrassed to discuss the drug behavior of their youth, but you have no choice.

I was thinking about this the other day, and I don't really think I was suited to heavy drug behavior, to be perfectly honest. But I don't mind talking about it. It's hard to believe that you did so many drugs for so long. That's what I find really hard. And didn't really consider it. You know, it was eating and drinking and taking drugs and having sex. It was just part of life. It wasn't really anything special. It was just a bit of a bore, really. Everyone took drugs the whole time, and you were out of it the whole time. It wasn't a special event.

But drugs definitely had a big impact on your band.

All these drugs had tremendous influence on behavior. I think half of starting to take drugs in that early period was to kind of place yourself outside of normal society.

Thinking about those days, do you feel this was a good use of time or a waste of time?

Good use of time. [Laughs] I'm reticent to go into a sort of dreadful reminiscence of the Swinging Sixties.

What about the contribution of Mick Taylor to the band in these years?

I think he had a big contribution. He made it very musical. He was a very fluent, melodic player, which we never had, and we don't have now. Neither Keith nor [Ronnie Wood] plays that kind of style. It was very good for me working with him — Charlie and I were talking about this the other day. We could sit down, I could sit down, with Mick Taylor, and he would play very fluid lines against my vocals. He was exciting, and he was very pretty, and it gave me something to follow, to bang off. Some people think that's the best version of the band that existed.

What do you think?

They're all interesting periods. They're all different. I obviously can't say if I think Mick Taylor was the best, because it sort of trashes the period the band is in now.

Why did Mick Taylor leave?

I still don't really know.

He never explained?

Not really. He wanted to have a solo career. I think he found it difficult to get on with Keith.

On musical issues?

Everything. I'm guessing.

After those four great albums, it seems like a weak period starts. There's *Goats Head Soup*, which has "Angie." And *Black and Blue* has got "Memory Motel" and "Fool to Cry." But these records are kind of weak after those big ones. What happened? Did it have to do with Keith's drug use?

Yeah, I think so. I find it so hard to remember, though, I don't want to commit myself to saying something. Everyone was using drugs, Keith particularly. So I think it suffered a bit from all that. General malaise. I think we got a bit carried away with our own popularity and so on. It was a bit of a holiday period [laughs]. I mean, we cared, but we didn't care as much as we had. Not really concentrating on the creative process, and we had such money problems. We had been so messed around by Allen Klein and the British revenue. We were really in a very bad way. So we had to move. And it sort of destabilized us a bit. We flew off all edges.

Everybody went in different directions?

We had all lived in London before this.

So for the first time you guys are not together all the time.

Not only couldn't we stay in England, we couldn't go to America because we had immigration problems. So we were limited. It was a very difficult period.

You came back, though, with *Some Girls*.

You are absolutely right!

Did that have to do, perhaps, with being in New York City?

Well done! I'd moved to New York at that point. The inspiration for the record was really based in New York and the ways of the town. I think that gave it an extra spur and hardness. And then, of course, there was the punk thing that had started in 1976. Punk and disco were going on at the same time, so it was quite an interesting period. New York and London, too. Paris — there was punk there. Lots of dance music. Paris and New York had all this Latin dance music, which was really quite wonderful. Much more interesting than the stuff that came afterward.

"Miss You" is one of the all-time greatest Rolling Stones grooves.

Yeah. I got that together with Billy Preston, actually. Billy had shown me the four-on-the-floor bass drum part, and I would just play the guitar. I remember playing that in the El Mocambo club when Keith was on trial in Toronto for whatever he was doing. We were supposed to be there making this live record.

That was the first performance of it?

Yeah. I was still writing it, actually. We were just in rehearsal.

But that's a wholly Mick Jagger song?

Yeah.

And "Beast of Burden"?

That's more like Keith's song. I wrote lyrics.

**It's got that really nice little lick on that.
And "Respectable"?**

Yeah, this is the kind of edgy punk ethos. Yeah, the groove of it — and on all of those songs, the whole thing was to play it all fast, fast, fast. I had a lot of problems with Keith about it, but that was the deal at the time.

**Keith told me that you kept trying to make a disco album,
and he didn't think that was the Stones.
Was that the problem?**

Not at all. I wanted to make more of a rock album. I just had one song that had a dance groove: "Miss You." But I didn't want to make a disco album. I wrote all these songs — like "Respectable," "Lies," "When the Whip Comes Down."

So most of the songs on this album are yours?

No, not most. I only mentioned half. I don't know what else is on there.

"Shattered."

That's one of Keith's and me in combination.

"Far Away Eyes"?

Combination. I wasn't out to make a disco record, making "Far Away Eyes." But "Miss You" really caught the moment, because that was the deal at the time. And that's what made that record take off. It was a really great record. I seem to like records that have one overriding mood with lots of little offshoots. Even though there's a lot of bases covered, there's lots of straight-ahead rock and roll. It's very brass-edged. It's very Rolling Stones, not a lot of frills.

On the *Some Girls* cover — and not for the first time —
the members of the band are in drag. This now seems
to have become a rock tradition. What are the origins
of the androgynous appeal of rock and roll?

Elvis. Elvis was very androgynous. People in the older generation were afraid of Elvis because of this. That was one of the things they saw in Elvis. They called it "effeminate." And they saw it straightaway.

I saw Elvis as a rock singer, and obviously you were attracted to him because he was a good-looking guy. But they saw an effeminate guy. If you look at the pictures, the eyes are done with makeup, and everything's perfect. Look at Little Richard. He had a very feminine appearance, but you didn't translate that into what Little Richard's sex orientation was.

When did you first start to incorporate all that into your own act?

Well, we did it straightaway, unconsciously.

But when did you get deliberate about it?

Oh, about 1960. Very early, before we made records. As far as I was concerned, it was part of the whole thing from the beginning. I couldn't have talked about it like I talk about it now. But it wasn't some new thing. You were copying all your idols. I always thought Buddy Holly was very effeminate. His voice, not necessarily his look. And you just incorporated it all. I just pushed it further because it seemed the natural thing to do. Plus, there was that whole culture of people you met who were gay, in the theater and so on. And everyone in show business talked in a very camp, English way: "All right, ducky," "Come along, dear." So as soon as you were in it professionally, that was the way people carried on, so it became even more camp.

The Beatles weren't like this. You were wearing heavy makeup and skirts.

I think you just pushed the whole thing because you thought it was sophisticated to be camp and effeminate. It was a thing you showed some of the time and then put aside. It was very English — guys dressing up in drag is nothing particularly new.

David Bowie told me that you were the master: "He taught all the rest of us."

Well, that's very nice. And it obviously worked and offended people, which was always the big thing, something new to offend them with. I think what we did in this era was take all these things that were unspoken in previous incarnations of rock and roll and intellectualized them.

**When were you first aware that you were this beauty,
that you had a power to attract both boys and girls?**

Oh, from the beginning.

The girls, then the boys?

Both, always.

In a sexual sense?

I didn't really think about it. Boys were a very essential part of rock and roll. The girls were more onlookers. When I was fifteen, sixteen, I used to play this old-fashioned rock and roll — like Little Richard, Jerry Lee Lewis, Elvis. And I always felt the boys were more involved than the girls. Boys, as far as England was concerned, were always the hard core. And you just know the guys like it. They want to be you. Some might be attracted to you without knowing it. The girls are more obviously reaching out to you. In those days, guys didn't reach out, put their arms around you, and kiss you.

**Pete Townshend wrote an essay that appeared in *Rolling
Stone* about your fortieth birthday: "When I am
with Jagger, I do love to look at him. He is still very beautiful
in my eyes; much has been said of his androgynous
attraction, and I suppose my response to his physical
presence confirms all that." What's your response?**

Gosh, it's nice to know, isn't it? Wow, Pete! You don't think of

Pete Townshend as someone who would respond to any of that, do you? To be honest, he would be the last person. But I think John responded to it, John Lennon.

In what way?

He responded to it in a different way. When you get a big response, you push it and so on, until you've really done it. And then you don't do it anymore. And it's great fun, dressing up and being this figure. It's wonderful.

What did John say?

He said something in your magazine. It wasn't to do with appearance, more with music. When asked about the Rolling Stones, he said, "I like the butch stuff, and I don't like the faggy stuff." But you don't want to be butch the whole time. It would drive you mad, wouldn't it?

Rock and roll is a very macho field.

Yeah, but the Rolling Stones isn't just a rock band.

**What does it say to you about rock and roll,
in what we've seen in Elton and Boy George?**

See, it's very confusing. In rock and roll, when I think of both sides of the coin or whatever you want to call it, I don't really think of Elton John. He doesn't spring to my mind, somehow. His appearance is flamboyant, always, but I don't think of him as a feminine stage persona. I'm not saying he was a great butch rocker. But he wasn't that feminine to me.

Boy George was a feminine persona in a way — the moves and so on. He was an overt homosexual. Apart from those two, where are we going with it? I can't think of hardly any others who are that well-known. Are there more who we've forgotten about?

**Well, David Bowie played with the same images
and themes that you have.**

But as you said, rock and roll mostly is a very butch thing, and it appeals to one hard side of the masculine character. But I don't think the Rolling Stones are only a rock band. They can be other things. They can be very feminine.

The Stones?

Yeah. Which tends to be overlooked because we don't show it that much because of the nature of the gigs.

———————

**After *Some Girls* comes *Emotional Rescue*.
Does it have a lot of resonance?**

No, it doesn't. You know, *Emotional Rescue* is a lot of leftovers from *Some Girls*. Really.

And then comes *Tattoo You*.

Yeah, that's an old record. It's all a lot of old tracks that I dug out. And it was very strange circumstances. I went through all the tracks from those two previous records. It wasn't all outtakes; some of it was old songs.

And then I went back and found previous ones like "Waiting on a Friend," from *Goats Head Soup*. They're all from different periods. Then I had to write lyrics and melodies. A lot of them

didn't have anything, which is why they weren't used at the time —
because they weren't complete. They were just bits, or they were
from early takes. And then I put them all together in an incredibly
cheap fashion. I recorded in this place in Paris in the middle of the
winter. And then I recorded some of it in a broom cupboard, literally, where we did the vocals. The rest of the band were hardly
involved. And then I took it to Bob Clearmountain, who did this
great job of mixing so that it doesn't sound like it's from different
periods.

I think it's your most underrated record.

I think it's excellent. But all the things I usually like, it doesn't
have. It doesn't have any unity of purpose or place or time. What
do you think?

**The playing is so precise on it, so sharp. The band sound is
very modern. And it's got "Start Me Up" on it.**

Which is a track that was just forgotten about, a reject.

And who wrote "Start Me Up"?

It was Keith's great riff, and I wrote the rest. The funny thing
was that it turned into this reggae song after two takes. And that
take on *Tattoo You* was the only take that was a complete rock and
roll take. And then it went to reggae completely for about twenty
takes. And that's why everyone said, "Oh, that's crap. We don't
want to use that." And no one went back to take two, which was
the one we used, the rock track.

What about *Undercover,* your next album?

Not a very special record.

And *Dirty Work?* I think that was the last album the
Stones made before you and Keith had a falling-out. How
was that record?

Not special.

I remember that when you made *Dirty Work,* you were
about to tour and then changed your mind.

Touring *Dirty Work* would have been a nightmare. It was a
terrible period. Everyone was hating each other so much; there
were so many disagreements. It was very petty; everyone was so out
of their brains, and Charlie was in seriously bad shape. When the
idea of touring came up, I said, "I don't think it's going to work." In
retrospect I was 100 percent right. It would have been the worst
Rolling Stones tour. Probably would have been the end of the band.

But, finally, it was your decision not to tour. Was Keith
upset with that?

Oh, yeah.

And the next thing you do is a solo album.

Yeah. He must have been quite unhappy with that. But when
we signed the recording contract with CBS, I had a provision to
make a solo record. Keith knew all about it, so it wasn't a bolt from
the blue. I don't want to excuse what happened; it was a very bad
period. Everyone was getting on very badly.

And then it turned into a public battle between you
and Keith, with all the sniping in the press.

I think that was Keith's way of trying to get back at me; he just liked to mouth off about it. He quite enjoyed it. He became very upset and overreacted when I wanted to do a solo record, which in retrospect seems a natural thing to want to do. But even before that, everyone was bored playing with each other. We'd reached a period when we were tired of it all. Bill [Wyman] was not enthusiastic to start with — there's a guy that doesn't really want to do much. He's quite happy, whatever he's told to do, but he's not suggesting anything, not helping…a bit morose and bored. You've got Charlie overdoing it in all directions.

He was getting drugged up and drinking?

Yeah. Keith the same. Me the same. Ronnie — I don't know what Ronnie was doing. We just got fed up with each other. You've got a relationship with musicians that depends on what you produce together. But when you don't produce, you get bad reactions — bands break up. You get difficult periods, and that was one of them.

**Do you feel like an underappreciated musician
vis-à-vis Keith?**

I don't think people really know or care that much about what really goes on. I don't think people care about the mechanics of songwriting, particularly. So they think, "Oh, well, Mick must write all the lyrics, and Keith writes all the tunes," which might have been true thirty years ago, but it really isn't true now. But that doesn't worry me very much. Keith might be underappreciated as a lyric writer. I don't think it worries him.

**I was listening to your last solo record, *Wandering Spirit*,
on which you play a lot of guitar, and there are songs
on there that for all intents and purposes could be
Rolling Stones songs.**

Yeah. You couldn't tell. That's me doing what I do, and you

think it's Keith. It's difficult not to do it. I didn't do it on every track. I would come out and go, "I don't want it to sound like that." Then I thought, "Fuck it. If they're good, they're good. It doesn't matter if they're too Stones-y."

Charlie says, "Mick is better with Keith Richards than he is with any other guitar players. I mean even a technically better guitar player — he's better with Keith."
Do you feel that?

Well, yeah, up to a certain point. I do enjoy working with other kinds of guitar players, because Keith is a very definite kind of guitar player. He's obviously very rhythmic and so on, and that works very well with Charlie and myself. Though I do like performing or working with guitar players that also work around lead lines a lot — like Eric [Clapton] or Mick Taylor or Joe Satriani. Whether it's better or not, it's completely different working with them. That's something Jeff Beck, to a certain extent, can do: a guitar player that just plays very careful lead lines and listens to what his vocalist is doing.

In the mid-eighties, when the Stones were not working together, did you and Keith talk?

Hardly at all.

A little while ago, Keith described your relationship like this to me: "We can't even get divorced. I wanted to kill him." Did you feel you were trapped in this marriage?

No. You're not trapped. We were friends before we were in a band, so it's more complicated, but I don't see it as a marriage. They're quite different, a band and a marriage.

How did you patch it up?

What actually happened was, we had a meeting to plan the tour, and as far as I was concerned, it was very easy. At the time [1989], everyone was asking, [whispers] "Wow, what was it like? What happened? How did it all work?" It was a nonevent. What could have been a lot of name-calling wasn't. I think everyone just decided that we'd done all that. Of course, we had to work out what the *modus vivendi* was for everybody, because we were planning a very different kind of tour. Everyone had to realize that they were in a new kind of world. We had to invent new rules. It was bigger business, more efficient than previous tours, than the Seventies drug tours. We were all going to be on time at the shows. Everyone realized they had to pull their weight, and everyone had a role to play, and they were all up for doing it.

Can you describe the time you spent in Barbados with
Keith, deciding if you could put this together?

Keith and I and [financial adviser] Rupert [Lowenstein] had a small meeting first and talked about business. We were in a hotel with the sea crashing outside and the sun shining and drinks, talking about all the money we're going to get and how great it was going to be, and then we bring everyone else in and talk about it.

So that was your reconciliation with Keith? Was there any
talk of putting your heads together and airing issues?

No, and I'm glad we didn't do that, because it could have gone on for weeks. It was better that we just get on with the job. Of course, we had to revisit things afterward.

Charlie said to me, "I don't think you can come between
Mick and Keith — they're family. You can only go so far,

and then you hit an invisible wall.
They don't want anyone in there."

Well, it sounds like one of the wives talking, doesn't it? I remember Bianca [Jagger] saying a very similar thing. But if that's what he thinks, that's what he thinks. It's funny he thinks that. I don't know why he should say that. I think people are afraid to express their opinions half the time.

In front of you and Keith?

Or just in front of me. They think they're going to go back to a period where people would jump down their throats for having an opinion. Drug use makes you snappy, and you get very bad-tempered and have terrible hangovers.

One more quote. Keith says, "Mick clams up all the time.
He keeps a lot inside. It was the way he was brought up.
Just being Mick Jagger at eighteen or nineteen, a star, gives
him reason to protect what space is left."

I think it's very important that you have at least some sort of inner thing you don't talk about. That's why I find it distasteful when all these pop stars talk about their habits. But if that's what they need to do to get rid of them, fine. But I always found it boring. For some people it's real therapy to talk to journalists about their private lives and inner thoughts. But I would rather keep something to myself.

It's wearing. You're on all the time. As much as I love talking to you today, I'd rather be having one day where I don't have to think about me. With all this attention, you become a child. It's awful to be at the center of attention. You can't talk about anything apart from your own experience, your own dopey life. I'd rather do something that can get me out of the center of attention. It's very dangerous. But there's no way, really, to avoid that.

After *Steel Wheels*, you took a couple of years off and came
back with *Voodoo Lounge*. What were your goals going
into both an album and tour? Is it a better album
than Steel *Wheels*?

I don't know if *Steel Wheels* is better than *Voodoo Lounge*,
actually. I don't think there's a huge difference of quality between
the two albums. I wish there was, but I'm afraid, in the end, I don't
think there is.

On *Voodoo Lounge* it seems like you've got better,
more distinctive songs.

I don't know. Perhaps if the *Voodoo Lounge* album had been
more successful commercially, I might have agreed with you,
because commercial success changes everything. It colors your
opinions. If it had sold five million albums, I'd be saying to you,
"It's definitely better than *Steel Wheels*."

Let's talk about it as two rock critics.

That's different.

You told me when you started to make the record that you
were going to spend a lot of time on this one, making
as good a record as you could possibly make, making sure
you've got the songs written in advance. You hired
a producer, which you hadn't done for a long time. Do you
feel that you've met that expectation?

Not completely. But maybe we should list the positive things
rather than the negative. I think there is a really good feeling of the
band on it — that the band is playing very much as a band, even
though it's got one new member [bassist Darryl Jones]. There's a

good variety of songs. It's not overelaborate. You get a feeling of really being there, and it's quite intimate in nature. The ballads are rather nice, and then the rock and roll numbers kick quite well and sound enthusiastic — like we're into it. I think it's a good frame of reference of what the Rolling Stones were about during that quite limited time in Ireland in that year.

It's very much a kind of time-and-place album. In that way I was quite pleased with the results. But there were a lot of things that we wrote for *Voodoo Lounge* that Don [Was, the record's producer] steered us away from — groove songs, African influences, and things like that. He steered us very clear of all that. I think it was a mistake.

What direction did he take you in?

He tried to remake *Exile on Main Street* or something like that. Plus, the engineer was also trying to do the same thing. Their mindset about it was just too retro. I'm not saying there's anything wrong with it inherently, but they went over the top; they'd gone too far. I didn't really fight it in the end. I gave up because there was no point in it. I think both Charlie and I didn't really like it. I don't think it really was that successful.

It always fascinated me that you are this great hands-on manager of these massive tours, really involved in the daily decision-making. And then you go out and perform, center stage, the consummate artist and songwriter. That's a very unusual combination of talent. Why?

There's really no one as experienced as I am doing it. And though I had huge arguments with [rock promoter] Bill Graham, he had fantastic qualities, especially being an impresario, making a show a real show. I learned a tremendous amount from Bill. He was fantastically difficult on a personal level, not only with me but with all the people working with him. He'd just scream and shout at everyone, which would start driving me crazy and everyone else. It makes for a not very good atmosphere. Much too prickly, and that was one of his big problems.

People who are involved in tour directing, they don't understand what it's like to be on the stage. And just on a very simple level like booking the rest of the tour of Europe: how many shows are you going to do in a ten-day period? My agenda is, can the band do this? Is this feasible? That is, making it a tour that the Rolling Stones can actually function, do, and have a good time on — not just a crazy skedaddle around with no time to think and eventually become totally exhausted.

How do you reconcile these two sides of yourself: your very artistic half and your very methodical, business half?

One is an extension of the other. I don't think of them as very different. It's being creative in another way. I find it very satisfying, the whole thing of designing a stage. One step from that it becomes real practicalities. It starts off as being a great design, but can it be made? And then who's going to pay for it? Well, the Rolling Stones, really. So can you make it for $30 million? And if you can't, you're going to lose. Now that's a kind of money decision, but who else is going to make that decision?

This passion for detail — does it come out of the same impulse as your artistic impulse?

It's the same impulse. It obviously divides itself up differently, but I don't separate them completely. I've learned that you have to just delegate. And once it's done, it's done. I'm not going to fret about the details. I used to, but I don't anymore. Don't fret, don't worry about it, and just enjoy yourself. I just leave other people to handle the day-to-day stuff.

Could you just describe how you see the show onstage evolve during the set? Particularly on the current *Voodoo Lounge* tour?

You open it with this big, grand gesture, an explosion of fire and with a drumbeat going. The first number's really simple as far as the musicians are concerned. Then we have fireworks going, which changes the light on the sides. It's rather eerie and smoky. It's supposed to be a dark beginning, a bit dark and slightly foreboding, not a big, happy, fun beginning. And then we cut to the beginning of the first rock section, which is "Tumbling Dice."

Why do you open with "Not Fade Away"?

Because we wanted something dark. It could be a bit moody, and then we thought that it would be good to revive this very ancient tune. And it's also rather short, which would be good. And that we could start off with this drumbeat thing we had.

So, you've got the rock section starting with "Tumbling Dice." Then what happens next? What's the next big mood you're trying to set?

There's quite a big move at the end of "Satisfaction" that becomes the high point of that set; then we start to slow it down. It changes mood again going into "Beast of Burden" and whatever ballad we do. When we constructed the set musically, I had in mind that it was in these sections — like breaking down a screenplay or, very simply, a plot. It starts off with this moody thing, goes into this rock section, breaks down into this power section, then we have what we used to call the grab bag section. Then it goes into Keith's two songs, it goes up at the end of that into this more audience-participation thing: "Honky Tonk Women." Then it goes into the *Voodoo Lounge* section, where we change the set. Then it goes to the end, the rock and roll run-out section.

How do you prepare for a show?

I like to have a peek, see what the audience is doing during the opening act, because it gives you a clue and gives you a good feeling of where you are — the air can be different in different places. And I like to see the place before, because some of them are very wide, and they're much more difficult to play. They tend to be baseball places, because they get so wide you have to work the outlying part of it a lot more, where the majority of people are.

When you go out to take a peek beforehand, what kind of things are you looking at?

Is the front section empty? Because that usually means that they're older and want to just show up at the time we go on. Or are they there only for the opening act or something? And just how do they respond? How loud they are, how enthusiastic they are. Of course, that's the opening act, too. Depends how good they are, whether they can communicate with them, which is not very easy. I'd hate to be a fucking opening act. You get out there, and you feel the temperature of it, really.

What's that moment like just before you go onstage? What's your energy like?

My energy's usually pretty good. Sometimes I think, "Oh, Jesus, do I really have to go on now?" You have to finally switch into the fact that you're just about to go on, because before it can be unreal. As you walk down to the stadium from the dressing room, you start to buzz a little bit. And you hear the audience, what their response is when the music starts. And then just before we go on, just while the music's really warming up, you get an extra buzz then. When you first walk on, I walk out to an empty stage; I'm very confident. This is what I do. I've done it so many times. I'm not at all nervous about going on. It feels very comfortable and like home. But having said that, there's certain feelings that you get, you know: "Jesus, all those people!" There's a few empty seats sometimes, I see, and you say, "Oh, God, how many empty seats?" And funny things that you think of — just silly things — and you must not think of those, because as soon as you start thinking, "I hope that the heavy rains that we've had in London don't block the gutters up [laughs] and the roof leaks again…" [Laughter] It's just — anything can come into your mind, but you have to throw it out because you just have to really concentrate on what you're doing.

> **When you're performing, what's that feeling? Can you describe that thrill of performing and dancing around and singing? Is that possible to describe?**

It's very high adrenaline. If you've ever been in this high-adrenaline situation — like driving a car very fast or being in a championship basketball team in the finals or whatever it was — it's really high adrenaline.

Our concerts do have a lot in common with sporting events. I mean, they're held in the same places and they have that kind of feeling. Obviously, what's lacking is the competition aspect, but there is a certain amount of the same feeling, that you're always present at an event. The event is important. I was at Super Bowl XVII or whatever, and I don't even remember who fucking played, but you were there. You might not remember what songs the Rolling Stones played when you saw them in the Astrodome, but you were there.

But it's quite hard to describe. I've sometimes tried to write it down. I have written it down — what it's like, what you feel like. But there's so much going on, it's hard unless you're really in a stream-of-consciousness thing. Because there are so many references: "Oh, I'm doing this, and I'm doing that," and you're sort of watching yourself doing it. "Oh God, look at that girl; she's rather pretty. Don't concentrate on her!" But it's good to concentrate on her, she's good to contact one-on-one. Sometimes I try to do that. They're actually real people, not just a sea of people. You can see this girl has come, and she's got this dress on and so on, and so you make good contact with one or two people. And then you make contact with the rest of the band. You might give a look-see if everyone's all right.

You're always checking everything?

The first number, I'm totally checking everything.

Now, you said you wrote down this other thing about feeling transported?

I don't let myself get transported on the first number, because that is very dangerous. I used to let myself do that, but it's not such a good idea, because there's too much to check. I mean, is everything working?

You seem to be split in various parts. There's part of you which is saying to you, "OK, don't forget this, don't forget that." And there's this other part of you, which is just your body doing things that it isn't really commanded to do, which I found is the dangerous part. You can hurt yourself if you don't watch out — because you've got so much adrenaline. That's why I rather like doing "Not Fade Away," because I don't do much physically on it. [Laughs] But if you start off with a number like, say, "Start Me Up," which we did on the last tour, your body starts to do all kinds of things on this adrenaline thing. You've got to watch out. You can really hurt yourself — or just tire yourself out too quickly in the first five minutes, and you're just wiped out.

I was standing down at the bottom of the stage in San Antonio, watching you do "Brown Sugar," and there was a look on your face kind of like ecstasy.

At some point in the show, you just lose it. You get such interaction with the audience that it feels really good. And it should be pushed. You should let yourself go. I have those moments when you really are quite out of your brain. But there's always a point where a good performer knows when —

To pull back?

Yeah, when they're allowed to happen, if they're going to happen, and when they're not allowed to really happen, if they start to happen. And it's all to do with concentration, really.

Is it sustained, or does it come in isolated moments?

It comes in isolated moments. It's just a transcendent moment — I don't know whether you can say it's joyful. Sometimes it can be joyful; sometimes it's just crazy.

Charlie said about you, "Mick Jagger is based on James Brown. He's a younger version of James Brown."

[Laughs] Well, that's a nice compliment. I mean, of course, I'm not anything like James Brown. I used to aspire to be like James Brown in his moves, and so I copied a lot of James Brown's moves in the early days. I don't do them, really, anymore. But I think what Charlie means is that James Brown is constantly attuned to the groove, to the drums. I'm also very attuned to the drums. It's just natural.

Charlie said that he's following you all the time and that the dynamic of his playing is based on a move that you'll make.

Well, that's probably the oldest thing in music or performing: the link between drums and dancing — before there was any other music, really. If you watch any folk music, if you go to Africa or you go to Asia, you can see it in Ireland or England. You'll see the connection between the performer who's dancing and the drums. In Balinese dancing or any of these things, they watch — very closely — the dancer. And there may be accents when the dancer moves, and they make rhythmic accentuations on them — turns and so on. That doesn't strictly go in all rock, because a rock drummer has to keep very basic time.

And then when you leave the stage, when you're done — how is it?

You just let yourself go, just tired, you know. And then you recover pretty quickly. After about ten or fifteen minutes, you feel okay.

What was the relationship between the Stones and the Beatles?

Super, highly competitive — but friendly. Because when you're very young, it's very hard. Looking back, thinking of all that competition, I hate it. But I suppose it's all right, because I won out. But it wasn't only between us and the Beatles but us and all the other bands.

The Beatles were so big that it's hard for people not alive at the time to realize just how big they were. There isn't a real comparison with anyone now. I suppose Michael Jackson at one point, but it still doesn't seem quite the same. They were so big that to be competitive with them was impossible. I'm talking about in record sales and tours and all this. They were huge.

Bigger than Jesus?

They were bigger than Jesus!

And there came a point where you were band two after that.

Yeah, we were band two. Like Avis. It's horrible being compared to a car.

What kind of a relationship did you develop with John?

I liked John very much to start. We all had a good relationship with John. He seemed to be in sympathy with our kind of music, so we used to go out to clubs a lot. We did a lot of hanging out.

Did you feel you were developing a special relationship with John? You're the leader of the one group, and he's the leader of the other group?

There was a professional thing above the friendship. You could talk about problems, bounce things off each other, and get a different take on it. Later, when John wasn't in the Beatles anymore, he was bouncing more ideas off me than ever before. I'm not saying I was the only person he bounced off of, but he used to bounce a lot off me — song choices and stuff.

He was educated and very smart and cynical and funny and really amusing company. He had a very funny take on the rest of the Beatles. If they boasted too much about how great they were, he had ways to shut them up. He'd say, "Don't worry, he's just getting used to being famous. Shurrup!" [Laughter] As if he'd been famous longer, you know. But I used to get on with Paul as well. Paul is very nice and easy to get on with. He didn't have the acerbic side. You always knew with John, you're going to be on the end of a lot of sarcastic remarks that you weren't always in the mood for.

What do you think was going on with him? What do you think motivated him?

Wanted to be the most famous person in the world [laughs].

He said as much.

Did he really?

Along that line. "We wanted to be bigger than Elvis."

Yeah. Elvis just did it all wrong, didn't he? Put all these silly ideas into people's heads. And John picked up on it.

Do you think that drove him?

It seems incredibly crass and superficial, doesn't it?

So now, looking back on his work, what do you think his contribution was?

He did wonderful things. John and Paul, because it's hard to separate this thing, and having been through a partnership, with people always asking you who did what, and, of course, you either exaggerate your own importance or you downplay it, but you never get it right. I think John himself was a very talented guy, very influential, and wrote some wonderful songs. And he was very funny. I think he really was larger than life.

But the rest of them took it more seriously than John.

You got that feeling, and that's why I told you that little story about him shutting them up. He knew it was all bullshit.

And he showed he could walk away from it. But don't you evaluate his contribution as greater than "He wrote some good songs"?

He obviously did more than just that, but he wrote really wonderful songs and performed them wonderfully. The stage performances were not mind-boggling, and after nineteen sixty-whatever-it-was, they didn't do any stage performances. So for all intents and purposes, Shea Stadium and the concert on the roof was it. But great songwriting, great personality, and he had all these other sides, which added to it: the writing, the drawing, the little books, the all-embracing, modernistic push, which was refreshing without being pretentious.

What was your thinking when you heard he was shot?

I was very sad and surprised. And it was all so horribly ironic. He thought he had found a place to be on his own, have this life, and he was quite taken with the idea that he was no longer in the Beatles, that he didn't have to have a lot of protection, bodyguards. He used to tell me how he would go in a cab in New York — go in a fucking yellow cab. Which, as you know, is probably to be avoided if you've got more than ten dollars. [Laughs] A London cab is one thing, but a New York cab is another. He wanted freedom to walk the block and get in the cab, and he felt in these big cities you can be anonymous.

**Did it have some deeper personal resonance with you
when he died?**

I just felt very sad for the loss of someone that I loved very much. I didn't write it up as a piece in *The Guardian*. I think journalists have this temptation to keep marking time lines. [Laughs] There are wall charts for children: dinosaurs end here, woolly mammoths here, and John Lennon dies here. You know?

**Do you think John deserves this huge reputation
he still has? The Beatles being the greatest group?**

They certainly were not a great live band. Maybe they were in the days of the Cavern, when they were coming up as a club band. I'm sure they were hilariously funny and all that. And they did have this really good onstage persona. But as far as the modern-day world, they were not a great performing band. But do they deserve the fantastic reputation? They were the Beatles. They were this forerunning, breakthrough item, and that's hard to overestimate.

What do you think of Tina Turner?

I was influenced by her. She's one of the first women performers I worked with who has the same aggressive thing that I've got. A lot of women performers are quite static — or certainly were in the Sixties. They did their best, but they weren't like Tina. She was like a female version of Little Richard and would respond to the audience, really go out and grab them.

Pete Townshend?

I always loved Pete. He's very bright, always thinking. He had this insane, rebellious, self-destructive streak. The first time we traveled with him, we were on the same plane going somewhere like Belgium. He got on the plane and got completely drunk in an hour — drunk and crazy. We just watched. But I love Pete. He was an exciting performer in the heyday of the Who.

Hendrix?

I loved Jimi Hendrix from the beginning. The moment I saw him, I thought he was fantastic. I was an instant convert. Mr. Jimi Hendrix is the best thing I've ever seen. It was exciting, sexy, interesting. He didn't have a very good voice but made up for it with his guitar. I first saw him at the Revolution Club, in London. I was one of six people in the club, and Jimi was playing. I couldn't believe it. It was insane — so good and the whole idea of this kind of English band behind him, this bizarre mixture between a blues performer and a rock player with an English touch.

Did you have any kind of relationship with him?

I was quite friendly with him. He was a really sweet guy. A bit confused. It's the same old story: Jimi Hendrix played all over the place with all these bands. He'd been a background guitar player for donkey years. And suddenly he gets what he wants, then has to play "Purple Haze" every night. He goes, "Uh, I don't want to play 'Purple Haze' every night. I don't want to burn the guitar." And then when everyone went off the deep end, he had to go off the deep end. He became a heroin addict.

What about today's music?

I'm not in love with things at the moment. I was never crazy about Nirvana — too angst-ridden for me. I like Pearl Jam. I prefer them to a lot of other bands. There's a lot of angst in a lot of it, which is one of the great things to tap into. But I'm not a fan of moroseness.

Can you define rock and roll for me? What is it about?
Is it about sex, violence, energy, anger?

All those things: energy, anger, angst, enthusiasm, a certain spontaneity. It's very emotional. And it's very traditional. It can't break too many rules. You have certain set rules, certain forms, which are traditionally folk-based, blues-based forms. But they've got to be sung with this youthful energy — or youthful lethargy, because youth has this languorous, lethargic, rebellious side to it as well. So they can be sung as an alternate mode of thrashing, this slightly feminine languor, the boredom of youth as well as the anger, because youth has those two things. To represent those emotions, this form seems to work very well.

Boredom and anger, which are both a form of rebellion.

Yeah, a statement of rebellion. Drawing the line where your generation is.

So the energy, the sexuality, is from this youthful aspect?

Yeah, but the sexuality is very potent and very obvious. There's nothing understated about it. That really comes from black music. The overt sexuality of black music was the precursor of all that.

And the violence?

Well, violence is mostly in the posing aspect of it. There's some in the lyrics, but it's also the attitude, the bad-attitude thing. It's very violent. Rock and roll in its very early days came with expressions of violence.

There were riots.

Not so much Elvis, but Bill Haley, when he was in *Blackboard Jungle*, do you remember? "Rock Around the Clock" was featured in this movie *Blackboard Jungle*. And when it was shown, there were riots everywhere. And rock and roll was associated with violence very early on.

Has your attitude toward rock and roll changed as you've gotten older? Do you still have the same feeling for it?

No.

What has changed?

Well, it's much older. Rock music was a completely new musical form. It hadn't been around for ten years when we started doing it. So we were playing with something new. I imagine it's a bit like walking into New Orleans after jazz had only been going eight years. I was there at the beginning. And we were going to change it — bring this rhythm and blues thing into it.

And at the beginning you felt like you were one of the chosen few, one of the only ones in the whole world who would get to play with this new toy.

We had evangelical fervor. So it was exciting, and no one knew where it was going, if it was going to last. When it first came out, people thought it was a dance craze like the cha-cha-cha or the calypso. Rock history is full of songs about hoping it would never die. It could have easily passed on.

I have a very different attitude now. It's forty years old. I still love performing it, but it's no longer a new, evangelical form. It's still capable of expression, and it's capable of change and novelty. But it's not as exciting for me. It's not a perfect medium for someone my age, given the rebelliousness of the whole thing, the angst and youth of it. In some ways it's foolish to try and re-create that.

Do you ever look back at your career and evaluate what you've done?

I'm afraid of doing that. Either you have this satisfied feeling, or you say, "What a bunch of shit. What a waste of time." You can say, "Well, it's something I should have done for a few years and given up, done something else."

Does that thought cross your mind?

Of course. It would be nice to have another shot. Instead of me being a rock singer, I could have done something else. You hope you've done something right, you've spent an awful long time on it, so you better be bloody right. "Did you waste a lot of time?" Yes, you've wasted a lot of time. "Did you use your intellectual and physical gifts?" Yes and no. Because I don't think rock and roll is as intellectually taxing as other things. It's not particularly challenging. So you get intellectually lazy. I don't think anyone is ever satisfied with what they've done.

Are the Stones the greatest rock band in the world?

It's just a stupid epithet. It just seems too Barnum and Bailey to me, like it's some sort of circus act. The first time we heard it said was to introduce us every night. So I used to say, "Will you please not use that as your announcement? It's so embarrassing.

And what does that mean? Does it mean the best, the biggest, the most long-lasting?" You know?

What does your new record, *Stripped*, tell you about the Stones today?

We tried to get a twist on a live record because I didn't want to go back and repeat the previous live record. I thought we just had to give something different — not original songs but reworked. I think "Like a Rolling Stone" was unusual to do. We've never done a Dylan song before.

What appeals to you about that song?

Well, melodically I quite like it. It's very well put together; it's got a proper three sections to it, real good choruses and a good middle bit, and great lyrics. It's a really well-constructed pop song, in my opinion. It's very much to the point, it doesn't waffle too much. I sang it a lot of times on the European tour, maybe fifty times. So I really got inside it, and I enjoyed it. I love playing the harmonica on it.

You said you liked time-and-place albums, ones that reflect the Stones at a particular period of time.

This is the Stones doing their small shows, doing a much more intimate show.

It's the Stones as a smaller club band; there's blues and country, and we're showing that side of the Stones rather than the big, huge stadium version.

Is there a version of the Stones that you prefer, one over the other — the stadium version versus this club version?

I like the club version of the band.

**In a general sense, what is in the future for the
Rolling Stones?**

It's a mystery. I don't know what's going to happen with the Rolling Stones. I mean, one is always very confident about the future. But what's actually going to happen is a mystery.

Why is it a mystery?

Because anything can happen in life and quite frequently does. We don't have set plans. But I daresay the Rolling Stones will do more shows together. But I don't know exactly what framework the next tour in the United States would take, nor do I know what form the next Rolling Stones music will take. But I'm sure there will be Rolling Stones music and there will be Rolling Stones shows.

**The Stones do seem a lot more stable than, say, ten years
ago.**

I think the Rolling Stones have always been mostly stable; they've got a terrific history, a long tradition. It's very steeped in all kind of things. The Rolling Stones are a very admired band, much copied, and so on. And [it's] very flattering — it always is.

How do you feel about rock's staying power now?

I'm kind of surprised by the resurgence of it as a young force.

Why would you be surprised?

Well, because there seemed to be a period when it was rather flat. It could have become dinosaur music. It's still very similar music to the music in the Sixties. It's got its own spin on things, but it's still very traditional. Maybe that's what makes the staying power work, because jazz went up such a difficult-to-understand alley when it went into bop; it lost a lot of mass audience. And rock hasn't really done that. It's kept its popular base by not only going into intellectual areas where it can't be followed by most people.

It stays with the beat.

Stays with that same beat, really. Rock has to absorb other rhythmic forms, because the underlying rhythm of music changes with fashion, and people like to move differently now than they moved thirty years ago, and the underlying rhythms have to be the ones that people want to dance to.

What about your own staying power?

I think it's a question of energy, really. I, personally, have a lot of energy, so I don't see it as an immediate problem.

How's your hearing?

My hearing's all right. But we worry about it because they play far too loud. Sometimes I use earplugs because it gets too loud on my left ear.

Why your left ear?

Because Keith's standing on my left.

BONO

[2005]

I WAS STANDING with Ali Hewson, the enchanting wife of Paul David Hewson — Bono — and mother of their four children, watching a U2 concert in Dublin, at Croke Park, an outdoor venue built on the site of the 1920 Bloody Sunday massacre. Bono was onstage, talking and preaching brotherhood, giant screens floating above the band, flickering with video images of human suffering and compassion, degradation and dignity. He wore a headband on which was drawn the crescent moon of the Muslim faith, the Star of David of the Jewish people, and the cross of Christianity. He was breathing fire and pain, ringing out hope and humanity, a call to salvation to eighty thousand rock and roll fans.

I thought of Martin Luther King Jr. Was Bono challenging fate, stirring the same dark and ancient forces that had struck down Reverend King? I asked Ali if she was scared, as I was. She said she was.

I was witnessing Bono as a preacher with some godly energy pouring out of him, a prophet from the land of rock and roll, a power that compelled me to want to understand where this miracle performer had come from.

Later that year I went to Cancún, Mexico, where the band was on a fortnight break in the middle of the U.S. leg of the *Vertigo* tour. The Hewson family had rented a beachside house at the edge of the coastal jungle. Jaguars had been prowling at night. I came at mid-afternoon, and when I arrived, an eighteen-foot boa constrictor was in the driveway. A storm was gathering outside. We set up for the interview in Bono's bedroom and emerged after dark. We continued the next day. In all, we talked for ten hours. "The collision of the Beatles and Bob Dylan gave us the galaxy that our planet is in."

When we got back to New York, where he lives around the corner from me, he helped edit the transcripts. We had discussed his bare-knuckle childhood and home-life, his early reckoning with religion and faith, how central and deep these matters were to the band and its goals, his own writing, and his evolution as a social activist, a global presence and conscience whose reach came to include prime ministers, presidents, and the Pope.

While U2's music is every bit as commercial, emo-tional, and drums/bass/guitar-grounded as traditional rock and roll, the songs are hymns, anthems, prayers, pleas. They come in settings of stately rhythms, chiming guitars, and magnificent chorale arrangements, slowly ascending melodies structured to reach crescendos of revelation.

Bono is Irish to the core, scrappy, charming, elo-quence in abundance. He is the star as statesman and advo-cate, an artist as moral leader, a phenomenon of our times, unprecedented in scale and accomplishment.

He has lifted his chosen profession and form to pur-poses and meanings that we could never have imagined, but in which we can all take pride, and with humility. "My job is catching lightning. If there's none around, my job is starting a fire. Once you see not only the problem, but also the solution," he told me, "there's no escape. You see it, you can't look away from it."

What was your childhood in Dublin like?

I grew up in what you would call a lower-middle-class neighborhood. You don't have the equivalent in America. Upper working class? But a nice street and good people. And yet, if I'm honest, a sense that violence was around the corner.

Mother departed the household early, died at the graveside of her own father. So I lost my grandfather and my mother in a few days, and then it became a house of men. Three, it turns out, quite macho men, and all that goes with that. The aggression thing is something I'm still working at. That level of aggression, both outside and inside, is not normal or appropriate.

> **You're this bright, struggling teenager, and you're in this place that looks like it has very few possibilities for you. The general attitude toward you from your father — and just the Irish attitude — was, "Who the fuck do you think you are? Get real." Is that correct?**

Bob Hewson — my father — comes from the inner city of Dublin. A real Dublin man, but loves the opera. Must be a little grandiose himself, okay? He is an autodidact, conversant in Shakespeare. His passion is music — he's a great tenor. The great sadness of his life was that he didn't learn the piano. Oddly enough, we kids were not really encouraged to have big ideas, musically or otherwise. To dream was to be disappointed. Which, of course, explains my megalomania.

I was a bright kid, all right, early on.

I get the sense that it was kind of a dead-end situation.

Its blandness — its very grayness — is the thing you have to overcome. We had a street gang that was very vivid — very surreal. We were fans of Monty Python. We'd put on performances in the city center of Dublin. I'd get on the bus with a stepladder and an electric drill. Mad shit. Humor became our weapon. Just stand there, quiet — with the drill in my hand. Stupid teenage shit.

Were there a lot of fights?

Oh, yeah. The order of the day was often being beaten to within an inch of your life by roaming gangs from one of the other neighborhoods. When they asked where you were from, you had to guess right — or suffer. The harder they hit us, the more strange and surreal the response.

You were the freaky kids?

Yeah. Gavin Friday was the most surreal-looking. He had an *Eraserhead* haircut; he wore dresses and bovver boots. Myself and my other friend, Guggi — we're still very close friends — were handy enough. We could defend ourselves. But even though some of us became pretty good at violence ourselves, others didn't. I thought that was kind of normal. I can remember incredible street battles. I remember one madser with an iron bar, just trying to bring it down on my skull as hard as he possibly could, and holding up a dustbin lid, which saved my life. Teenage kids have no sense of mortality — yours or theirs.

You were the smart-kid clique?

We were a collection of outsiders. We weren't all the clever clogs. If you had a good record collection, that helped. And if you didn't play soccer. That was part of it. Now, when you look back, there's an arrogance to it; it's like you're looking down, really, at the jocks, at the skinheads, at the bootboys. Maybe it's the same arrogance my father had, who's listening to opera and likes cricket. Because it separates him.

**When I spoke to Edge this week, he said that you're
turning into your dad.**

He was an amazing and very funny man. You had to be quick to live around him. But I don't think I'm like him. I have a very different relationship with my kids than he had with me. He didn't really have one with me. He generally thought that no one was as smart as him in the room. You know that Johnny Cash song "A Boy Named Sue," where he gives the kid a girl's name, and the kid is beaten up at every stage in his life by macho guys, but in the end he becomes the toughest man.

You're the boy named Sue?

By not encouraging me to be a musician, even though that's all he ever wanted to be, he's made me one. By telling me never to have big dreams or else, that to dream is to be disappointed, he made me have big dreams. By telling me that the band would only last five minutes or ten minutes — we're still here.

**It seems there's some power in this relationship
that's beyond the ordinary father-son story.
You were probably one of the most difficult
children to have around.**

I must've been a bit difficult.

He was trying to raise two children without a mother.
And here you are, unforgiving and unrelenting, showing
up at all hours, in drag and with all kinds of weird people.
I think it's amazing he put up with you and he didn't just
throw you the fuck out. Do you ever feel guilty about
how you treated him?

No, not until I fucking met you!

He loved a row. Christmas Day at our house was just one long argument. We were shouting all the time — my brother, me, and then my uncles and aunts. He had a sense of moral indignation, that attitude of "You don't have to put up with this shit." He was very wise politically. He was from the left, but you know, he praised the guy on the right.

The more you talk about it, the more it sounds
like you're describing yourself.

That is a very interesting way of looking at it, and I think there'll be a lot of people who might agree with you. I loved my dad. But we were combatants. Right until the end. Actually, his last words were an expletive. I was sleeping on a little mattress right beside him in the hospital. I woke up, and he made this big sound, this kind of roar — it woke me up. The nurse comes in and says, "You okay, Bob?" He kind of looks at her and whispers, "Would you fuck off and get me out of here? This place is like a prison. I want to go home." Last words: "Fuck off."

What were the first rock and roll records that you heard?

Age four. The Beatles' "I Want to Hold Your Hand." I guess that's 1964. I remember watching the Beatles with my brother on Saint Stephen's Day, the day after Christmas. The sense of a gang that they had about them, from just what I've been saying, you can tell that connected, as well as the melodic power, the haircuts, and the sexuality. Which I was just probably processing.

Then performers like Tom Jones. I'd see Tom Jones on Saturday night on a variety show — I must have been, like, eight years old — and he's sweating, and he's an animal, and he's unrestrained. He's singing with abandon. He has a big black voice, in a white guy. And then, of course, Elvis.

**Who else had a big impact on you, musically,
when you were young?**

I really remember John Lennon's "Imagine." I guess I'm twelve; that's one of my first albums. That really set fire to me. It was like he was whispering in your ear — his ideas of what's possible. Different ways of seeing the world. When I was fourteen and lost my mother, I went back to *Plastic Ono Band*.

The first song you learned how to play?

[Sings] "If I had a hammer, I'd hammer in the morning / I'd hammer in the evening / All over this land / I'd hammer out justice / I'd hammer out freedom / Love between my brothers and my sisters / All over this land."

Fantastic. A manifesto, right there.

You're still doing the same song.

[Laughs] Right. The Who: about age fifteen, that starts really connecting. In amongst the din and the noise, the power chords and the rage, there's another voice. [Sings] "Nobody knows what it's like behind blue eyes..." And the beginnings of what I would discover is one of the essential aspects for me — and why I'm drawn to a piece of music — which has something to do with the quest. I was in my room listening on headphones on a tape recorder. It's very intimate. It's like talking to somebody on the phone, like talking to John Lennon on the phone. I'm not exaggerating to say that. This music changed the shape of the room. It changed the shape of the world outside the room, the way you looked out the window and what you were looking at.

I remember John singing "Oh My Love." It's like a little hymn. It's certainly a prayer of some kind — even if he was an atheist.

[Sings] "Oh, my love / For the first time in my life / My eyes can see / I see the wind / Oh, I see the trees / Everything is clear in our world."

For me it was like he was talking about the veil lifting off, the scales falling from the eyes. Seeing out the window with a new clarity that love brings you. I remember that feeling.

Yoko came up to me when I was in my twenties, and she put her hand on me and she said, "You are John's son." What an amazing compliment!

Now, it's 1976. I was in school. It was the obnoxious-teenager phase. Schoolwork's gone to shite, angry, living at home with two men. My friends are all going to have big futures, because they're very clever. I'm probably not going to be able to concentrate enough to be that clever.

Then a note appears from this kid. Like, really a kid — he's fourteen, and I'm sixteen. He wants to start a band. He plays the drums. I go out to this suburban house, where Larry Mullen lives. Larry is in this tiny kitchen, and he's got his drum kit set up. And there's a few other boys. There's Dave Evans — a kind of brainy-looking kid — who's fifteen. And his brother Dik, even brainier-looking. Larry starts playing the kit. It's an amazing sound, just hit the cymbal. Edge hit a guitar chord which I'd never heard on electric guitar. I mean, it is the open road. Kids started coming from all around the place, all girls. They know that Larry lives there. They're already screaming; they're already climbing up the door. He was completely used to this, we discover, and he's taking the hose to them already. Literally, the garden hose. And so that starts. Within a month I start going out with Ali. I had met her before, but I ask her out.

That was a good month.

In the months leading up to this, I was probably at the lowest ebb in my life. I didn't know if I wanted to continue living — that kind of despair. I was praying to a God I didn't know was listening.

Everyone got to make suggestions about what music we should play. I wanted to play the Rolling Stones, from the *High Tide and Green Grass* era, and the Beach Boys. I was getting tired of the hard rock thing.

Hard rock being...

Big hair and extended guitar solos. I was saying, "Let's get back to this rock and roll thing." Then people said, "Oh, have you heard the Clash?" And then seeing the Jam on *Top of the Pops* in '76, just going, "They're our age! This is possible." Then the Radiators from Space — our local punk band — had a song called..."Telecaster" or something: [sings] "Going to push my Telecaster through the television screen / because I don't like what's going down."

How far into the band are you now?

It's just occasional rehearsing. We're playing the Eagles. We're playing the Moody Blues. But it turns out we're really crap at it.

We actually aren't able to play other people's songs. The one Stones song we tried to play was "Jumpin' Jack Flash." It was really bad. So we started writing our own. It was easier.

What role did religion play in your childhood?

I prayed more outside of the church than inside. It gets back to the songs I was listening to; to me, they were prayers. "How many roads must a man walk down?" That wasn't a rhetorical question to me. It was addressed to God. Who do I ask that to? I'm not going to ask a schoolteacher. When John Lennon sings, "Oh, my love / For the first time in my life / My eyes are wide open" — these songs have an intimacy for me that's not just between people, I realize now, not sexual intimacy. A spiritual intimacy.

I would rarely be asking these questions inside the church. Occasionally, when I'm singing a hymn like...oh, if I can think of a good one...oh, "When I Survey the Wondrous Cross" or "Be Thou My Vision," something would stir inside of me. But basically religion left me cold.

There was also my friend Guggi. His parents were in some obscure cult. His father was like a creature from the Old Testament. He spoke constantly of the Scriptures and had the sense that the end was nigh — and to prepare for it.

You were living with his family?

Yes, I'd go to church with them, too. We don't realize it, but we're being immersed in the Holy Scriptures. That's what we took away from this: this rich language, these ancient tracts of wisdom.

**So is that why you were writing such serious songs
when you're nineteen?**

Most of the people that you grew up with in black music had a similar baptism of the spirit, right? The difference is that most of these performers felt they could not express their sexuality before God. They had to turn away. So rock and roll became backsliders' music.

You never saw rock and roll — the so-called devil's music — as incompatible with religion?

Look at the people who have formed my imagination. Bob Dylan. Nineteen seventy-six — he's going through similar stuff. You buy Patti Smith: *Horses*. [Sings] "Jesus died for somebody's sins / But not mine." And she turns Van Morrison's "Gloria" into liturgy. She's wrestling with these demons — Catholicism in her case. Right the way through to "Wave," where she's talking to the Pope.

The blues are like the Psalms of David. Here was this character, living in a cave, whose outbursts were as much criticism as praise. There's David singing. [Sings] "Oh, God — where are you when I need you? / You call yourself God?" And you say to yourself, "This is the blues." Both deal with the relationship with God. That's really it. I've since realized that anger with God is very valid.

Soon after starting the band you joined a Bible study group — you and Larry and Edge — called the Shalom. What brought that on?

We were doing street theater in Dublin, and we met some people who were madder than us. They were a kind of inner-city group living life like it was the first century AD. They were expectant of signs and wonders. They lived a kind of early church religion. It was a commune. People who had cash shared it. They were passionate, and they were funny, and they seemed to have no material desires. Their teaching of the Scriptures reminded me of those people whom I'd heard as a youngster with Guggi.

But it got a little too intense, as it always does; it became a bit of a holy huddle. And these people — who are full of inspirational teaching and great ideas — they pretended that our dress, the way we looked, didn't bother them. But very soon it appeared that was not the case. They started asking questions about the music we were listening to. "Why are you wearing earrings?" "Why do you have a mohawk?"

If you were going to study the teaching, it demanded a rejection of the world. Even then we understood that you can't escape the world, wherever you go. Least of all in very intense religious meetings, which can be more corrupt and more bent, in terms of the pressures they exert on people, than the outside forces.

What draws you so deeply to Martin Luther King?

So now — cut to 1980. Irish rock group, who've been through the fire of a certain kind of revival, a Christian-type revival, go to America. Turn on the TV the night you arrive, and there's all these people talking from the Scriptures. But they're quite obviously raving lunatics.

Suddenly you go, what's this? And you change the channel. There's another one. You change the channel, and there's another secondhand car salesman. You think, oh my God. But their words sound so similar to the words out of our mouths.

What happens? You learn to shut up. You say, whoa, what's this going on? You go oddly still and quiet. If you talk like this around here, people will think you're one of those. And you realize that these are the traders — as in t-r-a-d-e-r-s — in the temple.

Until you get to the black church, and you see that they have similar ideas. But their religion seems to be involved in social justice: the fight for equality. And a *Rolling Stone* journalist, Jim Henke, who has believed in you more than anyone up to this point, hands you a book called *Let the Trumpet Sound* — which is the biography of Dr. King. And it just changes your life.

Even though I'm a believer, I still find it really hard to be around other believers: they make me nervous, they make me twitch. I watch my back. Except when I'm with the black church. I feel relaxed, feel at home; I can take my kids there. There's singing, there's music.

How big an influence is the Bible on your songwriting?
How much do you draw on its imagery, its ideas?

It sustains me. As a belief. These are hard subjects to talk about because you can sound like such a dickhead. I'm the sort of character who's got to have an anchor. I want to be around immovable objects. I want to build my house on a rock, because even if the waters are not high around the house, I'm going to bring back a storm. I have that in me. So it's sort of underpinning for me.

I let it speak to me in other ways. They call it the *rhema*. It's a hard word to translate from Greek, but it sort of means something that changes in the moment you're in it. It seems to do that for me.

You're saying it's a living thing?

It's a plumb line for me. In the Scriptures it is self-described as a clear pool that you can see yourself in, to see where you're at, if you're still enough.

After Live Aid, you and your wife, Ali, went to
Ethiopia. This was September 1985.
How did that experience affect you?

That's a big question. Your route here is interesting — whether conscious or unconscious. What you've got me to talk about is how I justify being in a rock and roll band. Going way back, I, for some reason, associate music with emancipation and freedom for myself. If rock and roll means anything to me, it's liberation. Not just for yourself — your sexuality, your spirituality — but also for others.

But sometimes the necessary narcissism of being a writer and performer conflicted me. You could be bought off by your success and forget your ideals. End up on the cover of *Rolling Stone* and forget who you are. And develop a knowing smirk, develop irony, develop layers of protection necessary to be a rock and roll star in the age of celebrity.

To the point of nearly breaking up the band a few times...

Yes, we thought at times there might be better tools to change the world than electric guitars.

What did you want to change?

First, ourselves, I suppose. To become better people. And second, the wickedness of the world. For a lot of people, the world is a desperate place. A third of the people who live in it cannot achieve sustenance. And there is no real reason for that, other than a certain selfishness and greed.

So Live Aid helped you justify being in a band?

Yes, it's fair to say that U2 were part of creating the climate in which the first Live Aid could happen. We were part of creating this kind of positive protest movement in the Eighties, encouraged and underpinned by people at *Rolling Stone* who recognized in us some of the idealism of the Sixties.

We were very moved to be a part of Live Aid. We see that this journey of equality, which had come through the civil rights movement in the United States, had now switched to what's going on in Africa: if we really believed that these people were equal to us, we couldn't let this happen.

So, Ethiopia?

That thought process brings Ali and I to Ethiopia, to study this up close. We worked in an orphanage. We lived in a little tent. The camp was surrounded by barbed wire. Woke up in the mornings as the mist lifted, and watched thousands of Africans, who had walked all night with the little belongings they had, coming toward us to beg for food and their life. We saw the everydayness of despair. People would leave their children in rags; some would be alive, some wouldn't. For a couple of kids from the suburbs, it was a very overwhelming experience.

But it begged bigger questions. Live Aid had raised $250 million — which felt like an enormous sum of money — and we were jumping up and down like we'd cracked it. Only to find out, years later, that that's what Africa spends every couple of weeks repaying the richest countries in the world for old loans taken out by dodgy dictators who were propped up in the Cold War to fight the commies. Suddenly, the penny drops: there's a structural aspect to this poverty. This was about justice, not poverty.

**You wrote "Where the Streets Have No Name"
about this camp?**

It's a sort of odd, unfinished lyric, and outside of the context of Africa, it doesn't make any sense. But it contains a very powerful idea. In the desert, we meet God. In parched times, in fire and flood, we discover who we are. That's my prayer, by the way, for the United States. Do you want to go to that other place...where the streets have no name, the place where you glimpse God, your potential, whatever? That's what it means at a U2 show.

No matter how crap a U2 show gets, we can be sure the gig will come off if we play this song. But all this stuff about deserts and the parchedness of the earth — I'd completely forgotten where it came from. I wrote those things on Air India sick bags and scraps of paper, sitting in a little tent in a town called Ajibar in northern Ethiopia.

How changed were your attitudes when you came back from that trip?

You promise that you'll never forget...but you do. You get back to your life, to being in the band. But something in the back of my mind told me there's something here I don't fully understand but that I will, at some point in my life, be able to help those people.

A father hands you his son and says, "Take him, because if he stays with me, he will surely die." I remember the look in that man's eye, what it took for a grown man to make that request. He's handing me his son — and you're saying "No." That's a very hard thing to walk away from. But there's part of me that didn't say no. And when I get a call ten years later from Jamie Drummond at Jubilee 2000 — a campaign to drop the debts of the poorest countries to the richest — I'm back there, immediately.

So you'd started the ascent or descent into rock stardom with *The Joshua Tree*?

A little, but not really. We were very earnest. Which explains those very iconic stony-faced photographs. I remember [manager] Paul McGuinness saying to me, "You're in danger of looking like the men too stupid to enjoy being at number one." We always have had a laugh, but in our public persona we're a little self-conscious, and we need to throw off a bit of moral baggage, which we got to do on Zoo TV. The duality, which has always been there in us, just came out more in the nineties. And then, it's fair to say, the sensory overload may have started to take over. And I needed to get back to where I was.

**So you got into the usual rock and roll problems
of money and drugs and success.**

Well, I'm not going to explain them in detail. I just...I had a taste of the pizza.

––––––––––––––––––––

**How do you submit yourself— and your intelligence,
and all this passion and stubbornness that you have —
to the will of a group?**

If it furthers the music that we make, I'm all in favor of it. If it furthers the personalities of the people making the music, I'm not. I am very aware of how much I need them. They make me a better singer; they make me a better writer. The idea of being in a room surrounded by people who agree with you is terrifying.

Sting says, "It's just a street gang — you should grow out of it." Enormous respect for Sting as a person and a musician, but I don't agree.

You can imagine how annoying it is to have someone like me come in with my head full of big ideas. But occasionally we get a little too easy and free with the criticism. These are motherfuckers. This is a tough crowd. I think you need to create an environment where people can take risks. If everything has to be brilliant from the word go, you're never going to get off the ground.

**Is there unhappiness in the group because you're away
so much on your various missions?**

This is a slight misconception. I'll tell you why, and it will make sense. My job is catching lightning. If there's none around, my job is starting a fire. I work very quickly, and it's the opposite of the way Edge works. Edge is the Zen master. He's like the guy that spends eight years mixing the inks to do the calligraphy. I'm restless and impatient with the process. The band are delighted to have a break from me.

**When you're onstage, what do you think about?
Who are you watching?**

You develop a kind of a third eye or a sort of reptilian sense of what's going on in the room. At your house I'm aware who's entered, who's walked out, what couple is having a row, if you're stressed — I pick all that stuff up. It's really a noise. It gets to be a terrible noise after a while, and you just wish you could turn it off. But it turns out to be the mark of a performer. When I go onstage and a song is not connecting, I can feel it. You can feel people going to the bathroom or to buy a T-shirt, and you're annoyed. Mick Jagger is one of those kinds of performers. So are David Bowie and Eddie Vedder. There are performers who don't feel that, don't know whether the place is empty or full. But I'm not one.

What are you thinking when you're singing?

If it's going the way you want, you disappear into the song and the song is singing you. At times it isn't, so you're very much aware of the sound in your earphones. For me, I have an advantage. I can't sing in the registers that I sing in. So I really have to step inside the song or else I'm not going to be able to hit some of those notes.

**So in other words, unless you're personally willing
to pour your feelings into the song, you're just not capable
of making that stretch.**

It's not any glorious dedication to the art. It's just a necessity.
I probably think if it wasn't that way, I might try to fake it, because
it's expensive.

Expensive in what sense?

On your emotional life. In a U2 show there's a lot of different
feelings you're going through. My family refers to "gig lag," where
the coming down off of a show can be unpleasant. I am as high as
a kite the day after, but the next day I can really hit a wall.

**Do you occasionally lose control when you're singing?
Not get out of control, but you just get so
transported into the song.**

That's when it's good. When it's good you don't know it's happening. It really is an extraordinary thing because it seems to
require no effort. And of course the other side of it is you can bump
into some aspects of your character that you'd rather not have
bumped into.

What are you trying to do with the audience?

To lose my own sense of self, self-consciousness — and theirs.
It's an amazing thing. We're not really a rock and roll band. We're
pretending to be a rock and roll band, and sometimes we get away
with it. Sometimes a song like "Desire" or "Vertigo" will arrive,
and you go, "Whoa! That's rock and roll!" But what we actually do
is something completely different. Our set list is designed in a kind
of three-act structure, to get people out of themselves and to get

ourselves out of ourselves. And to get to that place where every-thing feels possible and you want to call your mother, leave your wife, start a revolution, or crack open the piggy bank and go on holiday for a year.

> You have to open up and expose your deep fears,
> your ambitions, your heart.

Our definition of art is the breaking open of the breastbone, for sure. Just open-heart surgery. I wish there was an easier way. But in the end, people want blood, and I'm one of them.

> Do you ever get scared when you go onstage and preach?
> It's like listening to Martin Luther King.
> You're not scared by doing that?

I'm scared of embarrassing my bandmates and our audience, but it is my conviction that this is a generation that wants to be remembered for something other than the war against terror or the Internet. Your generation had a job to do in pursuing equality and civil rights, and you took to the streets and you accomplished a lot.

Our generation wants the same thing, and we recognize that the enemies are subtler. This business of equality is a pain in the arse because it won't lie down, and it won't let you lie down beside it. It keeps demanding to be redefined for a different time.

> But let me ask again: don't you feel you're making yourself
> a target? Doesn't it scare you to go out onstage
> and preach like that?

No, but maybe there have been times when certainly I should have been. In 1998, we were playing in Chile, in a stadium full of people and on national television. We invited the mothers and relatives of those who had "disappeared" and demanded that President Pinochet answer these people: where are the bones of these mothers' sons? At least tell them that.

All the police leave the stadium. There's no security and half the crowd is booing. I kind of respect that our audience who disagreed with us made itself clear. There was a "Gringo, go home, you don't understand this" aspect. But I did understand it. There have been moments when things have been scary.

**About Edge, what's his importance in U2?
Do you think he's getting the credit he deserves?**

I'm definitely overrated in the scheme of things for U2. It's just one of those things that comes with the turf. However, it is annoying to me that this genius of the guitar — and genius rarely comes with modesty — never pushes himself forward. Most guitar playing in the rock era is white guys redoing black riffs. Some amazing versions of that. But this man, this kind of Zen Presbyterian, has really redefined the emotional terrain that a guitar player can create.

There are feelings that Edge has brought with his guitar playing that didn't exist before. I'll see people rate some guitar player ahead of him in a list because they're faster. It's like saying Jackson Pollock was sloppy. Edge is a giant of guitar playing. He's right up there.

Can you describe the sound of his playing?

Those icy notes and those fragile arpeggios belie a rage beneath that calm surface. He has a lot going on in his head, but he doesn't speak about it like I do. He's a musician, and it comes out in these tones that no one's heard before, and it allows me to get to that ecstatic thing that I'm looking for. Without that, it's difficult.

Other songwriter partnerships are really tough: Lennon and McCartney, Jagger and Richards, Gilbert and Sullivan, and so forth. Yours keeps working, it keeps going. Why?

We're tough on the work, but not on each other. Edge deserves the lion's share of the credit. He has, in a sort of sacramental fashion, learned to sublimate his ego to his music.

And allows you to be the big ego?

I think he's delighted to be out of the line of fire. He's the clever guy who actually figures being the front man is hard work. Smart people know what he does, and he doesn't care about the rest of the world. I get annoyed and I say, "How do people not know?" An example would be "With or Without You." It was evident early on that this was a little bit special. The song is all one build to a crescendo. The song breaks open and comes down, and then comes back. Everyone in the room is, "Okay, Edge, let's see if you can let off some fireworks here." Three notes. Restraint. I mean psychotic restraint, and that is the thing that rips your heart out, not the chorus. Same at the end of "One." It's not the falsetto, it's the guitar running contrary to the opera. It's really extraordinary.

Can I get your quick thoughts on a few of your albums? Boy (1980).

One of the top ten debut albums of all time. No shadow of a doubt. Spoiled, or let's say soiled, by unfinished lyrics and an Irish singer with an English accent. But it has extraordinary themes and the same theme as our recent album. Innocence versus experience. It's very unusual subject matter for a debut rock and roll album because it's not about losing your virginity; it's about your virginity. One day, I want to finish off those lyrics.

War (1983).

Great collection of songs. Strong in content and ideas but poor in lyrical execution. We were trying to be the Who meets the Clash. I spent minutes on these songs rather than hours. So "Sunday Bloody Sunday," which was supposed to contrast Easter Sunday with the death of thirteen protesters in Derry on Bloody Sunday, didn't quite come off. And yet melodically and the suggestion of the lyrics stood up to the test of time. I've changed the lyrics when I sing it now just to make it more believable for myself. I don't think anyone else notices. But that's a great song, mostly Edge's song.

The Unforgettable Fire (1984).

Now getting toward some great stuff. Miles Davis's favorite U2 album and one of his top ten albums. We knew there was a more experimental side that was important. Enter Brian Eno and Danny Lanois. Even when the lyrics weren't strong, the subject matter was. So now the music starts catching up with the subject matter and beautiful sonic landscapes. The guitar playing starts to get very otherworldly.

"Pride" started out as an ecstatic rant. We looked for a subject big enough to demand this level of emotion that was coming out. We had discovered nonviolence and Martin Luther King, not just in relation to his use of the Scriptures and his church background, but also as a solution to the Irish problems.

The Joshua Tree (1987).

The lyrics are starting to kick in; now we're getting music, ideas, content, and lyrics that'll catch up. We're starting to spend more than an hour on the lyrics. Still, in the case of "Where the Streets Have No Name," not more than an hour. And I regret it. However, "I Still Haven't Found What I'm Looking For" is a great song, a great lyric. It's a very complete album, and yet the second half of it drops the ball a couple of times. We did a bad mix on "Red Hill Mining Town," and if anyone cares to, they should imagine Joe Cocker singing it. I was always imagining that he sang that song. There was supposed to be a brass section, but that isn't in it.

Achtung Baby (1991).

It's a great album. Like all great albums, it's almost impossible to figure out how you could've made it. It is way beyond the sum of its parts. Your enemies will define you. So make them interesting. In this case, it starts to be the hypocrisy in your own heart that you realize is the more interesting enemy. Before, it was railing against the world, and the wickedness in the world. The lack of justice, that bad things can happen to good people. Now, it's the havoc you're able to wreak in your own life if you allow yourself your heart's desires.

On *Rattle and Hum*, we sang about desire. On *Achtung Baby*, we were desire. We let it become us. We thought we were exorcising our demons. We might, in fact, have been exercising them.

**You were thinking that it was also time
to explore sexuality.**

Sex is a powerful subject. How is it that we've relegated the subject to pornographers and the dullest of minds? So our work became more eroticized at that time. It was a theme. We don't go after albums like rock bands. We go after albums like film directors: this is the subject, let's get into it. We improvise musically, not thematically.

People are always forcing you to make decisions between flesh and spirit. Whereas I want to dance myself in the direction of God. I go out drinking with God. I am flirtatious in the company of God. I am not a person who has to put God out of his mind to go out on the town. It's a key point. The divided soul of Marvin Gaye, Elvis, were conflicts that tore them apart. And they don't tear me apart. I reckon God loves all of me.

This is the central conceit of the song "One." I hate — just so you know — the concept of oneness. It's so hippie schtick. I tried to stop it being called the ONE Campaign. The reason a lot of the religious groups liked it is because they like that hippie schtick. But I wrote the opposite song — I wrote, "We're one and we're not the same." It was a bitter pill of a song.

**Was "One" about your relationship with your wife
or the band?**

It's a father-and-son story. I tried to write about someone I knew who was coming out and was afraid to tell his father. It's a religious father and son. [Sings] "You say love is a temple / Love's a higher law / You ask me to enter / But then you make me crawl."

I have a lot of gay friends, and I've seen them screwed up from unloving family situations. Which just are completely anti-Christian. If we know anything about God, it's that God is love. That's part of the song. And then it's also about people struggling to be together, and how difficult it is to stay together in this world, whether you're in a band or in a relationship.

So you're saying it's a song of anger?

It's quite an angry song. I cannot figure out why people get married to it. It's a song about splitting up.

Pop (1997).

An earnest band with political overtones kicks off their boots for dancing shoes. Supposed to be the return to pop from the experimental period that included Passengers and *Zooropa*. "Discothèque" was supposed to be what "Sledgehammer" was to Peter Gabriel. Great idea for an album. We just misfired — booked the tour before we finished the album.

All That You Can't Leave Behind (2000).

Great album. A complete set of ideas. It's an album about essence, about the casting away of the nonessential things and realizing what those essential things are: family, friendship. It all adds up, though the running order's a little odd.

The idea was: what is the essence of our band if you distill it? What do we have to contribute? For ten years, we'd been doing exactly the opposite. We'd been thinking, "What is it we don't have?," and going after it. Now, in order to keep it fresh, we say, "What is it we do have?," and let's go after that. We've done that for two albums.

I wanted to make a really raw record about the things you just cannot live without. And a really uncool album. I wanted to write a song called "I Love You." I never got to write that song. But it was that kind of thing. Who's going to write a song called "Beautiful Day"? You'd want to be unembarrassable. I think U2's often at its best when it's very uncool.

Tell me about Bob Dylan. How did you first meet him?

I went to interview him for the *Hot Press*, an Irish music paper, in 1984. We talked about playing chess. Van Morrison was there, too. Dylan was responsible for *Rattle and Hum* because he's the one who said, in that interview, that you have to understand the past, where the music comes from. He was talking to me about the McPeake family and the Clancy Brothers and then Hank Williams and Leadbelly, none of whom we knew. Bob came out on the *Joshua Tree* tour, played a few songs with us. During *Rattle and Hum*, he came down and played keyboards. We went out to his house in California and wrote a couple of songs together.

What was that like?

I think he was just keeping an eye out for me. I probably didn't realize what this meant, and I may not have respected his privacy the way I should have.

In what sense do you mean?

People say, "Oh, you've written with Bob Dylan," and I'd tell them what happened, not realizing that his privacy was sacrosanct. So I don't know why he continued to be my friend. He kind of comes and goes.

What's hanging out with him like?

I find him to be the least obtuse person in the world, except when there's more than a few people in the room. He's much better one to one.

The collision of the Beatles and Bob Dylan gave us the galaxy that our planet is in. I would consider myself to be more of a fan than a friend. He might call me friend; I would call me a fan. I find him very old-school — ancient values, ancient wisdom. For a man who helped to give birth to the modern era, he's really coming from a very old place. A pilgrim, a sojourner, a troubadour. It's almost a medieval way he sees the world, in terms of performing.

Your favorite Dylan songs and album?

"Visions of Johanna" and *Bringing It All Back Home*. I loved it as a teenager, and still love the humor and discovering some of the references as you get older, just realizing what that was about.

And the Beatles songs you like the most?

The White Album, because of the combination of the really experimental and the real songwriting craft. That's our yin and yang: really heavy, really soft. *The White Album* is probably my favorite album, although our last two albums are much more like *Abbey Road* or *Let It Be*.

What about Bruce Springsteen?

Bruce taught us so much — how to play arenas, and not rip people off, how to communicate to the back of the stalls, how to be emotional, how to be operatic and not overblown, how to have dignity.

Yet we couldn't be more different. Back in the Eighties I remember saying to Bruce, "All these characters in your songs. Why don't you write about yourself?" He looked at me and said, eyes darkened, "What's there to write about? What's my life? I play gigs, I go home." You know, chastising me with his humility.

What are your favorites of Bruce's songs?

"Darkness on the Edge of Town," the early Van Morrison–influenced stuff, *The Wild, the Innocent and the E Street Shuffle*. And his Elvis-like howl. It's a haunting, spooky music that he can make. I don't know the landscapes he's traveling through but I like when they're a little topsy-turvy and when you feel he might get lost.

If Dylan is Faulkner, then Springsteen is Steinbeck. He's one of the great guitar players, by the way. And I always admire a man who marries above his station — Patti is hot stuff, that red-haired woman. You can't not like a person who goes home to her.

U2 and the Rolling Stones are the only two bands to operate at a global stadium level and are similar in so many other ways. What did you learn from the Rolling Stones?

Swagger. Flirtation with an audience. Taking care of business. It's not sexy to not know what's going on. I always respected Mick for that. He made those guys very wealthy and they made him cool. It's worth remembering.

Keith always reminds me of that Bob Dylan line "To live outside the law, you must be honest." He has enormous personal integrity, the way he wouldn't talk about women, the way he would light a cigarette for you, the way he carries himself. He's much more graceful than people realize. I know he's got some demons, and I'm sure it's not pleasant to see that being worked out. It's a shame that he and Mick don't get on better. If they're doing this well without that kind of relationship, can you imagine how well they would do if they were actually ringing each other up to get a better verse, a better hook?

I like a lot of stuff from their later albums, like "Out of Tears," from *Voodoo Lounge*, "Out of Control." *Exile on Main Street* is one of the reasons why I live in the south of France part of the time. They made that album around the corner from where my house is, and there's humidity on that record and a certain free form that I relate to.

When you and Mick get together, do you have some laughs?

He's very funny, very charming, quite a conservative character. He's got the yacht club jacket on, or whatever it is. It's a relief to be around somebody not in the pursuit of groovy. And his kids have impeccable manners. One of his young children came up to me and said, "People think my daddy's the devil...and he lets them."

**By 2001, New York had become your second home.
"City of Blinding Lights" and "New York" are among
the classic rock odes to the city. Where were you
on September 11?**

I was in Venice. I'd gotten lost on the backstreets with my son Eli and a friend, and I was trying to find directions. It was just after the first plane had hit. I knew on that day that everything would be different from then on.

The vulnerability that was exposed in these events has helped Americans understand how others live with these vulnerabilities on a daily basis. The pictures of New Orleans, they look like Mozambique to me. There's an African word, *ubuntu*, which means something along the lines of "I am because we are" — the interconnectedness of people and things. That time of America behaving like an island is over. If there was some kind of plate glass around the country, it smashed on September the eleventh.

I saw you play Madison Square Garden one month later.

That was one of the most extraordinary moments of our lives. When "Where the Streets Have No Name" went off, and the lights went up, I think half the house was in tears. New York had let us into a very private moment. We did not feel in any way like visitors or tourists. We were the same people.

When you have a shock like what happened in Manhattan, you face your mortality in a very real way. You're living with the chance that any moment something else can happen and take you or your loved ones away.

A lot of people told you that you shouldn't play New York. It's too soon, it's too dangerous.

Yes, they told us not to play, and our own people begged me not to put up the names of all the men and women who died there. But I felt it was so important to do that because these people weren't statistics. They were real people. I was looking around from the stage and seeing the names of brothers and sisters and fathers, and it brings it home.

It sounds like September 11 raised the stakes for you.

It completely changed everything. The mood at the shows was very different. People were holding on much tighter to our band — as I do myself when things are going on in my life. I put on music. It changes the music you listen to. Bob Dylan's *Love and Theft* and *All That You Can't Leave Behind* are the two albums that people associate with that time. We are proud to be in that company.

You were touring America with your social crusade during one of the most vulnerable moments in American history.

Here's an Irish rock star, who has lots of ideas about what he thinks America is and isn't, and what it should be, and won't shut up. You could be forgiven for wanting to turn that radio down. Except after 9/11 a lot of people were asking the same questions. Not just, "How could this happen to us?" But very big questions about, "What is America?" I was touring the country at the time, saying America is not just a country, it's an idea, and that idea is under attack. When you're under attack, you have to rethink things. You have to make sure of what you believe in.

When you're going to go sit down with George Bush, how do you prepare? Not in terms of policy, but psychologically?

I have no fear of politicians or presidents or prime ministers. They should be afraid, because they will be held accountable for what happened on their watch. I'm representing the poorest and the most vulnerable people. On a spiritual level. I have that with me. I'm throwing a punch, and the fist belongs to people who can't be in the room, whose rage, whose anger, whose hurt I represent. Their moral force is way beyond mine. It's an argument that has much more weight than I have. So I'm not feeling nervous.

Do you say to yourself, "I'm going to curse less, keep certain things in check"?

Am I going to watch my mouth? Yes, I am. I'm trying to be respectful. Remember, before I'm going in there to meet the president for the first time, I know he's already set to double aid to Africa. So I want to shake this man's hand.

You've been getting criticized for making a deal with Bush. There's cynicism about that, that maybe you've made a deal with the devil here.

First of all, I don't support any president, whether from the left or from the right. I support, or do not support, what they do in the area that we are discussing. I can't criticize a man who has doubled, tripled aid to Africa — especially after we asked him to, and he said yes. To get along with someone, you don't have to agree on everything, but just one thing if it's important enough.

Do you feel now you can't criticize him on the war in Iraq?

Everyone in the administration knows how I feel about the war in Iraq. Everyone. I criticize it to Tony Blair as well. Do I campaign against the war in Iraq? No.

Why not?

That's the compromise. I feel I gave that up when I started to work for other people whom I will never meet, those 400,000* people in Africa who now owe their lives to American money, which paid for these lifesaving drugs. I work for them. If me not shooting my mouth off about the war in Iraq is the price I pay, then I'm prepared to pay it. Others have been eloquent on this issue.

Does it frustrate you not to be able to say what you think?

I'm a bigmouthed Irish rock star; of course it frustrates me. Look, I don't bring the subject up, but when it does come up, I've been very clear.

What are the fundamental lessons that you've learned about the art and nature of politics?

Anything's possible in politics as long as it's not your idea. That's what I've learned. Share authorship. Same thing I learned in the band. And that bipartisanship may take longer but it will get you a lot further.

---

* As of 2023, that number has risen to twenty-five million.

**What tools do you have to use in there,
besides your fame and your charm?**

A relentless and rigorous argument that unless we deal with the enormous inequality that exists in the wider world between us and them, we're not going to have the life we enjoy now. I mean that spiritually, I mean that economically, and I mean it politically. I've rarely met an American or an Irish or an English person who doesn't somehow know that.

**Your manager, Paul McGuinness, said to you once
that the duty of an artist is to illustrate the problems
of the world, to bring them before his audience,
but not to solve them.**

Artists won't be able to solve it, but this generation will be able to eradicate extreme poverty. Not poverty, but extreme poverty. I call it stupid poverty: kids dying of starvation. This should not happen, and does not have to continue to happen. The people have to give the politicians their permission to spend what is, after all, their money.

I'm tired of tin-cupping, begging for the beggars. We have now two million people signed up to the ONE campaign to make poverty history. By 2008, we'll have five million — that's more than the NRA. That's real firepower.

————————

**You think your duty as an artist now is to help make
that happen?**

I wish it wasn't, because I'd much rather be in a studio writing a song. When that song forms something that didn't exist ten minutes ago, and now it looks like it's heading to be played on the radio in Tokyo, that is a thrill. I enjoy my work campaigning as an activist, but my gift is, I'm a singer, a songwriter, and a performer. And I just happened to have learned other skills to protect that gift, and those skills seem to suit an activist.

> **What drives you? Is it fear of failure or to show you can do anything? What's the source of that energy?**

Fear of a missed opportunity. I can see a way through to what my friend Jeff Sachs calls the end of poverty. This is not wide-eyed Irish rock star nonsense. These are achievable goals. I seem to be able to communicate them and so if I don't do it, I've walked away from an opportunity to really effect some change in a world that badly needs it.

> **You've been on this never-ending peace and nonviolence crusade since you've been seventeen years old. Do you feel anointed or chosen to do this? Do you have a messianic complex, like Bruce teasingly said?**

That's fair enough. As regards anointing, I put my hand up for this job. I've probably just worn the good Lord out. "Okay, you can have the anointing, then." I'm sure it wasn't in the cards. It's like the two brothers, Jacob and Esau, who go to Isaac for the blessing and the younger brother, Jacob, pretends he's Esau in order to take the blessing before Isaac passes. I'm like that guy. Why does God Almighty stand over the blessing if it was stolen? Only recently I figured it out. Jacob wanted it more than Esau. He knew how powerful the blessing was.

Once you see not only the problem, but also the solution, there's no escape. You see it, you can't look away from it. I want it to feel like an adventure, not a burden. I don't mean just for me, I mean for the movement. This is an extraordinary thing, an uplifting thing. This is not, "Oh, my God, all the poor starving Africans with flies around their faces." They are very noble, royal people, full of easy laughter and very innovative. This is about us, too. It's about, who are we? What are our values? Do we have any? It's exciting.

How do the guys in the band feel
about the way that your crusades are shaping the
perception of the band?

They were very, very worried for the first few years. It's very unhip work. They thought our audience would tire of it, but our audience has ended up feeling more powerful themselves as a result of me raising my voice for them.

How do you feel about getting older and playing to older
audiences? Does it affect your perceptions of yourself?
You know there's a golden circle out there.

There's a golden circle because rich people have feelings, too [laughs]. We have a vital audience from the colleges, but we also have an audience that has been with us for a long time, and that brings with it a real weight.

And there's a resonance to that?

The us-against-them situation in the Sixties isn't the case anymore. I know seventy-year-old men who are much more radical than their seventeen-year-old grandchildren.

There is a power that comes from age. You see the face of Johnny Cash before he left this world and you hear that voice. Or you see Mick Jagger these days, who looks like Nureyev. Their faces are more interesting. They're much more dangerous men as they get older. They know their way around the world, and they have more to say.

Where do you see yourself in twenty years?

I'd like to return to fiction and poetry. I'd like to just be a writer, and a singer, and a performer. At sixty I'm going to be much better looking than I am now. I'm sure of that. I don't hope I die before I get old. A lot of my heroes tend to be people who are alive, not dead, and living long.

In other words, you want to be doing the same thing but in a more pure form, maybe without all the outside work?

Words are becoming more and more important to me. I was never a guy who listened to the words. I just wrote them. And I'm really enjoying writing, whether it's speeches or letters, or prose poems, scripts, or lyrics. Maybe it's because I stop talking when I start writing.

If you hadn't been in U2, what would've happened to you?

I would've been a journalist.

Why do you say that?

Curiosity. I like writing. I'm attracted to things I'm afraid of. Disaster groupie, journalist, scriptwriter. The media plays a really valuable role in a free society. The United States has the best-quality journalism in the world, though your television really sucks.

Can rock and roll contain everything that you want to do?

It's so exciting, music. It really is. I believe that old adage that all art aspires to the condition of music.

What does that mean?

It's such an extraordinary thing, music. It is how we speak to God, finally — or how we don't. Even if we're ignoring God. It's the language of the spirit. If you believe that we contain within our skin and bones a spirit that might last longer than your time breathing in and out — if there is a spirit, music is the thing that wakes it up. And it certainly woke mine up. And it seems to be how we communicate on another level.

I just came back from one of the most moving experiences of my life: playing Poland, hearing huge audiences singing every word of a language they weren't born into. They felt them before they understood them. It's humbling as a lyricist and hugely uplifting as a musician.

The thing that drives me on is a sort of curiosity about the world and people. Occasionally I lift the stones and find a few creepy-crawlies under there. The access that I've had through music to other artists in other fields — economists, novelists, doctors, nurses in the field — it's been amazing for me.

When we were in the middle of punk rock, I wanted to hang out with Johnny Cash. I wanted to know what was going on under his hat. And I got to. And Frank Sinatra — I got to know what was going on under his hat and in his heart, and he shared things with me. That blessing that I was talking about — I've been chasing that blessing all my life from all different sources and places. From Bob Dylan to Willie Nelson to Billy Graham.

Do you have any regrets?

I have loads. I won't speak about them, but yes, I do. Musically, that I didn't finish those songs in the Eighties. That's why I get a kick out of playing them live. I'm finishing them every night.

Have you found what you're looking for?

I used to think that one day I'd be able to resolve the different drives I have in different directions, the tension between the different people I am. Now I realize that is who I am, and I'm more content to be discontent. I do feel I'm getting closer to the song I hear in my head, getting closer to not compromising that melody with some crap words. I mean that on every level. I wasn't looking for grace, but luckily grace was looking for me.

BOB DYLAN

[2007]

NEARLY FORTY years had passed since I interviewed Bob Dylan in 1969. Despite his disdain for the press, after that first interview he began to sit down with *Rolling Stone* writers with regularity. I had my own ideas about Bob, but the complexity and density of his talent, the many worlds he encompassed and described, were beyond any one inquisitor. To do fuller justice to his work, and the volume of it, I sent many different interlocutors, with their different points of view, expertises, disciplines, and theories: Jonathan Cott, Ben Fong Torres, Jonathan Lethem, Kurt Loder, Mikal Gilmore, and Doug Brinkley, among others.*

I think that Bob came to respect *Rolling Stone* for how intelligently and reverentially we treated him. We put him on many covers, of course, and we insisted on his genius and centrality to our times and his place in rock and roll and in our history. *Rolling Stone* became important to him. He would never admit as much — in fact, he would take a stance that he never read his press, that he was indifferent to it all.

---

* *Bob Dylan: The Essential Interviews,* edited by Jonathan Cott, contains these and many other of the best Dylan interviews over the years.

However, whenever we talked or met, he was always up to speed on whatever had lately been written about him.

Our relationship was easygoing and mutually entertaining, as we would try to outwit each other, upping the laughs especially in the company of others. We also had opportunities to get into what was deeper and more personal. He was a gentleman with me, old-fashioned, thoughtful, fascinating. I have remembered every minute of being with Bob, as the years rolled by. Once we sat in chairs on the banks of the river on a farm I owned, talking for hours and "watching the river flow."

Rolling Stone decided to mark its fortieth anniversary with a special issue in which we would ask our heroes — artists and activists, presidents and poets, scientists and sages — what we had learned in the past forty years. We wanted to present a generational retrospective and assessment to understand where we now found ourselves. I knew it was time to talk to Bob again.

In October 2007 I flew to Amsterdam, where he was on tour. It was the only way to make deadline, just two days away. This was making me nervous, because sometimes interviewing Bob is like playing Ping-Pong, which is always fun but not when the presses are about to roll and there is no time for a second match. Which, of course, he knows. Bob began with one of his evasive, head-bobbing runarounds. I had no time to play and no choice but to bust him on it, which I have included here, and then he became expansive and forthcoming.

America is Bob's great passion, the subject of his studies and his songs, and second only to his songs of the human soul and spirit. He is the greatest poet of our times, and like Walt Whitman, he became the voice of America.

His new record, *Modern Times*, seemed to me a bookend to his 1965 album *Highway 61 Revisited*. We were still on the same highway. The advertising signs were different now, the pretty girls had wrinkles, but the road was still headed in the same direction. In "Workingman's Blues," the sun has set further on the unions. In the beautiful dirge "Nettie Moore," he sings, "I loved you then, and ever shall, but there's no one left to tell." And in an overlooked minor masterpiece, "Ain't Talkin'," the ten-minute-long album closer, we are back on Desolation Row, but the ambulance has long since departed. There's no point anymore, just "hand me down my walkin' cane." The chorus contrasts who we are inside to what we see in front of our eyes: "Heart burnin', still yearnin' in the last outback at the world's end."

Bob spoke of "the old America," and how the atomic bomb changed all that when we discovered that we had the power in our hands, as if we were God Almighty, to destroy all of creation.

What had Bob learned? What remained true? "Nature," he told me. "Just elemental nature. And I'm still tramping my way through the forest."

––––––––––

You've been on the road pretty steadily for forty years.

I like the originality of being on the road. It's real life, in real time.

What is it that is so enjoyable?

The groupies and the drinking and the parties backstage…[Laughs] Why would anybody? Performers are performers. Why do you still edit your magazine?

It's something I do well, and one gets pleasure
out of something one does well.

Exactly. It's the one thing in life you find you can do well.

You said that going out on the road makes you write more.

Yeah. That would be true, to a certain degree. But if you don't have to write songs, why write them? Especially if you've got so many you could never play — there wouldn't be enough time to play them all, anyway. I've got enough where I don't really feel the urge to write anything additional.

You just released this amazing new record.
The title, *Modern Times*, seems to be a very
deliberate statement.

Well, I don't know. Can you think of a better title?

***Highway 61 Revisited?* How did you decide**
on *Modern Times*?

Titles are something that come after you've done whatever it is you've done. I don't set out with a title. It was something that probably just passed through my mind. Why, does it have some impact?

It seems that you set out to assess America
right now. Is there a general theme
to the record?

You would have to ask every individual person who hears it what it would mean. It would probably mean many things on many levels to many different kinds of people.

To me, it seems that it's about war and corruption.

Well, all my records are, to a certain degree. That's the nature of them.

Your records are about power, knowledge, salvation.

That would be not so easy for me to relate to, what a record is about. It is a statement, it's its own statement, its own entity, rather than being about something else. If I was a painter...I don't paint the chair, I would paint feelings about the chair.

You're a student of history. If you were to put the current moment in a historical context, where do you think we are?

That would be hard to do, unless you put yourself ten years into the future. It's not the nature of a song to imply what's going on under any current philosophy any more than...How can I explain it? Like all the music that came out of the First and Second World Wars. Did you ever notice how lighthearted it was? If you listen to the songs from that period, you would think that there's nothing gloomy on the horizon.

Do you think it's gloomy on the horizon?

In what sense do you mean?

Bob, come on.

No, you come on. In what sense do you mean that? If you're talking about in a political sense...

In a general political, spiritual, historical sense. You're talking about the end of times on this record, you've got a

very gloomy vision of the world, you're saying, "I'm facing the end of my life and looking at all this..."

Aren't we all always doing that?

No, some people are trying to avoid it. But I'm trying to interview you and you're not being very helpful with this.

Jann, have I ever been helpful?

You have been in the past. You have given some really great interviews in the last several years.

Yeah, but I wasn't on tour when I was doing them; I could be fully present. But now, I'm thinking about amps going out and...

You don't have people taking care of those for you?

You would hope.

You can't find a good road manager? Is that the problem here?

Yeah [laughs].

What can I do to get you to take this seriously?

I'm taking it seriously.

You're not.

Of course I am. You're the one who's here to be celebrated. Forty years... forty years with a magazine that obviously now has intellectual recognition. Did you ever think that would happen when you started?

I was taking it seriously.

Look how far you've come. You're the one to be interviewed. I want to know just as much from you as you want to know from me. I would love to have you on our radio show and interview you for an hour.

I'm going to do that as soon as we're done with this.
We'll just turn it around and flip it and do that.

You've seen more music changes than me.

Oh, please.

No, no please. You please. You've seen it all from the top. I've seen it maybe from...also near the top.

From the bottom up, what's the view today? *Modern Times*
is not lighthearted. And it seems like you are worried
about the times we're in and what we may or may not have
learned as a country. It seems not distant from *Highway*
61 or earlier records where you describe a difficult
situation in the country, but nothing in this record
indicates anything has gotten better —
indeed, it's gotten worse.

Well, America's a different place than it was when those other records were made. It was more like Europe used to be, where every territory was different — every county was different, every state was different. A different culture, different architecture, different food. You could go a hundred miles in the States, and it would be like going from Stalingrad to Paris or something. It's just not that way anymore. It's all homogenized. People wear the same clothes, eat the same food, think the same things.

This style of music, which punctuates my music, comes from an older period of time, a period of time that I lived through. So it's very accessible to me. Someone who was not around at that period of time, it wouldn't be accessible to them. For them, it would be more of a revivalist thing or a historical thing. You're from that time, too. I'm sure you know all these same things.

The first time I ever went to London, which was in the early Sixties, '61, they still had the rubble and the damaged buildings from Hitler's bombs. That was how close the complete destruction of Europe was to the period of time when I was coming up.

Robert Johnson had just died, three years before I was born. All the great original artists were still there to be heard, felt, and seen. Once that gets into your blood, you can't get rid of it that easily.

What gets in your blood?

That whole culture, that period of time, that old America.

You mean the 1920s and 1930s?

It wouldn't have made sense to talk to somebody who was, say, in their Fifties [back then], to ask him, "What was it like in the late 1800s or 1900s?" It wouldn't have interested anybody. But for some reason, the 1950s and 1960s interest people now. A part of the reason, if not the whole reason, is the atom bomb. The atom bomb fueled the entire world that came after it. It showed that indiscriminate killing and indiscriminate homicide on a mass level was possible... whereas if you look at warfare up until that point, you had to see somebody to shoot them or maim them, you had to look at them. You don't have to do that anymore.

With the atom bomb, mankind — suddenly,
and for the first time — had the power to utterly destroy itself.

I think so. I'm sure that fueled all aspects of society. I know it
gave rise to the music we were playing. If you look at all these early
performers, they were atom-bomb-fueled. Jerry Lee, Carl Perkins,
Buddy Holly, Elvis, Gene Vincent, Eddie Cochran...

How were they atom-bomb-fueled?

They were fast and furious, their songs were all on the edge.
Music was never like that before. Lyrically, you had the blues singers,
but Ma Rainey wasn't singing about the stuff that Carl Perkins and
Jerry Lee were singing about, nobody was singing with that type of
fire and destruction. They paid a heavy price for that, because obviously the older generation took notice and kind of got rid of them as
quickly as they could recognize them. Jerry Lee got ostracized. Chuck
Berry went to jail. Elvis, of course, we know what happened to him.
Buddy Holly in a plane crash, Little Richard, all that stuff...

Then in this new record,
you're still dealing with the cultural effects of
the bomb?

I think so.

But doing it in the musical styles of earlier generations?
I don't hear much rock in there.

You don't hear any rock in there, because I'm not familiar
with rock music. It's not something that I feel assimilated into. It's
too spacey, there's too much space in it. It doesn't get to the point
quick enough, if there is a point. It's what's taken over, but the rock
and roll element's been kind of taken out...I don't know how to

put it. It either reaches you or it doesn't reach you. I just like the older music better.

**What do you think of the historical moment
we're in today? We seem to be hell-bent on destruction.
Do you worry about global warming?**

Where's the global warming? It's freezing here.

It seems a pretty frightening outlook.

I think what you're driving at, though, is we expect politicians to solve all our problems. I don't expect politicians to solve anybody's problems.

Who is going to solve them?

Our own selves. We've got to take the world by the horns and solve our own problems. The world owes us nothing, each and every one of us, the world owes us not one single thing. Politicians or whoever.

**Do you think America is a force for good
in the world today?**

Theoretically.

But in practical fact...

The practical fact is always different than theory.

What do you think the practical fact is right now?

With what's going on? Human nature hasn't really changed in three thousand years. Maybe the obstacles and actualities and daily customs change, but human nature really hasn't changed. It cannot change. It's not made to change.

Do you find yourself being a more religious person these days?

A religious person? Religion is supposedly a force for positive good. Where can you look in the world and see that religion has been a force for positive good? Where can you look at humanity and say, "Humanity has been uplifted by a connection to a godly power"?

Meaning organized religion? At one point, you took on Christianity in a very serious way, and then Judaism. Where are you now with all that?

Corporations are religions. It depends on what you talk about with a religion. Anything is a religion. Religion is something that is mostly outward appearance. Faith is a different thing. How many religions are there in the world? Quite a few, actually.

What is your faith these days?

Faith doesn't have a name. It doesn't have a category. It's oblique. So it's unspeakable. We degrade faith by talking about religion.

When you write songs where you say you walk in "the mystical garden," there's a lot of religious imagery.

In the "mystic" garden. That kind of imagery is just as natural to me as breathing, because the world of folk songs has enveloped me for so long. My terminology all comes from folk music. It doesn't come from the radio or TV or computers or any of that stuff. It's embedded in the folk music of the English language.

Much of which comes from the Bible.

Yeah, a lot of it is biblical, a lot of it is just troubadour stuff, a lot of it is stuff that Uncle Dave Macon would sing off the top of his head.

What do you take faith in?

Nature. Just elemental nature. I'm still tramping my way through the forest, really, on daily excursions. Nature doesn't change. And if there is any war going on a big level today, it's against nature.

On *Modern Times* it seems like you're dealing with the forces of reckoning.

Reckoning? You mean every day is a judgment? That's all instilled in me. I wouldn't know how to get rid of it.

How is it instilled in you?

It's instilled in me by the way I grew up, where I come from, early feelings...

Is it something you see as coming, or something that's happening right now?

We really don't know much about the great Judgment Day that's coming, because we've got nobody to come back and tell us about it. We can only assume certain things because of what we've been taught.

**What do you assume is happening in the world
around us when you walk in the mystical garden?**

You see things closing in, you see the darkness coming.
"Mystic" garden. I could have come up with that line thirty
years ago. This is all the same thing from different angles.

**It's like the landscape of "Desolation Row," only you've
changed from outrage to acceptance.**

I think as we get older, we all come to that feeling, one way or
another. We've seen enough happening to know that things are a
certain way, and even if they're changed, they're still going to be
that certain way.

Therefore, we have to accept it?

I've always accepted that. I don't think I've thought about
things any differently in the whole time I've been around, really.

**You've resisted talking about your past for years.
In *Chronicles* you're writing about
and considering your legacy. Why are you
doing it now?**

Well, it probably was because enough things have resolved
themselves, and I had an editor who was a good ally. I could have
probably done it earlier, but I just didn't have the encouragement.

Did you enjoy it?

When I did it, I did, yeah. What I didn't like about it was the constant rereading and revising, because I'm not used to that. A song is nothing compared to some kind of literary thing. A song, you can keep it with you, you can hum it, you can kind of go over things when you're out and around, you can keep it in your mind. It's all small. But you can't do that with a book. If you want to check it, you have to reread what you've done. It's very time-consuming, and I didn't like that part of it.

If I wasn't inspired to do it, I wouldn't do it. Great flashes would come to me. These waves would come, and I would have to either mark things down or have to go back to where I could write things, and keep typewriters here and there, and do that. But it was enjoyable in that I only did it when I was inspired to do it and never touched it when I wasn't. I never tried to manufacture the inspiration.

> **I was struck by your account of coming to New York when you were young, going to the public library, and by the very deliberate and methodical fashion in which you went about learning your craft and building your knowledge.**

But I was learning everything I needed to learn from real live people who were really there at the time, so it was firsthand. I think that's where my feelings came from, in terms of all of them early songs. Even songs at later dates, it's "What is human nature really like?" Not "What am I like, what do I like, what don't I like, what am I all about?" Not that kind of thing, but "What are all these invisible spirits all about?" I think that's where songs like "Blowin' in the Wind" come from. It's a more ancient struggle than what might currently be seen as the fulcrum of where the lyrics are coming out of.

> **Are you surprised that you made a record today that's as vital and as important and as creative as any you've made in the past?**

No. No, I knew I was going to make it. I'm surprised that it sold as many records as it did, so a lot of people must feel a similar way.

Why do you think people reacted so strongly to you in the 1960s? What did you reach in people that resonated so deeply?

Because I had — and perhaps still do have — that originality that others don't have. Because I come from a time when you had to be original, and you had to have some kind of God-given talent just to begin with. You couldn't manufacture that. Just about everybody and anybody who was around in the Fifties and Sixties had a degree of originality. That was the only way you could get in the door. That was just a necessary part of your makeup, which needed to be there.

My thing was never heard or seen before, but it didn't come out of a vacuum. There's a direct correlation between something like *Highway 61 Revisited* and "Blue Yodel No. 9," by Jimmie Rodgers. It just doesn't spring out of the earth without rhyme or reason.

Nobody had heard stuff said that way or spoken that way.

But nobody had heard the stuff that we heard. You came up in the Fifties. There was more freethinking then, there wasn't such mass conformity as there is today. Today, a freethinking person gets ridiculed. Back then, they were just sort of ostracized and maybe avoided. The popular consensus at the time, in this time we're speaking about, was a very mild form of entertainment; it was boring and uninteresting. Beneath that surface, though, there was an entirely different world.

And you tapped into that world?

We all did. Some of us decided we could live in this world.

Others decided, well, they could visit it once in a while, but it wasn't necessarily their thing.

So you lived in it.

I did.

And everybody else was just visiting?

Yeah, like tourists. Like at the sock hop.

**So people entered your world and were awed by it,
but couldn't live in it?**

No, I don't think you could, any more than...Did you ever see Little Richard perform? You could be awed by it, but you were not a part of it. Unless, of course, you wanted to be a part of it; then it was open to you.

———————

Last night, you chose to close with "All Along the Watchtower," which has now become an anthem of yours.

Who knew?

Did you rediscover that song because of Hendrix?

Probably.

**Had you heard that before, in your mind,
what he did with it?**

No, that record's kind of a mystery to me, anyway. When he

made it, it caused me to sit up and pay attention. Like, "Oh, there might be more to that than I had dreamed."

> What did you do from *Highway 61 Revisited* last night?
> "Just Like Tom Thumb's Blues"? How did you choose
> that one? I love the rearrangement.

You know, it's not rearranged. There's a different dynamic. The dynamic on all of those songs can change from night to night, because of the style of music that I've grown accustomed to playing, which I always could play. But you can't do everything. You can't just display everything at the same time.

> You change them to make it more fun for yourself?

Well, it's more contrived than that.

> Why is it more contrived?

It's because I have so many different types of songs, speaking musically: fast ballads, slow ballads, minor-key twelve-bar things, major-key twelve-bar things, twelve-bar pieces that differ greatly in the dynamics of the rhythm, which causes the lyrics, the way you deliver them, to change from night to night. It's based on an infinite system where you don't necessarily have to feel good to play it, but if you just follow the rules, you can do different things every night.

> Take "It's All Over Now, Baby Blue," for instance, which
> you did last night. Don't people come to the show
> and want to hear that original, mournful version?

I don't know who would, unless it's somebody who bought that record in nineteen sixty-what. But it's the same song, and I'm the same person, and it's always been there. Those early songs I made with just an acoustic guitar. In a way, those are like demos, because that's what people do when they demo a song: they just go in and play it with their acoustic guitar, and that's what it is. Then they develop the song later.

Do you think your performance of it in this way gives it a different meaning? Originally it was lost and sad; now it's assertive.

Yeah. Astrologically, you're dealing with a different day every day of the week. Every day is a different color, a different planet rules it. You could say the same thing, you could feel the same way, you could write the same thing, but if it's on a Tuesday, it's going to be different than if it comes out on Friday. That's just a fact. You can ask any astrologer.

When you see Bono do his Africa relief work or Bruce Springsteen go out and do the Vote for Change tour, do you think that rock music can be a voice for change?

Maybe to some people it can. A person feels good when they do charity work. What Bono does is a good thing. Bruce has got a certain degree of power. He can use that power any way he sees fit. You have to applaud him for it. He's not playing around, and he means what he says.

But do you think rock music is a voice for change?

It's a change in lifestyle. I don't know. I've never been affected by it that way, so I can't really say.

When you heard music as a young kid, there was a calling of your talent, but wasn't there also a calling of "My life can be different"?

Yeah, but that was a calling. People who have a calling play it different than people who just play it for frivolity, people whose motives aren't sincere. You talk about musicians — maybe one in a thousand are worth listening to, in terms of what they have to say, in terms of what they're putting forth, in terms of the world they're involved in, in terms of moving you from here to there. There's not many musicians capable of that.

A few of your friends and contemporaries:
what do you think of Neil Young?

Neil is very sincere, if nothing else. He's sincere, and he's got a God-given talent, with that voice of his, and the melodic strain that runs through absolutely everything he does. He could be at his most thrashy, but it's still going to be elevated by some melody. Neil's the only one who does that. There's nobody in his category.

Tell me about George Harrison.

George got stuck with being the Beatle that had to fight to get songs on records because of Lennon and McCartney. Well, who wouldn't get stuck? If George had had his own group and was writing his own songs back then, he'd have been probably just as big as anybody. George had an uncanny ability to just play chords that didn't seem to be connected in any kind of way and come up with a melody and a song. I don't know anybody else who could do that either. What can I tell you? He was from that old line of playing where every note was a note to be counted.

You were very close, right?

Yeah. We'd known each other since the old days, really. I knew the Beatles really early on, all of them.

**What was your relationship with John Lennon like?
Somewhat competitive?**

Yeah. Only to a certain extent, but not really. Him and McCartney both, really, they were fantastic singers. Lennon, to this day, it's hard to find a better singer than Lennon was, or than McCartney was and still is. I'm in awe of McCartney. He's about the only one that I am in awe of. He can do it all. And he's never let up. He's got the gift for melody, he's got the rhythm, he can play any instrument. He can scream and shout as good as anybody, and he can sing a ballad as good as anybody. And his melodies are effortless — that's what you have to be in awe of. He's just so damn effortless. I just wish he'd quit [laughs]. Everything that comes out of his mouth is just framed in melody.

**What do you think accounted for that period
in the Sixties that was so remarkably creative?**

It was a more singular time. I think what we talked about in the early part of the interview is something to be thought about, the first atom bomb that went off. That was explosive, and it gave rise to a different type of personality. You had fiery people, whereas before, everything was more in the backwoods and more secretive. The same things were going on back then; they were just more isolated or taking place in the upper rooms. That's what I think, anyway. I don't know why it was a more powerful period of time. I don't feel it was any less uncomfortable than it is today.

**What does it feel like to grow older? Do you feel wiser?
Happier? More creaky in your bones?**

Things begin to happen that you never considered before. You realize how fragile a human being is and how something insignificant, like what happened to your finger or your toe or something like that, may be enough to really sit you down for a while. I've certainly had trouble in those areas. As you go on, you realize life goes by at a very fast pace, so you've got to slow everything down, because it's going by too quick. I think we all realize it's still going down fast, and we're just not quite as agile as we used to be.

Do you feel wiser?

Wiser? Not necessarily.

Happier?

I don't think happier. Happiness to me is just being able to breathe well.

You seem happier to me, less angry and amped up and pissed off.

Oh. It depends what hour of the day you catch me in, though. It'll get better before it gets worse.

Do you still try to reach your audience every night, every listener there?

In the same way that the Stanley Brothers would have done or Chuck Berry would do: try to display talent in a way that could be conceivable.

Are you thinking about that person in the last row or up there in the balcony?

No, I'm not. I know a lot of performers say they do, but I don't know how much they really do. To me, the relationship between a performer and the audience is definitely anything but a buddy-buddy thing, any more than me going in and admiring a van Gogh painting and thinking that me and him are on the same level because I like his painting.

So you're there to do your art, and they're there to appreciate it and try to understand it.

I would hope so. I think so.

How do you describe your influence when you first came out?

Maybe just like what the books say: that my stuff allowed people to write and perform stuff they felt like singing, which hadn't been done before. But I don't think about that as much of an influence.

You just gave them the opportunity to open up their own thinking?

Yeah, but I never opened up my own thinking. My stuff was never about me, per se, so everybody who came after who thought it was about me, per se, or them, per se, they took the wrong road.

Do you think you have any influence on things right now?

Well, how many performers are out there doing what we do night after night? How many shows are you going to go to? We play at some of these festivals, and me and my band are the only performers there doing anything remotely close to what we're doing in the type of music that it is. It's almost like Tony Bennett or something; it's, like, archaic. You have to be thankful that you still have a generous audience.

BRUCE SPRINGSTEEN

[2023]

T HE FIRST I heard of Bruce was the prophecy "I have seen the future of rock and roll and his name is Bruce Springsteen," in a review written by Jon Landau, then recently retired after nearly a decade of duty as the resident music guru of *Rolling Stone*. The words were career-altering for Bruce and life-altering for Jon, who became Bruce's mentor and manager. The prophecy was right, and Bruce became the biggest American rock star since Elvis.

The first record that Bruce made with Jon's counsel, *Born to Run*, in 1975, was a revelation, containing within it everything that rock and roll music could be. Bruce was more rock and roll past than future: Elvis, Roy Orbison, Phil Spector, the Beatles, the Rolling Stones, Otis Redding, Bob Dylan could all be heard in those performances. Bruce had marshalled the whole lot and catalyzed the future of rock from its past.

Fifty years of American history have elapsed — our own life spans nearing fulfillment — since his appearance as an insurgent rock star. He is now a revered icon of American society, a standard of artistic and moral integrity, the poet laureate, decorated with the Presidential Medal of Freedom, a national treasure.

In all that time, I had only interviewed Bruce once, at his request, to explain his decision to endorse the Democratic presidential candidate, John Kerry, in 2004. It was a carefully considered choice, breaking his precedent of partisan neutrality. The interviews he had already done in *Rolling Stone* (with Kurt Loder and Jim Henke) and his own wonderfully written and intimate autobiography had said about all there was to say by then. His twenty studio albums had also been the story of his life.

Nevertheless, there is no way of putting out a collection of the great masters without Bruce. And I think both of our careers and rock and roll music had now reached a new inflection point. It was coming time to look back and reflect. So, five years after leaving *Rolling Stone*, I went down to Bruce's farm in rural New Jersey — ten minutes from where he grew up — and talked with him at length. At seventy-four, he was on a break from his first tour since the Covid epidemic shut down the concert business. Bruce was doing three and a half hours onstage each night, down from four plus, a concession to the facts of life.

The conversation was a fitting place to bring my search for rock and roll to its destination. In Bruce I had found someone whose tastes and path to discovery in music was so like my own. I also listened to *Highway 61 Revisited* at least one hundred times when it came out, and still regularly do. Favorite guitarists: Mike Bloomfield, Mark Knopfler, check. R&B and soul were the River Jordan.

We shared the same politics and passions and wanted our voices to be heard. We saw broad purpose in the spiritual power and social responsibilities that were potential in rock and roll. We saw it, embraced it, and lived by it.

Bruce was the very embodiment of that vision. He read his first issue of *Rolling Stone* at the newsstand across the street from his uncle's radio repair shop in Freehold. "If you were young, alone in the far lands of New Jersey, *Rolling Stone* was a dispatch from the front, carrying news of a bigger world and another life awaiting."

It was Bruce's calling, to be of service. "I go back to the people who influenced me and they manifested different visions of the country in their own work. I said, 'Yeah, I want to work in the vein that these people who'd affected me so greatly worked in.' I saw that self to be somebody who was engaged in the daily life of their country. I wanted to be a part of that discussion that was occurring. I wanted my audience to be a part of it. It became a part of who I am and what I do."

All these many years later, when I leave a Bruce Springsteen concert rocked out, uplifted in my heart, I feel lucky to be alive.

––––––––––––––

You're on tour again — after five years off the road.
What are you getting out of it now? What's changed
with your audience and what you see?

The actual answer to that question would be more likely in the things that haven't changed that are essential. Which is your attitude about doing the job, what the job still means, what it still means to you, what it means to your band, what it means to the relationships that you have with people you've been working with for fifty years.

Outside of experiences in my personal life with my family,

what happens between being onstage with the band and with the audiences just takes me to my highest self. That's the fundamental and essential thing that remains the same from when I was sixteen years old doing the same job. There's an element of finiteness that everybody recognizes, like, "Hey, we can do some more of these, but not a whole lot more." That's just the way that it is. The unusual thing is that the band can be at such a high place in its own development.

I think the show we have right now, it's one of the best shows we've ever done. It's seemingly the most unrelenting. We hit the button at three hours, nothing stops till then. You're taken and transported, that's our hope. For the guys, it's relishing this period of our work life together.

After fifty years, when you go out there,
do you think the audience you're looking at is a new
audience or is it the same audience and they're grown up?

The majority of the audience is younger than the band. But that's not hard to do. I look out into the eyes, these twenty-something-year-old kids sometimes in the pit, and they're going out of their minds and for me it's just like, "Okay, this is where I'm supposed to be, and this is what I'm supposed to be doing until I don't do that anymore." That's inspirational.

What do you want to communicate to those new faces?

It is not a question of something different from twenty years ago or ten years ago or forty years ago, I think that we had our code worked out really early on, when we were very young in our twenties. There was a certain sort of reverence for the work itself. We're less about what's new than the things that don't change. Our thing is that nightly, the congregation gathers around, the things in life that are permanent. Your family, your work, your friends, lovers, wives, husbands, children. That's all we've done since the beginning. We try to make it entertaining and exciting, and bring intensity of presence, which is really what people are paying for when they buy your ticket and come in.

You live here in New Jersey within miles of where you grew up. Why do you stay here?

Initially, my thoughts about staying here were that I was not worldly, not a cosmopolitan person, not a city person. I was provincial, it was in my nature, I felt it was protective of my own spiritual self and my own emotional life.

There wasn't somebody looking over your shoulder constantly, as if you lived in New York or Los Angeles and you were disassociated from the things that you wrote about and the things that you came up living. My idea was to not lose that association, as a form of defense against the nature of fame and success, where there can be a stripping away of your core self and it can be replaced with — I don't know — a Ferrari. Those trades haven't worked well for the people who've come before me.

It's where I have made sense of my life and provided context for my experiences. This is where I understand myself. I know who I am here. You're navigating from a place where you know who you are, who you've been, who you want to become, who you want to be. All of those things were at the core of all my decisions that I made from the minute I started playing to now, and they remain the same. Once again, it's not something that's changed.

As a teenager you were a Top 40 kid. Right? What were your favorite songs then, and who were the artists who were most influential on you?

I was fourteen in 1964 with the British Invasion, so that was very shaping. I was a big Animals fan, probably because they had a certain class consciousness that I wanted to include in some of the music that I was writing. "We Gotta Get Out of This Place." "It's My Life." Those are huge, huge songs of self-determination. The bands that spoke to that side of yourself really meant a lot to me at the time.

I think when you're young, you wanna be the Rolling Stones. And then, of course, as you get older, you realize, "Well, I don't think I would fit in the Rolling Stones very well." I was interested in artists who manifest worlds and manifest places in time. You can't hear Frank Sinatra without thinking of New York in the Forties.

The Beatles ushered in an entire world that we're living in right now. They created a culture that didn't exist previously. The Beatles had a broader conceptual purpose and a sense of themselves. Artists like the Stones would've felt that was too pretentious for themselves. We are what you call a counterculture, alternative culture, or whatever. Everybody's gotta take a moment and kneel down in front of the Beatles.

What of Bob Dylan did you listen to most?
When I listen to your early records, I hear *Highway 61*
and *Bringing It All Back Home* all over them.

Those were my Dylan records. I didn't know anything about Dylan as a folk performer until long after I was into him for "Like a Rolling Stone." Those were definitive. They were showing me a version of my country that I knew was true but had not been whispered to me previously.

Bob was the guy that came in, pulled the veil away, and said, "This is where and what I'm living really looks like to me," and it feels like, "I know that person and I know this place. This place is my home, and this is who I am." It gave me a context to begin to build my own aesthetic world. My first connect was "Like a Rolling Stone." Heard it first on Top 40.

What's the impact of *Highway 61*?

First of all, that album cover is one of my all-time top two or three album covers. And the record itself simply was on constant play on my little box record player in my bedroom. I played it a thousand times — every night, just round and round and round. I lived in that record for a long time.

Were you taking any drugs at this point?

No. I never took any drugs. I never had a drink till I was twenty-two years old. I was not a part of the drug culture for one reason: I didn't take any drugs. Two, I wasn't sure they were such a good idea. Personally, for me anyway. So my little environment was relatively drug-free because I commanded this little area where we had the band. I left the guys to their own devices. As long as I didn't feel it negatively inflicting itself on the work we were doing. I was only superficially a part of a counterculture. I grew up in a small town. There were drugs, but there weren't a lot of them. I was frightened of drugs. I didn't want anything that was not within a reasonable amount of my control. I had experienced a young life that was very out of control, and was not interested so much in things that are going to open me up in a way that I don't know if I have any control over. I felt I'd lived in that world where you don't have control over your daily life, and I didn't like that. I didn't really drink, either.

All I knew at the time was this would not be right for me. I'm in the process of trying to sort out this world that I want to communicate, and manifest for people who are coming to see my show. It was a situation that didn't involve drugs. It was purely about the music.

That's how I received a lot of the abstractness of *Highway 61*, or *Sgt. Pepper* for that matter. I didn't personally experience them as drug records. To me, the basic message of all those records was "pull open the blinds." That was the essential lesson of all the poetry that was on those records.

When did you realize that you had something special?

When I was twenty, I was playing to three thousand, four thousand people with no record. No one outside of Monmouth County knew who we were or where we came from. I'm not sure how much it mattered because I was really locked into internal choices and internal battles. I wasn't somebody who was sitting around waiting to be validated by the outside world.

I had my own little world that I was working in very successfully for my money, I was writing and we were performing. We weren't recording, but we were doing everything else. Where that was gonna lead I didn't know, but I knew I was as good as anybody I'd seen. I knew that.

Rolling Stone, and all the music that was out there, were informing this act of self-creation that you were involved in. You were interested in becoming a part that world. It was like when you did the magazine: I wanna be a part of this. Where do I fit? This seems progressive and humane, and that's the world that I wanna assist in shaping. How can I steer my best efforts into helping bring that culture and that world into being? On a larger scale, I thought it was a real possibility that you could do that. That was a big part of what was motivating me.

Your first three records, *Greetings from Asbury Park,*
The Wild, the Innocent & the E Street Shuffle*, and *Born
***to Run*, let's characterize as a group. Where is the author**
at? What were you trying to say as a writer, as a seeker?

I was very influenced by Dylan. I always say he's the father of my country. He initially provided me with a picture of a country that I recognized. One that feels real, that feels like the truth. My early-twenties writing, certainly *Greetings from Asbury Park,* was influenced by Dylan, though if you go back to it now, it had its quirks and that made it sort of its own record.

> Rhyming "mumps" with "in the dumps"
> is really kind of cringey.

It really was youthful. I immediately started to move away from that toward my soul influences. When I realized I was going to be compared to Dylan, as I was at the time, because people didn't have any other reference, I immediately went for a rocking soul record. "E Street Shuffle" comes from Major Lance's "Monkey Time." "Kitty's Back" is just swing, blues. All of my black influences kind of came and took me to another place than where Bob was going in his work.

> Your second album — *The Wild, the Innocent & the E Street Shuffle* — has three outstanding songs you still play regularly today. "Kitty's Back," "The E Street Shuffle," and "Rosalita." What is your favorite song from that?

With my second record, I really let my musical influences exert themselves as a way of pulling back from the Dylan comparisons. "Rosalita" has got to be one of the best rocking soul songs I've ever written. It's fundamentally Latin-based. I don't know of anything else like it in the entire rest of my work. There's only one "Rosalita." There's things that are somewhat related, but no, it doesn't really happen twice.

I had been playing soul music and R&B and blues for the past ten years of my life. So I had all of these influences that I turned to as a way of making what I was doing distinctly different than other things that were there. That was a big decision when I really let my musical influences go on that second record.

Looking back on *Born to Run,* what's your attitude about it today? What do you think of it today?

Born to Run would've sounded a lot more like *The Wild, the Innocent* without Jon Landau producing. This was probably John's greatest act of production, and he's done plenty of great things since. I had really long versions of "Thunder Road." I can remember us working on it in the little warehouse twenty miles away from where we sit here today and editing it down to the version that's on the record, and "Backstreets" and I'm sure little "Jungleland." I caught the editing bug. Jon also said, "Look, let's not overdo it." He was streamlining my influences into something that packed a real progressive and hard punch musically. *Born to Run* is still a modern-sounding record. Jimmy Iovine did a really good job.

What's special about that record to you?

There's a group of songs that just were unique in a certain place and time. It has only eight songs. I really came into my own identity on *Born to Run,* to a point where I didn't sound like anybody else. You could read the influences in the music, whether it was Spector or Roy Orbison or Bob Dylan, or big groups, but it was distinct — something that hadn't previously occurred. I came into my own. I was just trying to make music that entertained me personally. I wanted to make a record that felt like the last record you'll ever need to hear. Simple as that.

So when you go to do *Darkness on the Edge of Town,* working in that same area musically, you've gotta be constrained by thinking about, what am I doing as the follow-up to *Born to Run?*

You're having a new experience and the new experience is a

post-success experience. *Darkness* was sort of a reactive record in the sense that "I'm not gonna make *Born to Run* again, because I don't know how that was even possible." Part of the onslaught of the success feels like an aggressive attack, even though you've pursued it your entire life. So I said, "Well, I'm tucking back in and I'm going back to my town and the people that I knew, the circumstances in life that I understand, and the stakes of living that I can write about." That became *Darkness on the Edge of Town*. It received a lot of criticism for not being enough like *Born to Run*.

Darkness is intensely personal about your own childhood. This is deep stuff about your private self.

Once again, I'm circling myself and trying to find what I want to say and what I want to be about. And once again I move back in the direction of home. Whatever the reasons were — whether they were my own nervousness about having the kind of success that I had — I knew that it was very important that I remain very connected to who I've been, who I am, where I come from. I want to do meaningful work, "Where am I going?" is the thing that I'm most interested in. Am I interested in making money, looking good, traveling the world or whatever? No, I'm interested in doing the most meaningful work that I can. Am I making my stand right now? And it ended up being kind of where I came from. I said, "Okay, I'm at the crossroads." All right, *Born to Run* and *Darkness* are my crossroads moment. I'm down at the crossroads, I can go this way, or I can go that way. This way, this road looks pretty good, pretty appealing. I'm not sure what's down that other way. The direction I took was moving back to the roots of my own life. It was food for inspiration. And the town I grew up in, and people that I know, was my crossroads moment. That's where *Darkness on the Edge of Town* came from.

**It doesn't seem like a defensive mode, it seems like you
make yourself even more vulnerable. Especially
when you're going to be vulnerable to criticism after *Born
to Run* because it's not *Born to Run Part II.*
It's just not going to be good enough.**

That's what happened. People don't really remember this part
of its history, but it was not immediately successful. But we went on
tour, we played all across the country, I met every DJ from the East
Coast to the West, we played every town and city. When people
came and saw that music performed live, they understood it. That
record's success really has a lot to do with the ability of the band to
take that music and make it such a powerful live performance.

**And then you do *The River*, which is even more personal
than upbeat *Born to Run* with its pace and mood.
Now you're weary and now it's your family.**

By the time *The River* came around, I knew a couple of things.
I knew I wanted to include music that was just fun and exciting. I
wanted that to be a part of what I was doing, the full range of my
catalogue. I also wanted to keep my lyrical and conceptual intensity. You can't get any more personal than the very title of that
record. That was my sister, my brother-in-law. The baby that I
wrote about in that song just passed away last week. So that song
is at the center of a lot of my work. I don't play it regularly on a
nightly basis, though I could. It's got the great opening stanza "I
come from down in the valley."

The River was finished as a single album, handed in, taken
back, and another year goes by while I turned it into a double
album. So, once again, basically, I'm lost and I'm looking for
"Where do I go from here? How do I maintain my sense of self
and aesthetic relevance?" It took me two years. *Darkness on the
Edge of Town* also took two years.

Once again, I was just into a record that conjured a world, a world with the veil pulled back, one that allowed people to get a truer sense of where they live, who they are, what's being done in their name. I'm always pursuing this particular vision. I'm like a dog with a bone. I just chase after it until I feel like I've gotten enough of it to present to my audience.

The River is a record of acceptance. And that's what you get at the very end, which is why I ended with "Wreck on the Highway." Very strange little song to end the record. People ask on a daily basis, "How do I live with this?" We learn how to live with these things, and in doing so, we attempt to alter them and create a more understandable life and society, culture. You're just trying to help people get to the next house on the block.

What was happening to you then?

I was thirty-one when *The River* came out. Thirty-one is not twenty-one anymore. At thirty-one, you're attempting to wrestle with issues of adulthood. *The River* was really — and *Darkness on the Edge of Town*, too — an adult record. It dealt with marriage, relationships, and work, and death, joy, despair. I wanted to make sure it had all of it in there.

The River itself is their metaphor for life.
It often makes me cry.

Mission accomplished.

So you do *Nebraska*. On the surface it's decidedly uncommercial.

It's got "Atlantic City," "Mansion on the Hill," it's totally acoustic. I was confident it would find its audience and have a life of its own. It's ended up being one of the most meaningful records

I've ever recorded and is the record that is mentioned most to me by young people. Maybe it's the do-it-yourself nature of the sound or something. But obviously, it was a big departure.

It feels almost like there's a deliberateness about following that up with the extremely commercial *Born in the U.S.A.*

Once I did *Nebraska,* I had plenty of room to do anything I wanted. I'd made my point. *Nebraska* gave me a lot of license to do something unapologetically commercial. *Born in the U.S.A.* is still my most commercially successful record.

The Ghost of Tom Joad was another big change of subject. You're not writing about yourself anymore. You're dealing with the underclass: migrants, immigrants, refugees, homeless, oppressed, marginalized.

The key to good writing is you always have to draw out of yourself the commonality that you feel between you and your subjects to make those songs real and so you're not just a reporter. You've got the final living, breathing characters that you respond to. The key to the success of that kind of writing is you've got to have your detail really right. The part of you that feels a commonality with the person you're writing about has got to be up front and forward. You must have both of those things.

Tom Joad came from living in California through the nineties and through there being such an enormous amount of border reporting in your daily newspaper. Reading these stories of people struggling just to stay alive. I wrote that record pretty quickly in my writing room in Los Angeles. And the trick was getting the details right and then making the emotional connection. Those are the two things you've got to have right on top of one another, if you want to write a successful topical song.

Were you influenced by Steinbeck?

The Latin American songs were pretty Steinbeck-influenced. I look at the sort of characters he wrote about fifty years down the line and that was part of the influence. I like getting people to walk in other people's shoes. And also to see just what it tells me about myself or about the place that we're living. That was a very enjoyable record for me. I've done a certain amount of writing in that vein, and it's not that easy to do and get it right. I get really attracted to it, and like it a lot, when fiction is also not-fiction. I think where I get kind of deep into narrative story writing. It's a different style than writing rock and roll music.

It seems incredibly cinematic. The whole thing. That makes me want to ask you, do you cry at movies?

Do I cry at movies? Yeah. The last movie that I cried at was *Fried Green Tomatoes* — I had a two-day headache after I saw that one from crying so much while the film was going on. And then there was another one called *Resurrection* that starred Ellen Burstyn and Sam Shepard. She becomes a faith healer, and I don't know if you've ever seen it but if you're bored some night, it'll turn the faucets on.

Do you believe in God?

I'm a tricky one here because I had so much orthodox Catholicism growing up. I was really well indoctrinated as a child with the Catholic faith, which I don't regret. It was terrible at the time. The first thing every single day, religious studies, every single day, first thing in the morning for eight years. Eight years of it from when you're six years old. A lot of the spirituality and religious references come out of my studies as a child at St. Rose of Lima, ten minutes away from here.

I was back in that church singing two days ago when my

nephew passed away. I sang "I'll See You in My Dreams" in St. Rose of Lima Church with my sister and my brother-in-law from *The River*. He was their child. He was a construction worker his whole life. And he went to work one morning, stepped outside, and fell over and died at fifty-three years old. We're all still very connected to that community, that church, the priests that are there, it's still a part of my life and my sister's life and that's why we had the funeral there. It's still very evocative and a very intense environment for me. It's where a lot of "Promised Land," a lot of *Nebraska* goes, where characters are in this existential, spiritual crisis. That's where all that music came from.

Looking back on it, I don't regret all the years I put into religious studies. I get a lot out of it now. It's come back around, and it serves me well. I'm not at Mass every week, but I'm still somewhere deeply connected to that religion and the role it plays in my community, and in my life. I'm seventy-three years old, I'm ten minutes from the house I grew up in. I've just always had a big spiritual curiosity as to how the spiritual part of your life plays out if you're not orthodox. I'm always still trying to figure that part out. Where do I figure all life's questions out? Through my music. If you're wondering what I'm thinking about, what I'm concerned with.

The Rising seemed to contain all that.

The Rising was a religious record. It's about life after death, how our communities are impacted by what end up being spiritual events. The first song I wrote for *The Rising* might have been "The Rising" — and really the record probably should have started off with that. I look back on that record and it had too many songs and the sequence probably wasn't exactly right. It contains a couple of my really greatest songs. "The Rising," certainly one of my top five. That record was filled with the idea of being of service. What good am I? How can I be of service to my audience, to my fans, to my community, to the people that I've grown up with? I'm always in pursuit of where that leads me. I had the classic experience of a guy rolling his car window down and yelling out, "We need you." Well, that's a pretty clarifying statement. It's like, "Okay, I do something that events of the day call upon me to react to and to be a part of, and to fulfill a certain need at a certain moment."

Who do you think you are, to take on this profound national event [the terrorist attacks of September 11, 2001]? Nobody else did.

All right. That's a good question. I guess I just did it because I thought I could and because someone kind of asked me to. On a Sunday afternoon or something, simply driving past me and rolling his window down reminded me of who I was and what I do for a living and what my purpose was within our community. That's what I live for. That's what I live for.

You wrote "Paradise" from the bomber's point of view. "Mary's Place" also is an unexpected choice.

I was trying to take on all points of view. It was, for lack of a better word, a concept record. "The Rising" is simply one of my best songs. As for "Mary's Place," the classic example is my nephew's wake the other day. I don't know if you're hip to the Irish Italian wakes, but they involve an enormous amount of talking, laughing, joking around with the body right in front of you. "Mary's Place" was about a certain type of joy that exists at the center of some of our most tragic life experiences. Death's last gift to the living is an expanded vision of the world that you're living in. It's a reaffirmation. In death, there is a need of a reaffirmation of life.

Eight years later, *Wrecking Ball*.

Wrecking Ball, definitely. I mean that was "Okay, this is a political record."

Brendan O'Brien, the producer, who brought us into the modern era of recording. We moved into *Wrecking Ball* when I started to work with Ron Aiello, who Brendan O'Brien sent over to work with me on the record that became *Western Stars*. I didn't know what record it was going to be at the time. I drove into Red Bank, and on the way back I started to sing, "You put the dog out, I'll take out the cat, easy money." That was the first song I wrote for *Wrecking Ball*. And I came back, ran into the studio right there, recorded a rough of it, and then totally sidelined *Western Stars* and made *Wrecking Ball* in the next three weeks.

I made it very quickly, and it's a good record. I listened to it just a couple of weeks ago. As for doing what it was called on to do, [it] worked really well. I thought it was going to be received a little more popularly than it was. For whatever the reason, there was a toughness to it. I have anger in my music, but it's not the first word that someone would call to mind when they start talking about me and my music. But that record? Absolutely an angry record.

What were you angry about?

On that record it was the crash of 2008, and the effect it had on so many people's lives in the country. That was me trying to sort out "Where are we taking ourselves with this?"

**You're also fixing the blame here. We're calling
out the names.**

That's unusual for me.

**In "Jack of All Trades" there is this astounding line:
"If I had me a gun, I'd find the bastards
and shoot 'em on sight."**

That was a throwback to *The Grapes of Wrath*. The scene at the beginning of the movie where the bank is coming to take the farmer's home and land, and I believe he says something like this. I don't remember the scene exactly, but that was my recollection.

People lost their lives. We knew a lot of people that lost a little bit of everything, or most of everything they had. And people whose fault it was walked away scot-free. We had Tom Morello with us on *Wrecking Ball*. Talk about the Angry Young Man. He plays the guitar on "Jack of All Trades." He's great at it, so that was a real plus for us having him.

**Another standout is "Death to My Hometown."
The line there is just unbelievable. "Send the robber
barons straight to hell, the greedy thieves that came
around and ate the flesh of everything they found, whose
crimes have gone unpunished, who walk the streets as free
men now —"**

That's one of my favorites. "They brought death to my home-town." There were a lot of really good things on that record that I thought people might respond to a little more than they did. But that's the way it goes.

You close with "Land of Hope and Dreams."

That's a big song for me. I wrote it in 1998 for the reunion tour of the E Street Band. We had no new music. I wrote that song to say, "Okay, this is our statement of purpose in 1998. This is what we're hoping to accomplish. This is what we want to be about. This is who we want to be." It comes up last on that record. "Land of Hope and Dreams" is certainly one of the best songs I've written in the past thirty years.

I call it the Church of Rock and Roll. How important is it to
you to lift up the audience like that? To bring an auditorium
or an arena together in a kind of communal sharing?

That's what I like to do, and in doing so, I am lifted.

"We are alive." You walk outta the show on the march.
When did you discover that the rock show could be that
transcendent or should be?

I always had that experience myself, that I was lifted, just being
with an audience, with my peers, with my family, with my neighbors, with my friends together in an event that lifts the entire town,
the entire city, the entire country. I always felt that music can do this
if you do it well enough, and with the correct intent and purpose. I
want my band to have that kind of response from their audience.

Who did you see do that?

What comes first to my mind? Elvis, Little Richard, incredibly transcendent. "Wop bop aloo bop!" Transcendent and very
religious. Richard had an enormous religious background, and
that background is essential to his work. Of course, Elvis, I count
him in there also.

These were people with gospel roots. They sang religious
music in their spare time. These were people who were looking for
a way to incorporate their beliefs. I find that to be essential in their
work and also in mine. The pure imagery in the Bible that I stud-
ied for one hour every day just took you there. And it became very
important to me in my own writing, lost in the flood.

It still remains. I still go there. I still go to the religious, to the
well, to draw me into the highest part of myself and to do my best
work.

Why did you stay away from being actively involved in partisan politics for so long?

I didn't grow up in a very political household. The only politics I heard was from my mother. I came home from grade school, where someone asked me if I was Republican or Democrat, and I asked my mom, "Well, what are we?" She said, "We're Democrats, cause Democrats are for the working people." I was politicized by the Sixties, like most of the other people of that generation at that time. I can remember doing a concert when I was probably in my very late teens, helping to bus people down to Washington for an anti-war demonstration.

But still, basically, I wanted to remain an independent voice for the audience that came to my shows. We've tried to build up a lot of credibility over the years, so that if we took a stand on something, people would receive it with an open mind. Part of not being particularly partisan was just an effort to remain a very thoughtful voice in my fans' lives.

I always liked being involved actively more at a grassroots level, to act as a partisan for a set of ideals: civil rights, economic justice, a sane foreign policy, democracy. That was the position I felt comfortable coming from.

Did it make you more credible if you avoided endorsing an individual?

It makes people less likely to marginalize you or pigeonhole you. Our band is in pretty much what I think of as the center. So if I wrote, say, "American Skin," which was controversial, it couldn't easily be dismissed, because people had faith that I was a measured voice. That's been worth something, and it's something I don't want to lose. But we have drifted far from that center, and this is a time to be very specific about where I stand.

I think that a more complicated picture of who you are as an artist and who they are as an audience emerges. The example I've been giving is that I've been an enormous fan of John Wayne all my life, although not a fan of his politics. I've made a place for all those different parts of who he was. I find deep inspiration and soulfulness in his work.

Your audience invests a lot in you, a very personal investment. There is nothing more personal, in some ways, than the music people listen to. I know from my own experience how you identify and relate to the person singing. You have put your fingerprints on their imagination. That is very, very intimate. When something cracks the mirror, it can be hard for the fan who you have asked to identify with you.

Pop musicians live in the world of symbology. You live and die by the symbol in many ways. You serve at the behest of your audience's imagination. It's a complicated relationship. So you're asking people to welcome the complexity in the interest of fuller and more honest communication.

The audience and the artist are valuable to one another as long as you can look out there and see yourself, and they look back and see themselves. That's asking quite a bit, but that is what happens. When that bond is broken, by your own individual beliefs, personal thoughts, or personal actions, it can make people angry. As simple as that. You're asking for a broader, more complicated relationship with the members of your audience than possibly you've had in the past.

Now you're at the Lincoln Memorial every four years.

It wasn't by accident. I say Bob Dylan is the father of my creative country. I looked at that and I asked myself, "Hey, you want to be a truth-teller?" I want people to get the same experience from listening to one of my records as I had when I listened to *Highway 61*. The idea that something was being revealed to them that was fundamentally true, and essential, and gave you a view of your world, your country, your town, your neighbors, your family.

That was fundamental to me doing the kind of work that I wanted to do.

Having said that, you now are enshrined in a certain sense. I used the Lincoln Memorial, where Bob had played, as symbolic of your being kind of the official rock and roll star of the United States, or the poet laureate or something. My question to you is, if that is a weight you're carrying?

It was a recognition of a certain conceptual aspect I had about my job that goes back to my early twenties. I was applying for that position. From the beginning I said, "Yeah, this is a job that seems to be somewhat vacant at the moment and also seems necessary and useful, and I have the range of skills that might allow me to have something valuable to say. At certain moments."

It's always sitting there on the side as a part of what I'm doing. I always experience my work at some point as to how I'm contextualizing myself at a given moment, you know? Whether it's around 9/11 or whether it's *Wrecking Ball* in 2008. I can feel myself in that place, and I try to do it as well as I can.

And you feel at ease with that?

I do. I do. I do feel pretty at ease with it.

Do you feel in awe of it in any way?

You do feel the responsibility with it, so I'm careful with it and I don't place it on my plate as something that I must do or must have. I remember around the L.A. riots, in the early nineties we lived in Los Angeles, I tried to write about it. I didn't have the right song. I didn't do it well enough, and so nothing came out. At the end of the day, you've got to have a good song. It has to be entertaining. It has to be meaningful. But I'm pretty comfortable with taking on those topics now.

**What do you think of the new version of "Tom Joad"
that Tom Morello and you came up with?**

That thing is just a hurricane. The very first time we played it together, the roof came off the L.A. Sports Arena. People just went ballistic. When Tom played with the E Street Band for one tour it was just tremendous. He just brought an enormous amount of intensity, not just to his guitar playing, but to his vocal on that cut — it was just, rage. It's one of my favorite reconstitutings of one of my songs.

Like you did your own "All Along the Watchtower"?

Yeah, exactly.

I rate _High Hopes_ as one of your better records.

That was a funny record, one of those records that you don't plan. It just happened.

**The commentary was that it's got some good songs but
there's no obvious thread to the whole thing. But I hear
a lot of unity, there's a level of sophistication, even maturity
to the cynicism on it. Take a lyric like "You don't fuck with
Harry's money, you don't fuck Harry's girls."**

I had a great song called "The Wall" about the Vietnam Memorial in Washington, D.C. Really one of my best songs about war. I wrote it in the nineties.

"American Skin."

It's a continuous toxic part of our American life. That was a really well-written song.

> **You're writing about America as your identity,**
> **as a passion, as an idea. Are you consciously writing**
> **this long narrative about America?**

I guess I am. In the sense that it's a part of what I do. I go back to the people who influenced me and they manifested different visions of the country in their own work. I said, "Yeah, I want to work in the vein that these people who moved me so greatly worked in." It was a part of being in the middle of this act of self-creation. I saw that self to be somebody who was engaged in the daily life of their country. I wanted to be a part of that discussion that was occurring. I wanted my audience to be a part of it. It became a part of who I am and what I do.

> **Your twentieth studio album is *Letter to You*. It's painful,**
> **it's mournful. It's a farewell.**

I would say *Letter to You* is my summation E Street Band album in the sense that I felt like I was coming to terms with everything over the past fifty years, starting with my original little band and ending, of course, with our tour and the E Street Band and *Letter to You*, the record. That's as good an E Street Band record as I'm gonna make right now.

> **"Rainmaker" has to be about Trump, right? He was such**
> **a fact of our lives. What do you think of him?**

That's an older song that I wrote a long time ago and just happened to cut. It's not a central part of the album. It's a bit of an outlier on that record, I happened to have it laying around. It was nice musically on the album, and so I put it on. He was the accidental president. That's all. You know, it was an accident that happened and we had to live with it for four years and then some. I don't put a lot of significance on him beyond that. I don't want to oversignify Trump because I don't think he deserves it or is worth it.

Bush was the worst president we have ever had.

To that date.

And probably still the worst.

Yeah. I think I agree with you on that one.

You sing, "Big black train coming down the track." That can only be death. As an adult in your seventies, this is what you're dealing with?

It's just a part of life now. I have no idea as a songwriter where I'm going from here. I don't know the answer to that yet. That's why I say the record was a summation record of the past fifty years.

What themes are left? What is worth writing about?

After mortality, there's not a lot of themes left. You start backing up and find some of the old ones again. I truly don't know. I don't know what I'll be writing, when I'll be writing, what it'll be like, if I'll be writing again. I had tremendous joy making *Only the Strong Survive*. I got to flex my musical muscles, my voice, and the arrangements of the band. And without having to deal with the issues of writing. I don't know exactly where, as a writer, I'm going to go next. So I'm enjoying recording and singing and making records right now without being overly concerned with where conceptually or thematically they fit along the arc of my creativity.

What are the common qualities of your best songs?

A musical richness. A lyrical richness. When I'm at the top of my game, I'm carrying both of those things in my sheath. When I get those things going right, I'm pretty proud of what comes out. What do my best things have in common? There's two separate kinds of writing. There's the narrative songwriting and, for lack of a better word, rock songwriting. They're very different things.

The piano is a basic instrument.

We're very unusual for a rock band. We had two leading keyboards, organ and piano, and the only bands that had that are Procol Harum and the Band. Roy Bittan was such an imposing figure when he sat at the piano. He had such a richness in his playing, we used to say, "We have to remember to leave room for the guitar somewhere." We are not at the service of any one instrumentalist or anybody's shining presence on their instrument. We were really an ensemble that played at the service of the song. Roy was a wonderful ensemblist, whether it's "Jungleland" or "Backstreets." The richness of the piano is wonderful. The piano was a big thing because I wrote all of *Born to Run* on the piano.

I would play the piano, come up with the melodies and the themes, play them for Roy, and then Roy would enrich them and make them sound great. We were always an ensemble group. We're not really a bunch of soloists, even though we tip our hat on "Kitty's Back" and stuff in the live show now.

Just about playing the guitar, how good are you?

I'm an excellent guitarist. It's a tremendous source of expression. I made my living as a lead guitarist, not a frontman, not a singer. I was a lead guitarist in this area for a decade, where that was how I literally stayed alive, by being that fastest gun in town. And so that was my career before *Greetings from Asbury Park*. I took the guitar very seriously, and I still do. I love solo playing, and I do it a little bit at night, just enough to use those muscles. You're the gunslinger.

Have you been listening to Bob Dylan's recent work?

I love it all, I like *Modern Times* and *Rough and Rowdy Ways*. There's tremendous writing and playing, and the production on them is terrific. "Murder Most Foul" is a masterpiece, a real classic Dylan masterpiece. To come along with that at eighty years old, that's pretty damn impressive.

What's your relationship with him? When you inducted him into the Hall of Fame, you referred to him as "the brother I never had." Explain that a little more.

We don't communicate all the time. We're always friendly. Bob's always very sweet to me. He's been very kind as a champion. He obviously holds a big place in my heart. There's that position in your family of someone who just is kind of the tip of the spear. Bob's out front, in front of everybody. It's courageous. It's a great gift. It's lovely to have someone like that in your life. That's how I feel about him. I just feel very touched that Bob's in my own work and in my life in general.

Why did you write a book? How did that affect you in terms of the way you looked at yourself?

It happened by accident. We played the Super Bowl and I wrote an essay on playing the Super Bowl. I found a voice that I could write in, and then I just kept pursuing it. I'd put it away for two years and not come back. So during the next seven years, that's where it all came from.

Once you found that voice and find that muscle, then you experience the tremendous joy of creativity. Pure pleasure. I felt that if it was over tomorrow, my children, as they became older, would have a way of getting to know me a little closer, and it would be always there for them to have a picture of Dad's life. It was just really purposeful in that sense. I'm glad it exists.

What did you discover about yourself?

I had to write a lot about my personal life and the difficulties I had in creating a home and a family. That was really hard for me to do when I was young. I really struggled. What I'm proudest of is Patti and the children and who they've ended up being and the person that they drew out of me.

Tell me about Patti.

I don't know how to do that.

Tell me about her voice.

Patti is just a powerful presence, with a unique and singular voice, unique writing talents that are really her own. She's made three terrific records and has another really great one in the can coming. She was just a formidable presence to deal with as far as someone who is helping you get your lives together on track.

Her power was really important to me and remains important to me to this day. Not just her creative power, but her personal power, a loving partner and friend. We still knock ourselves in the head at night and we go, "We're pretty lucky."

Your voices work amazingly together —

We're working on some country-influenced stuff that we sing together a little more on. We haven't exploited it at all yet. It's kind of a nice thing that's waiting there. We're going to get the right record and do a lot of singing together. That would be fun.

Why do you stay onstage so long?
Is it a drug to you or —?

It's the endless question, why do you do it? There's a switch that gets pulled. Theoretically, you go into some higher part of yourself, and you try to communicate that to the audience, with the idea of bringing out the best in you. That's kind of a big part of what we do at night.

Do you get to point of just exhaustion?

You have those nights where that happens, but you depend on your mission. If I get up there, and I'm just getting towards the end of the night, or maybe it could be in the middle of the night, sometimes you get fatigued really early. You just have to settle down, settle yourself into it, and the music itself just revives and resuscitates you on its own on a song-to-song basis.

Do you feel spirits emerging from your body?

That's exactly what you feel. And entering the room, and reentering yourself, and entering your audience. And there's this exchange of spiritual grace between you and the people that you're working for. You can feel incredibly high from it. At night, you come offstage just elevated. It's wonderful, wonderful. One of the greatest feelings of my life. You've gone into some spiritual high place. If things are right, you're inhabiting that space and assisting your audience in achieving and reaching that space themselves.

How does it feel being up there as an older rock and roller? When we were young, we didn't think it was possible. Does it still make sense to you?

Yeah, it does. What we didn't take into consideration is the fact that time and space are altered during the three hours of the concert. Time itself literally ceases for a moment. What age are you? I'm not sure. You're indeterminate in that area at night. It's not even essential information. You experience it in a way that bypasses your normal understanding of time and age. I don't know radically what the difference would be between the way I feel now at seventy-three and the way I did at forty or at fifty. I don't feel dramatically different. Lucky enough, physically I've been blessed, being able to do what I need to do. How long that'll last, I don't know. At this point, there's only one thing we know, which is that none of us know.

I have a theory that in the great periods of art there was a simultaneous burst of creativity with a handful of people working on the same stage at the same time.

There was a bit of a golden age here. I tell Steve, "We're old men, but we're lucky old men because we came along at a time when what we do is valued and was valued." The second half of the twentieth century obviously was the rock and roll moment. It's a form that came out of nowhere. We had an enormous amount of incredibly talented people to study and to learn from. Steve says it was a Renaissance period for popular entertainment and popular music. We've been very, very fortunate.

**What accounts for the longevity? It wasn't supposed
to be adult music.**

There's an enormous joy in it. Why do people go to see the Rolling Stones? It's fun. They're fun. They're still fun. I love to see the Stones. They're playing terrific right now. They play great. Mick does a great job and he's seventy-eight years old.

He's eighty this year.

Is he? That's hard to believe.

I always tell my children, "Kids, you're lucky. In another place and time, I'd be wearing a clown hat in the front of a cart with a donkey, and you'd be in the back." And that's who we'd be for our entire lives. So we timed it exactly right.

**Do you think of yourself as a baby boomer, encompassing
an awareness of the atomic bomb, a rebellion against your
parents, the rejection of racism, the hypocrisy of society?
Rock and roll seems to have addressed all those themes.**

The country had gotten to a point where there were some untenable circumstances, like civil rights, that had to be addressed. It's funny that you had this incredible popular cultural renaissance going on at the same time. All of these things, mixing with one another, creating a different way of living, a way of life. It's a fascinating period of time. We're old men, but we're lucky old men.

**Your rock and roll army has marched in this enormous
time of change. Did we change things?**

Some people say, "The whole countercultural thing flamed out," and the classic *Easy Rider* thing, "We blew it." All of that. I don't look at it like that personally. I look at it like it was a tremendous success in altering the way the country saw itself and addressing some of the issues that needed to be addressed. You can't expect miracles overnight. Change is slow, it moves slow. An enormous catalyst for altering culture, society, and the country came out of a popular cultural movement of the second half of the twentieth century. Being a small part of that has been a wonderful part of my life.

ACKNOWLEDGMENTS

Mick Jagger, Bono, and Bruce Springsteen each took me in as a fan, a fellow traveler, and a brother in arms. And thanks to Patti Scialfa and Ali Hewson, who welcomed me into their families and also joined ours.

Jonathan Cott, my longtime friend and colleague, had the idea for this book and then meticulously edited it. Roger Black, a pivotal RS art director, designed it cover to cover. The photo portraits are contemporaneous to the interviews. Annie Leibovitz (John Lennon, Jerry Garcia) and Mark Seliger (Bono) graciously let me have the photographs they took for the interviews. My assistant, Susan Kerner, patiently and diligently wrangled tapes, transcripts, manuscripts, and me.

At Little, Brown, Bruce Nichols provided smooth sailing, Michael Noon helped me with the loose knots and dangling modifiers, Sabrina Callahan spread the good word.

Lynn Nesbitt, my friend and agent, as ever.

INDEX

"Black Muddy River" (Grateful Dead), 137

Blackboard Jungle (film), 228

Blind Faith, 37

Blonde on Blonde (Dylan), 35, 52, 58–60

Blood, Sweat and Tears, 68

Bloomfield, Mike, 296

"Blowin' in the Wind" (Dylan), 54, 285

"Blue Yodel No. 9" (Rodgers), 286

Bonavena, Oscar, 115–116

Bono, 233–271. *See also names of specific albums and songs*
  Africa, 245–248, 264–265, 268
  aggression, 235
  aging, 268–269
  America, 263–264
  "anointing" for peace crusade, 267–268
  art and nature of politics, 265–266
  art as open-heart surgery, 252
  art aspiring to the condition of music, 270
  band's opinion of missions, 250, 268
  Beatles, 239, 259–260
  being journalist instead of artist, 269
  childhood of, 235–240
  Chile concert, 252
  drugs, 249
  duty as an artist, 266–267
  Dylan, 258–261, 263, 289
  early musical influences, 239–240
  early song writing, 242–243
  eradicating extreme poverty, 266–267
  father of, 235–238
  fear of a missed opportunity, 267
  finding what he's looking for, 271
  formation of U2, 240–241
  gangs and street fights, 236–237
  getting transported while singing, 251
  gig lag and emotional expense of shows, 251
  hard rock, 241
  Jagger and the Stones, 241–242, 261–262
  learning to play first song, 239
  liberation as meaning of rock, 246
  Live Aid, 245–247
  losing sense of self, 251–252
  Martin Luther King, 244–245
  personal future, 269
  potential breakup of band, 246
  preacher and prophet, 233–234, 252
  regrets, 270–271
  religion and spirituality, 242–245, 257
  September 11, 262–263
  sex and sexuality, 256–257
  songwriting partnership with Edge, 254
  Springsteen, 260–261
  stepping inside songs to reach notes, 250–251
  submitting self to will of the group, 249
  thought process when performing, 250
  three-act structure, 251–252
  Who, 239–240

Booker T. & the M.G.'s, 21, 50

"Boots of Spanish Leather" (Dylan), 54

Born in the U.S.A. (Springsteen), 307

Born to Run (Springsteen), 294, 302–305, 321

Bowie, David, 203, 206, 250

Boy (U2), 254–255

Boy George, 205

"Boy Named Sue, A" (Cash), 237

Boyd, Pattie, 84

being fisherman instead of artist, 115–116
best and favorite songs, 108–109
Bono, 239–240
breakup of the Beatles, 63–65, 71–76
Brian Epstein, 72, 90–92
campaign for peace, 78–79
clean image, 93
concerts, 98–99
covers of songs by others, 99–100
current state of business, 121–122
Davies' biography, 91–93
death of, 224–225
desire to be bigger than Elvis, 81–82
devices and tricks, 98
drugs, 83–89, 110, 119
Dylan, 36–37, 131–133, 291
falling in love, 78
falling out between Taylor and Epstein, 90
first solo album, 63–67, 107–108, 113, 121
future of rock and roll, 96
George Harrison, 124–125, 131
guitar playing skills, 69–71
harmonica, 98
having afflicted and obnoxious people thrust upon them, 113–115
"hidden" messages in songs, 103–104, 120
"I don't believe in the Beatles," 67, 124
identity of "the walrus," 104–105
impact of the Beatles in America, 116–117
impact of the Beatles on history, 116
influence of Liverpool, 130
inhibiting each other, 65
interactions with fans, 24
Jagger and the Stones, 93–94, 186, 205, 222–225
learning from each other, 127

Manson's quotation of "Helter Skelter," 96
meaning of rock and roll for so many, 96–97
music and sound of the Beatles, 97–98
musical preferences and listening habits, 68, 125–126
Paul McCartney, 73, 99–100
people seeking cures and miracles, 113–114
personal feelings for rock and roll over the years, 68, 97
personal future, 133–134
possibility of recording with the Beatles again, 122–123
potential live album, 98
psychotherapy, 63
realization of personal genius, 126–128
recording on tape at home, 102–103
religion and spirituality, 64, 67, 82–83, 103
reviews, 94–95
revolutionary songs, 107
Rolling Stone covers, 63
Rolling Stones, 93–94
simple music and lack of imagery, 66–67
sitar, 102
Townshend, 24
transition from performing to recording, 69
true songs, 65
view of self as genius, 75–76
who or what the Beatles are or were, 123–124
Yoko Ono, 63, 71, 76–81, 90, 100–101, 104, 108, 110, 122, 127–129
"Leopard-Skin Pill-Box Hat" (Dylan), 55–57

ABOUT THE AUTHOR

JANN S. WENNER was born in New York City and raised in San Francisco and Marin County. He founded *Rolling Stone* in 1967. Over the ensuing decades, *Rolling Stone* won many awards for its design, photography, public service, and journalism, and was instrumental in launching the careers of many groundbreaking journalists and photographers. He also founded and published *Outside, Us Weekly, Family Life*, and *Men's Journal*. A member of the Rock and Roll Hall of Fame and the youngest inductee into the American Society of Magazine Editors' Hall of Fame, Wenner has also been awarded the John Lennon Peace Prize and the Norman Mailer Medal for Lifetime Achievement. Wenner lives in New York and Idaho. He is married and has six children.